NEW
EUROPEAN
POETS

NEW
EUROPEAN
POETS

— General Editors —

WAYNE MILLER AND **KEVIN PRUFER**

Graywolf Press

SAINT PAUL, MINNESOTA

Publication of this volume is made possible in part by a grant provided
by the Minnesota State Arts Board, through an appropriation by the
Minnesota State Legislature; a grant from the Wells Fargo Foundation
Minnesota; and a grant from the National Endowment for the Arts,
which believes that a great nation deserves great art. Significant support
has also been provided by the Bush Foundation; Target; the McKnight
Foundation; and other generous contributions from foundations,
corporations, and individuals. To these organizations and individuals
we offer our heartfelt thanks.

A Lannan Translation Selection
Funding the translation and publication
of exceptional literary works

Published by Graywolf Press
2402 University Avenue, Suite 203
Saint Paul, Minnesota 55114
All rights reserved.

www.graywolfpress.org

Published in the United States of America

Printed in Canada

ISBN 978-1-55597-492-3

2   4   6   8   9   7   5   3   1
First Graywolf Printing, 2008

Library of Congress Control Number: 2007925196

The general editors wish to thank Mary Byers for her work on this book.

Cover design: Kimberly Glyder Design

REGIONAL EDITORS

CHRISTOPHER BAKKEN . . . . Cyprus, Greece, Turkey

PETER COVINO . . . . Italy, Switzerland (Italian)

CHAD DAVIDSON . . . . Italy, Switzerland (Italian)

MICHAEL DUMANIS . . . . . . Bulgaria, Czech Republic, Macedonia, Slovakia, Russia

MARELLA FELTRIN-MORRIS   Italy, Switzerland (Italian)

ROGER GREENWALD . . . . . . Denmark, Norway, Sápmi

MARILYN HACKER . . . . Belgium (French), Luxembourg, France, Switzerland (French)

BRIAN HENRY. . . . . England, Northern Ireland, Republic of Ireland, Scotland, Wales

JOHN ISLES . . . . Estonia, Finland (Finnish), Latvia, Lithuania

ILYA KAMINSKY. . . . . Belarus, Russia, Ukraine

JASCHA KESSLER . . . . Hungary

JOHN KINSELLA. . . . . England, Northern Ireland, Republic of Ireland, Scotland, Wales

RIKA LESSER . . . . Finland (Finland-Swedish), Sápmi, Sweden

ALEXIS LEVITIN . . . . Portugal

WAYNE MILLER . . . . Albania, Iceland, Kosovo, Malta

MURAT NEMET-NEJAT . . . . . Cyprus, Turkey

D. A. POWELL . . . . Estonia, Finland (Finnish), Latvia, Lithuania

KEVIN PRUFER . . . . Iceland, Malta

ADAM J. SORKIN . . . . Moldova, Romania

IGOR ŠTIKS . . . . Bosnia and Herzegovina, Croatia, Montenegro, Serbia, Slovenia

JOVANKA ULJAREVIĆ. . . . . . Montenegro, Serbia

ALISSA VALLES . . . . Belgium (Flemish), The Netherlands, Poland, Spain

SAM WITT . . . . Estonia, Finland (Finnish), Latvia, Lithuania

ELIZABETH
    OEHLKERS WRIGHT . . . . Austria/Lichtenstein, Germany, Switzerland (German)

— *This book is dedicated to all who translate* —

CONTENTS

⤞ ITALY ⤝

INTRODUCTION

Since the middle of the nineteenth century, when the French Symbolists were influenced by the poems of Edgar Allan Poe, American and European poetries have had an intertwined relationship. In the early twentieth century, many American Modernists famously chose to live in Europe rather than in the United States, drawing inspiration from the long histories and bustling internationalism of cities such as Paris and London—and more generally from the atmosphere of experimentation pervading the European artistic and intellectual milieu. Although World War II shifted the center of American poetry back to the U.S., strong poetic ties continued.

After World War II, confessionalism cast a long shadow in American poetry, just as, in European poetry, surrealism and what Carolyn Forché has called "poetry of witness" (inverting the title of Czesław Miłosz's essay, *The Witness of Poetry*) cast long twin shadows. In the late 1950s and early 1960s, dissatisfied with the legacy of Imagism, Robert Bly, James Wright, W. S. Merwin, Galway Kinnell, and Donald Justice, among others, sought alternative, surrealist (or surrealist-inspired) models in the works of poets such as Georg Trakl, Federico García Lorca, Juan Ramón Jiménez, Antonio Machado, Tomas Tranströmer, and César Vallejo. Along the way, they translated these poets, bringing them to an American audience. Other American poets, such as Forché, while attempting to balance personal and socio-political subject matter, found themselves frustrated by the inelasticity of confessionalism, and so looked to European and Latin American writers as models. Still others, such as Charles Simic, immigrated to the United States as children at the end of World War II; as they developed poetically they sustained a strong interest in European poetry. And a number of prominent Central and Eastern European writers, Czesław Miłosz and Joseph Brodsky among them, lived in exile in the West for extended periods of time, bringing with them reading lists unfamiliar to Americans and exerting their own influences on American poetics.

For all these reasons, many European poets who lived and wrote during the first two-thirds of the twentieth century—poets who lived through the world wars, the Spanish Civil War, and the Russian Revolution, experiencing firsthand the heyday of European totalitarianism—have occupied a significant place in the American poetic imagination. Most American poetry readers have at some point encountered poets such as Czesław Miłosz, Paul Celan, Anna Akhmatova, Federico García Lorca, Wisława Szymborska, Eugenio Montale, Zbigniew Herbert, and Osip Mandelstam. As the world got smaller throughout the twentieth century, the divide between American and European poetries got smaller as well.

How strange, then, that when we conducted a poll (an admittedly unscientific one) of poets of our generation, few knew much of anything about today's European poets. We ourselves had little sense of the exciting work and aesthetic range we would discover in the process of editing this anthology. Excluding perhaps those few American poets who have lived overseas for extended periods of time, and despite the best efforts of journals, presses, and programs focusing on translation (*Circumference, Two Lines,* Green Integer Press, Archipelago Books, the Field Translation Series, the Lannan Foundation, PEN, ALTA, and the Iowa International Writing Program, to name a few), the poetic dialogue that blossomed throughout much of the twentieth century seems to have wilted today. This is a shame, because, to put it mildly, a lot has happened in Europe—and European poetry—over the past forty years. It seems high time that our transatlantic poetic conversation be reinvigorated.

We've chosen 1970—twenty-five years after the end of World War II—as the cutoff date for this anthology, meaning that all the poets we've included published their first books after that year. Of course, all cutoff dates are imperfect, and ours is especially so, given that each European country has its own watershed moments, both historically and poetically. We've particularly wanted to emphasize poets who gained prominence in the 1980s and 1990s, during the slow (and then sudden) dissipation of the Cold War. Nonetheless, using 1970 as our cutoff has allowed the many editors who worked on this project the flexibility to dip all the way back to the early 1970s in cases where important European poets have remained largely unknown in the U.S. And, from a historical perspective, 1970 means that nearly all of the poets we've included were born after the end of World War II, and all the poems in the anthology were first published after the tumultuous period of the 1960s.

By the 1960s, postwar divisions that had initially appeared temporary now looked to be permanent. Europe proper was adjusting to its secondary role in the context of the Cold War, and Western Europe was still getting used to the end of its colonial period. In contrast to Eastern Europe, which was stagnating economically, the West had grown prosperous after its postwar economic recovery. Nonetheless, the possibility of an economically unified Western Europe seemed to have faded when French president Charles de Gaulle vetoed Britain's entry to the European Economic Community in 1963—and again in 1967. England consequently remained at a remove from the Continent, where France and West Germany had only recently begun to warm toward each other.

Nonetheless, throughout the 1960s, opposition to the Vietnam War helped unite Western Europe in a growing skepticism toward the United States' military and economic power; in the East, the Soviet economy was failing to fulfill its people's basic needs, forcing President Leonid Brezhnev tacitly to allow the black market to fill in the gaps. Then, in 1968, massive student protests and riots erupted in France and Italy, drawing attention (and imitations) throughout Western Europe. Similarly, news of the Prague Spring (and the Soviet tanks that shut it down) spread across Eastern Europe and, less immediately, to the West. Given the failure of the student protests and the Prague Spring to sustain themselves, it might not have been obvious that Europe was on the edge of a period of massive reconfiguration.

The 1970s found worker revolts in Poland; the additions of the UK, Denmark, and Ireland to the European Economic Community; and, after António de Oliveira Salazar's appointed successor was ousted, a new era of democratic reforms in Portugal. Also, the Greek dictatorship of Georgios Papadopoulos and his colonels faded away, allowing Greece to return to democracy, and the death of Francisco Franco brought a bloodless transition to democracy in Spain, marking the effective end of European fascism. In 1980, the shipyard strikes in Gdansk, Poland, opened up obvious fissures in the Eastern Bloc. When, in 1985, Mikhail Gorbachev took power, the reforms he instituted in an attempt to save the Soviet empire ironically hastened its collapse. Then in 1989, the Berlin Wall came down, ushering in a new era in European history.

Although the 1990s were a chaotic and complicated period of further upheaval—especially in the East—today, Europe has emerged more unified than it has ever been in its history. The European Union now has twenty-seven member states, thirteen of which share the euro as their currency. The UK, which for a long time was more closely connected to the United States than to its European neighbors, now has a center of gravity that has shifted nearer to the Continent. And while France and Germany—because of their sizes, advanced economies, and early leadership roles in the EU—continue to serve as the confederation's heavyweights, other countries, such as Poland, are quickly becoming more politically important, thanks to large populations, strengthening economies, and the EU's policy of subsidizing economic growth in new member states.

Much has been made of the idea that the European Union now offers a political and economic "third way," distinct from the United States' relatively unfettered corporate capitalism and China's oddly hybrid command economy; and, despite growing pains, "European" has increasingly emerged as a significant identity alongside—or in addition to—European national identities. This is aided by the fact that Europeans—and European writers—now move between countries more or less as easily as Americans move between states. And European countries have been socioculturally diversified by a rapid growth of immigration from outside of Europe—primarily from former European colonies.

All but the youngest poets in *New European Poets* grew up in the midst of the Cold War, and thus all except the Russians lived most of their lives in the shadowy though warless space beneath the potential arcs of American and Soviet missiles. The oldest poets in this anthology generally were adolescents during the 1960s and emerged as writers during the upheavals of the 1980s and 1990s. The youngest poets in the book were still children when the Cold War ended, and several of the poets—especially from France, Germany, and the UK—are relatively recent immigrants to Europe from the Middle East, Africa, and the Caribbean. Numerous poets have lived in multiple European countries. A number of others have spent significant periods of time in the United States.

Also, starting in the 1970s, long-suppressed or hegemonized minority groups—particularly in Western Europe—began vying for cultural and/or political representation. Thus, in Spain, we find the growth of a Basque identity movement—most visible perhaps through the terrorist activities of ETA, but also present in the arts—as well as similar movements in Galicia (in the northwest of Spain) and Catalunya (with its center in Barcelona). A number of important poets from each of these regions pointedly write in their respective regional languages, just as Italian poet Raffaello Baldini writes in the Romagnolo dialect and Irish poet Nuala Ní Dhomhnaill writes in Irish. In Scandinavia, the nomadic Sami People of the far north, for whom the national borders of Norway, Sweden, Finland, and Russia are largely irrelevant (their transnational geographic region is called "Sápmi"), gained their own independent parliament in 1989. In Eastern Europe, former Soviet states such as Belarus, Ukraine, Modova, and the Baltic States have reemerged as discrete nations with their own national languages and literatures. Other Soviet-era countries, such as Czechoslovakia and Yugoslavia, became divided according to earlier national boundaries. Even as Europe as a whole has moved toward political and economic confederation and unification, within a number of European countries there has been a push toward exploring and engaging (or reengaging) local cultures, traditions, and histories.

Given these complexities, there was no one ideal way for us to organize the many languages, nations, and national identities represented in this book. To do so by language group—though in some ways this might have been more precise than organizing by nation—would have yielded numerous one-page sections such as Romagnolo dialect or Galician, which might have been counterintuitive for readers inclined to search for those poetries under Italy or Spain. Yet, to organize alphabetically by nation would have divided language groups arbitrarily, and would have separated geographically and/or culturally proximate nations. Consequently, we have struck upon a wholly imperfect compromise: we've organized by nation (while noting language in the translation credits), beginning the book in Iberia and moving eastward toward Russia, eventually looping northward and back toward the UK and Ireland—resulting in something of a linguistic and geographic tour of Europe. This organizing principle has allowed us to keep the poetries of similar language groups and cultures as close to each other as possible. Thus, the Romance languages begin the book; we then move through the Slavic languages and end with the Germanic languages. Those languages that don't easily categorize into these groups—Maltese, Albanian, Greek and Turkish, Hungarian, the languages of the Baltic countries, and Irish—have been fit in this organizational scheme as best as possible with regard to cultural, geographic and/or political connections.

In terms of poetics, it's still possible to find strains of surrealism in the work of many of the poets in this anthology. But other influences—sometimes surprising ones—also emerge. Several writers, such as Hungarian poet Ákos Szilagyi and Ukrainian founders of the Bu-Ba-Bu movement Yuri Andrukhovych and Viktor Neborak, combine Dadaism with the carnivalesque. Others, like Spanish poet Roger Wolfe, Romanian poet Radu Andriescu, and Ukrainian poet Yurko Pozayak write a noirish poetry informed in part by the American Beat writers and the French Symbolists. Portuguese poet Adília Lopes and Basque poet Kirmen Uribe have both been influenced by American confessionalism. The work of Belgian Francophone writer Werner Lambersy is informed by Asian philosophies, and others, such as Greek poet Haris Vlavianós and Danish poet Niels Frank, have been reading (and translating) the New York School poets—especially John Ashbery. The Russian Acmeists continue to influence various poets in the anthology, and the included poem by Evgenii Bunimovich argues with Mayakovsky. A surprisingly large number of European poets are writing long—often book-length—poems, practicing a sort of poetic maximalism. And of course "poetry of witness" is still very much alive in the works of numerous Eastern European poets who bear witness to the chaos of the Soviet collapse, the prison camps of Enver Hoxha's Albania, and the genocidal violence of the Yugoslav Wars; examples include Russian poet Irina Ratushinskaya, Kosovar poet Abdullah Konushevci, Albanian poet Visar Zhiti, and numerous others from Serbia, Croatia, and Bosnia.

Our goal in putting together this anthology was not to pretend to present a comprehensive view of European poetry today—that would be impossible. Europe has nearly 750 million inhabitants and, depending how you count, more than forty languages. In organizing an anthology simply of *one* nation's poets, it's difficult enough to determine, without the benefit of hindsight, which writers are important and will one day be influential. An anthology of European poets presents a whole host of additional problems—questions of national representation, translations, intranational languages and identifications, the politics of national boundaries, and so on. Nonetheless, we felt that it was important to bring this wholly imperfect endeavor to an American audience for three primary reasons: (1) the trajectory of European poetry has continued beyond the European poets known to an American audience; (2) culturally and historically Europe is radically different than it was just a few decades ago, and thus a reexamination of Europe's poetry seems due; and (3) American poetry readers and poets seem to be less engaged with European poetry than they once were, which is a shame.

Given the scope of this project, our methodology was necessarily complex and, in many ways, evolved as the anthology progressed. Since no one (or two, or ten) people can possibly contain the breadth of knowledge required to complete a project of such scope, we knew we'd need help. So, we began by inviting the participation of many other poets, translators, and scholars capable of bringing with them energy and resources particular to the poetries we hoped to collect, people whose skills as poets and/or abilities as translators we admired. In the end, we brought together twenty-two talented regional editors, each of whom scouted assigned language groups, arranged for translations of those poems that had not yet appeared in English, communicated with editors abroad, and in many cases provided original translations of their own. To each, we assigned a page count based roughly on population, with no language receiving more than twenty or fewer than two pages. (As the book progressed, these page counts proved somewhat malleable, as editors discovered some areas of Europe of surprising vitality and others of more limited poetic output. Nevertheless, they stayed largely faithful to our original plan.)

Each regional editor also had the following very general instructions: Be as generous and open to various aesthetic schools and styles as possible; try to focus on poets who have not yet had significant work published in the United States (which is why poets such as Eavan Boland, Vénus Khoury-Ghata, and Adam Zagajewski aren't included).

Since we asked the regional editors to decide for themselves how best to represent the range of work in their categories, the results suggest something of their many perspectives. Some elected to offer just one poem each by many poets. Others selected two or three poems by a smaller number of poets who seemed to them to be most representative of their region. Some focused attention on poets who came of age during the Cold War, while others became more interested in the generation that emerged just afterward. Since every regional editor was asked to discover what was both most exciting and most representative of the work of poets in their area, the result is an anthology that is, we hope, clear in its intentions, but also kaleidoscopic and unpredictable, reflecting the deep knowledge and sensibilities of a great many committed editors, poets, translators, and nationalities.

WAYNE MILLER and KEVIN PRUFER

NEW
EUROPEAN
POETS

→¦ PORTUGAL ¦←

— ROSA ALICE BRANCO (b. 1950) —

Mornings on the Ground

To accept the day. What will come.
To pass through more streets than houses,
more people than streets. To pass through
skin to the other side. While I make
and unmake the day. Your heart
sleeps with me. It wraps me up at night
and the mornings are cold when I get up.
And I'm always asking where you are and why
the streets no longer are rivers. At times
a drop of water falls to the ground
as if it were a tear. At times
there isn't ground enough to soak it up.

translated from the Portuguese by Alexis Levitin

The Highest Branch

I cling to the day by its hair. Yours flies with the waves.
My clothes are wet. An autumn beach. I remember
that I have no other place. The consistency of the sand
on my feet and the birds that settle on the highest
branch for the highest flight. What other place?
Perhaps the desert, a palm tree in the south.
Dates rain down. To let the pit roll around in one's mouth
from wave to wave. Who receives my voice?
I undress as if you're waiting for me to tell you all.
Silence works within my flesh. The city at night
seen from the other side. We walk along in each other's
breath. We know nothing. Ignorance
like a flower in the desert. Do you know that you've arrived?
Don't leave your mouth at the door, your smile.
Help me to become your thirst.

translated from the Portuguese by Alexis Levitin

Between Yesterday and Your Mouth

I will spend the night with those days.
With the smile you left in the sheets.
I still burn with the remains of your name
and see with your eyes the things that you touched.
I am here between the bread and table, in the glass
you lift to your mouth. In the mouth that holds me.
And I don't know what I am between yesterday and what will come.
Yesterday I was the river at evening, the gaze that caressed the light.
My son writes on pebbles on the beach and I invent
steps for deciphering them. They all roll far away.
That's how the sea is. I am learning with the waves
to melt away to foam. There is always a seagull
that cries out when I come near, there is always a wing
between the sky and my floor. But nothing belongs to me,
not even the words with which I cement the hours.
Perhaps love is just a small difference in time zones
or a linguistic accord that only exists
deep in the flesh. But here where I am not
what grounds me is the certainty that you exist.

translated from the Portuguese by Alexis Levitin

— ADÍLIA LOPES (b. 1960) —

Elisabeth Doesn't Work Here Anymore

(with a few things from Anne Sexton)

I've already walked from breakfast to madness
I've already gotten sick on studying Morse code
and drinking coffee with milk
I can't do without Elisabeth
why did you fire her madam doctor?
what harm was Elisabeth doing me?
I only like Elisabeth
to wash my hair
I can't stand to have you touch my hair doctor
I only come here doctor
for Elisabeth to wash my hair
only she knows the colors and scents and thickness

I like in shampoos
only she knows how I like the water almost cold
running down the back of my head
I can't do without Elisabeth
don't try to tell me that time heals all wounds
I was counting on her for the rest of my life
Elisabeth was the princess of all the foxes
I needed her hands in my hair
ah if only there were knives for cutting your
throat madam doctor I'm not coming back
to your antiseptic tunnel
once I was beautiful now I'm myself
I don't want to be a ranter and alone
again in the tunnel what did you do to Elisabeth?
Elisabeth was the princess of all the foxes
why did you take Elisabeth away from me?
Elisabeth doesn't work here anymore
is that all you have to say to me doctor
with a sentence like that in my head
I don't want to go back to my life

translated from the Portuguese by Richard Zenith

— JOSÉ TOLENTINO MENDONÇA (b. 1965) —

Calle Príncipe, 25

Without warning we lose
the vastness of the fields
singular enigmas
the clarity we swear
we'll preserve

but it takes us years
to forget someone
who merely looked at us

translated from the Portuguese by Richard Zenith

The White Road

I walked with you through the exact afternoon
you gave me your hand, life seemed
hard to establish
above the high wall

leaves trembled
under the stronger invisible weight

I could die for just one of those things
we share and have no words for saying:
stars cross paths at a frightful speed
unmovable glaciers at long last shift
and in the only way it can accompany you
my heart beats and beats

translated from the Portuguese by Richard Zenith

Stonecrop

What do the explorers,
the wayfarers, pilgrims we'd thought had long since disappeared,
the Berbers, the nomadic herders
and the exiled
say to people like us whose law is of the letter and testament
not of the unknown necessity
which moment by moment
is revealed

Beyond us, where they live, there's a ghost language
which accommodates what no language
can say:
the photons generated by the stars' clashing
how the antelope wends its way through the orthography
the yellow that returns to the rugged slopes
after the heavy snows

translated from the Portuguese by Richard Zenith

Polish Restaurant

The night is sustained by its decor
like a dead man linked to his machines.
Customers leaf through books, all Poles
from the same block. We suddenly
realize: there is something beyond words
that resists deciphering. In foreign cities
we make better use of our senses, we are bolder
in our intuitions. And after the soup and the warm
tea, going out into the street, we can discover
that we are still alive and that, after all,
we have never known any other condition.
This is the hour that reveals us.
And what we call reality
heads off with us in the same direction.

translated from the Portuguese by Alexis Levitin

Lost Friends

Friends carried off by life
are the most difficult to appease, the most
tyrannical. Barbarians of an unknown land,
they sip the poison of silence and they grow
beyond all limits in the distance, a blind eye
to our loneliness. And to think that we were
brothers in arms, that we dug up buried treasure
from the same islands, from the most
barren of books. How things turn out.
Could all have been in vain? It seemed
that we were destined for the same
songs, for a more certain kind of love.
Well, well. And we cannot even understand
what happened.

translated from the Portuguese by Alexis Levitin

This Way Out

But is there a way out? Imagine
in insomnia the forests that grow
at such hours in other regions, the trains
that cross them to reach a destination
in the future of others.

Is there a way out? Imagine
night filled with violent cities,
the rumbling of engines in the subways
and rain falling on the black plastic
of strawberry fields, all the suffering
and uncertainty of the world.

And in the morning, look, it's a beautiful
day. Your friends are getting up in the other room,
they're heading down to the kitchen to make coffee.

But is there a way out?

translated from the Portuguese by Alexis Levitin

Our Turn

It's the cold that cripples us on a winter
Sunday, when hope is at its
rarest. There are certain fixations
of consciousness, things that wander
about the house searching for their place

and secretly they slip into a poem.
It's envelopes from the water
company, a knife smeared with butter
on the tablecloth, that trail we leave
behind us and decipher without effort
and to no advantage. It's the wait

and the delay. It's the streets so still
at newscast time and the clinking of
neighborhood cutlery. It's the nighttime

aimlessness of memory: it's the fear
of having lost, quite casually,

our turn.

translated from the Portuguese by Alexis Levitin

City of the Missing

There were lots of times I didn't love Lisbon,
didn't know how to love her at dusk
on a work day, when she was used up,
slow and dirty, and
the deep-set sorrow of the world,
my first and most
precocious intuition, traveled,
lights on, in the almost empty buses. Great city
of the missing, so often I didn't have
the vigor to take pleasure in
your small, deserted
gardens. When in the cafés
they were already disconnecting the coffee machines
and from the other end of the line no one
would ever answer
the way I wanted, how often
did I fail to find the place and the serenity
to forget and sleep? Even so,
I didn't do you justice, Lisbon, when
I complained of you: I wasn't a good example,
I had always felt a bit uneasy in the bed of life.

translated from the Portuguese by Alexis Levitin

⤜ SPAIN ⤛

— BERNARDO ATXAGA (b. 1951) —

The Tale of the Hedgehog

The hedgehog wakes up in his nest of dry leaves
his mind suddenly filled with all the words he knows.
Counting the words, including the verbs, more or less, they come to twenty-seven.

Later he thinks: the winter is over,
I'm a hedgehog, up fly two eagles, high up,
Snail, Worm, Insect, Spider, Frog,
which ponds or holes are you hiding in?
There is the river, this is my kingdom, I am hungry.

And he repeats: this is my kingdom, I am hungry,
Snail, Worm, Insect, Spider, Frog,
which ponds or holes are you hiding in?

But he remains still like a dry leaf,
because it's just midday and an old law
forbids him sun, sky and eagles.

But night comes, gone are the eagles; and the hedgehog,
Snail, Worm, Insect, Spider, Frog,
disregards the river, attends to the steepness of the mountain,
as sure of his spines as a warrior
in Sparta or Corinth could have been of his shield;
suddenly, he crosses the boundary
between the meadow and the new road
with a single step that takes him right into my and your time.
And given that his universal vocabulary has not been renewed
in the last seven thousand years,
he doesn't understand our car lights
or see his death coming.

translated from the Basque by Amaia Gabantxo

Life

Life knows only
thorny extremes.
When not Jungle,

Desert.
It dreams no more.

And so, this September of
Red Ferns
wants only
Snow,
and Wolf;
aims at being bare,
frozen Immensity.

And Sun dreams
of Light pure and sharp,
blinding memory
of Bees.

While Night
remembers fondly
that first moment
of only night.

And so
Never, Never,
or,
Always, Always,
loudly beats my Heart.
Measuring
against those two words, unfortunately,
all desires.

translated from the Basque by Amaia Gabantxo

— CHUS PATO (b. 1955) —

[you can't see the battle because it's far off, in Eritrea]

you can't see the battle because it's far off, in Eritrea
the painting's monstrous, three or four times bigger than an opera
backdrop. The mother, one of the lad's four mothers, will speak and does. There's
no way, no symbolic place where the mushroom can turn into a maiden
—just look at her little hood and lepiota cloak
intuit her body, svelte and tiger-striped, her touch, cold. How icy it is in the
mushrooms when night falls. Surprised and glad because you can pull your
hand away and glove your fingers or warm them in your pockets. She's mute,

naturally. There's only the perfect name of God, the name of Antonin Artaud where someone bears the stone. Great sheets of rain into it, miles down, deep with damp dead leaves and since you're late you crouch in chestnut husks where children sleep with solar tiaras and rock themselves and one of the four mothers seems about to speak and does in this bedroom dedicated to Stern because that's where we are, in the grimoire of a poet, and Julia Moesa tells how she had to wade through twenty-five yards of barn manure to find a lost bit off the milking machine,

and everyone gazes, miles down, the pages of the Outre-tombe frozen to kill bookworms, to cure it of evil, and they all breathe and the stone must be cloaked again

what we'll never figure out is if we're inside or not, if the teardrop is jet or basalt, if inside are the three dancing witches, if we'll someday tunnel to the open. The stone compacts itself, as in a zigguri ritual. Just notice the initials, white and red initials, of the royal male-sun, and the female-sun, royal. We'll never find out if our nerves are solar emanations, if the page is parasitical on the secretions of my brain

our nerves radiant with saffron in the letters of the betyl

Especially when the losses are so violent and close

Veracruz, May 1947.

translated from the Galician by Erín Moure

[and now the panopticon is a ruin]

and now the panopticon is a ruin

never mind for i can imagine the landscape however i want
if a desert, it'll be a tell
if rich with vegetation, wisteria will grow over the building
if in Antarctica, it'll be a phantasmagoria of ice

some folks (working women, crazies, schoolchildren, poets)
still live there, they don't realize no one guards them

for in times of plenitude, systems of domination don't pay
attention anymore to populations, they don't have to feed
them

just as you were saying, "capital is illiterate"

i have to get out:

exit biology, remain in my body

translated from the Galician by Erín Moure

— LUIS GARCÍA MONTERO (b. 1958) —

Poetry

Poetry is useless, it serves only
to behead a king
or seduce a young woman.

Perhaps it serves also,
if water is death,
to part the water with a dream.
And if time grants us its unique matter,
it serves possibly as a blade,
because a clean cut is better
when we open memory's skin.
With broken glass
desire
leaves ragged wounds.

You are poetry,
a clean cut,
a part in the water
—if water is the reason for existence—,

the woman who submits to seduction
in order to behead a king.

translated from the Spanish by Katie King

Poetics

There are also moments when we leave behind
words of love and silences
to talk about poetry.
You rest your voice in the past
and recall the title of a book,
the story behind some verses,
adolescent nights of the singer songwriters,

the importance that poets and protesters
hold in your life.
I speak to you of commas and case,
of images that exceed or that lack,
of the need to find the rhythm
that will support the story,
just as hands support
the dampness and the walls of a sand castle.
I also recall some verses
in the nights where commas and case,
metaphors and rhyme,
warmed my home,
kept me company,
knew how to convince me
with your same power of seduction.

I know that other poets
disguise themselves as poets,
they go to their offices of silence
they manage with their banks of brilliance,
they calculate with essence
the balance of their internal assets,
they are the torchbearers of the kings and gods
or they are the tongue of hell.

Do they have souls?
I am content to have you
and to have a conscience.

translated from the Spanish by Katie King

— JOSÉ MANUEL DEL PINO (b. 1958) —

The Evening

Your shadows stand out at the bottom of the street.
It is raining.
The stones, the eaves, the lightning rods,
the darks from the parks are wet.
The narrow alleyways have had enough
of pounding student footsteps,
of laughters, of fritters and wine.

I look at you, you move on,
I contemplate the steady rhythm of your gait,
nymph sandals: pink,
black.
You walk before the bulk of this cathedral
of sword and horse.
The ease with which you roll your hips,
the shape of your buttocks
conjure up the enormity of these carved blocks,
the atlantean heaviness of the flagstone.

The fountain in the plaza spouts
four jets of water,
its multiple arms shining snakelike.
Blood sculpted the stone
despite being softer,
like all you girls
who disappear from the city
leaving only a strange disquiet in the air,
a memory of young breasts heaving
to the beat of tourists strolling by.

Flesh smells like air, like burnt wood
and, albeit briefly, its scent persists
tangled up among the stern statues
out from which, on some evenings, the figure of an angel
reaches its hand to caress
the thighs of young girls looking at these stones,
indifferent, serious.

translated from the Spanish by G. J. Racz

The Sweet Arms of Inspiration

Lyric poetry is a bite on the neck,
a burning kiss planted right on tender cheeks,
a caressing of the silkiness of forms,
a panting tangled up in a head of hair.

Poetry is made, and ever has been made
in front of wine glasses and lascivious
gazes.

The sensuality of the game
surpasses the harsh construction of the hendecasyllable.

Youths also make poetry, and have made it
in the past by painting in bright letters their
howls of false rebellion on the whitewashed walls
(they are dadaists, they are office workers).

Paros, Ios, and Mikonos are islands;
one puts aside moussaka and lets it sit;
bathing suits and parasols with the mellow
rhythm of a tango wafting in the breeze.
There, heraldic panoplies with bright sabers
and foils ornament beds of nocturnal love.

Lechery is the rule in the new cycle
of romances, while a horse's white trotting
disturbs, off and on, the blank face of the page,
spilt blood flowing out now for the sacrifice.

High-sounding, overly mannered madrigals
take their shape in the sparkle of gleaming eyes,
a happy smile above the lashes and lips
of any old laura wearing tight-fitting
black pants, sandals that are eternally black
and a bodice that allows us all to catch
a glimpse of the sweet arms of inspiration.

translated from the Spanish by G. J. Racz

— ANNA AGUILAR-AMAT (b. 1962) —

Orpheus

My keys, when they fall on the ground, make the noise
of a gong or the bell of some religious
ceremony with a God I do not know.
Because the ground was wet, I saw the gleam
of the safety pin that had been dropped
on the pavement, and a bit before that the mattress
soaking up last night's rain. My hands
trembled when I wanted to open the door.
A God I don't know and who sports a cap and,
why not, a moustache, and punches the tickets

on the *vaporetto* that was making Venice recede.
Your pass and mine, joined by a hole
of synchronicity that afterward was going to make us
vanish. You were not supposed to fall
until you were outside the underworld. No looking,
as simple as that. And now you are four or maybe
forty, and your eyes are full of sand. You squeeze
your pain, your eyelids are hate, and a voice
from nowhere rebukes you, demands that you open them; now,
they tell you to weep. "Look," they repeat, "look":
Eurydice isn't there, she cannot be lost again.
Yes, these damaged, bloodshot eyes are still
yours. And the narrow pass that leads to Hades.

translated from the Catalan by Anna Crowe

Relativity

(Homage to Maurice Cornelius Escher)

Picking up green bottle ends and golden shells
on the beach may be an innocent act, full of beauty
for the walker who uses his eyes. But it can also be
a treacherous episode, if your wandering thoughts frame
an alien face, unknown to the bodies that are yours
and which concern you.
But that does not make less beautiful or strange your objets trouvés,
stored in the tubular glass belly of your hope.
Now, the figures you see when you rub your eyes
are green snow crystals, a negative looked at through the microscope
of a hurricane's eye. Your life like a drawing
where you see two faces: an old woman and, afterward, the woman when young;
a rabbit if you look at it with the left eye (and this is love
entirely); if with the right, a duckling's beak aimed
directly at the open heart of a patient in theater.
Even so, although we stayed on the edge, we were afraid
of the trucks backfiring.
Today, a calm mind sees how past and future rush by
haughty and utterly opposed. Let us not cease to thank the man
who painted it: spring, the present, the dividing line.

translated from the Catalan by Anna Crowe

Wisdom

A woman
rides by on a bicycle
at two o'clock in the morning,
her beautiful dark legs
pumping the pedals
while a breeze lifts her dress
to reveal
a perfect miracle
of feminine flesh in motion.

Our eyes
meet for a moment
and she is gone.

There are things like that
which make you realize
what little you really know
about anything.

translated from the Spanish by Gary Hawkins

Words

Words are useless, stubborn, twisted
like screws that won't go in straight.
And they tire me. But they are all I have.
The playthings of a poor boy.
They lie gutted all around me.
All their magic spills out of their open bowels.
Their inner workings long ago stopped being
intriguing or attractive.
There's no challenge. There's no spark. There's no color.
The world is as gray as my disgust.
Words are the columns of my fatigue.
But they are—I have said it, I repeat—all I have.

translated from the Spanish by Gary Hawkins

The Last Night of Earth

The blackbird of ages has returned to visit my house
and I still remain here.
His music does not change, and I have already written it down.
But my work is to state the obvious
and that the blackbird draws me to remember.
Time passes, people grow old, die,
by their own hand or with assistance.
Words are going down the drain
of what someone has called intrahistory.
Everything flows on and is lost, the rivers to the sea,
the sea into the incommensurable immensity of the cosmos,
the cosmos into the nothing from which it cannot leave.
Meanwhile we type on.
A mute tapping against centuries of programmed death
and a future of precise uncertainty.
A battalion of pathetic forgetful amanuenses
calling for two shirts for the journey to the gallows.
But the problem isn't the cold but our fear.
And it is the blackbird, in his ignorance, who knows the truth.
Not the least bit shrill he completes
the ritual that biology has conferred on him.
Soon he will die. Without epitaphs, like this one,
that fall apart, an indifferent face
within the flames of the last night of Earth,
when no one understands any meaning anymore,
if anything made sense once before.

translated from the Spanish by Gary Hawkins

— VIOLETA RANGEL (b. 1968) —

[I pray to heaven your house]

I pray to heaven your house
falls on you—you lousy rat!
a thug busts open your skull
and your children eat your guts,
though with all this you still

wouldn't pay—you filthy hyena!
It consoles me that you're scum,
pure scum, scummy scum,
nothing but scum, and that
sometime ago I helped you
toward your death.

I drink to it.

translated from the Spanish by Frank Bergon and Holly St. John Bergon

[Night, every night,]

Night, every night,
spreads onto the rug.
I finish another cigarette, another coffee.
I spread out like a corpse
and enjoy myself.

A ray of sunlight lashes my back
like a spiteful teenager after an all-nighter.
This light is coming home from a party,
bitch daylight.

translated from the Spanish by Frank Bergon and Holly St. John Bergon

[It's true everything you touch]

It's true everything you touch
sours and vanishes,
every memento your hands caress
brings no feeling,
those you loved
have slipped away down the street
mounted on a horse made of wood.

It's true, but this evening,
at least this evening, celebrate it.

translated from the Spanish by Frank Bergon and Holly St. John Bergon

[Spidery light scratches the crystal]

Spidery light scratches the crystal
and the little table of flickering wicks.
The wharves, coughs, pipelines rumble.
With the slam of a door a rock
rolls down toward the jail.
Outside, bus doors
fold like leaves.

This is life
turning and returning like a chained prisoner.

translated from the Spanish by Frank Bergon and Holly St. John Bergon

— KIRMEN URIBE (b. 1970) —

Visit

Heroin had been as sweet as sex
she used to say, at one time.

The doctors have been saying now she won't get worse,
to go day by day, take things easy.
It's been a month since she failed to wake up
after the last operation.

Still and all, we go every day to visit her
in Cubicle Six of the Intensive Care Unit.
Today we found the patient in the bed beside hers
in tears, no one had come to visit, he'd said to the nurse.

An entire month and we haven't heard a word from my sister.
I don't see my whole life stretching before me the way I did,
she used to tell us.
I don't want promises, I don't want repentance,
just some sign of love is all.

Our mother and I are the ones who talk to her.
Our brother, with her, never said too much,
and here doesn't make an appearance.
Our father hangs back in the doorway, silent.

I don't sleep nights, she used to tell us,
I'm afraid to go to sleep, afraid of the bad dreams.
The needles hurt me and I'm cold,

the serum sends the cold through every one of my veins.
If I could only escape from this rotten body.

Meanwhile take my hand, she implored us,
I don't want promises, I don't want repentance,
just some sign of love is all.

translated from the Basque by Elizabeth Macklin

Cardiogram

—Describe, if you would, his heart for me.
—It's like a frozen lake,
    and the face of the child that he once was
    is erasing itself in there.

translated from the Basque by Elizabeth Macklin

Loren

The boats have come in,
the kids race down.
Loren has got red hair now,
wears spike heels.

Whiskey and Coke,
in her pocket, snow.
No one's been born on Earth
to keep up with her.

How, they ask her,
did you make that dress?
On black cloth with white chalk
I drew the stars.

The wind from the North
hurts my face.
The new world as yet unmade
hurts, too.

translated from the Basque by Elizabeth Macklin

Ford

like a bear waking up lethargically
bit by bit our ford melts the windshield of snow
I pack the suitcases in the backseat review the road map

now you arrive half asleep
without paint without repair broken down for the night passage
night of questions of fear of clothes that float

in and out of the closets night of the disconnected refrigerator
but today is different and with you beside me it feels like before when we traveled
    without haste
through forests and fields of corn those nights
the bright headlights burned in search of the sea

slowly the ford climbs the hill
I want to travel south south of all the projects

translated from the Spanish by Brian Barker

Father

in the ford on the northern highways
traveling with my nine-year-old daughter sara
cold service stations long cafés with plateglass windows

where time and again she blows out the candles on a birthday cake

I see her growing losing herself between the tables talking with strangers
staying out later past eight o'clock past ten o'clock past twelve
and I'm looking for her in mcdonalds in hospitals in police stations
and she's shouting furiously that I'm a motherfucker

bastard son of a bitch

too much of a coward
to look for home to pay taxes one day I stopped the car
in the middle of the snow I put the steering wheel in her hands

I took my baggage and my few belongings
and she pulled away in my ford

translated from the Spanish by Brian Barker

✳ FRANCE ✳

— PAUL DE ROUX (b. 1937) —

Figure in a village

What is he thinking of, what
is he dreaming? Black city shoes,
shirt neat as a pin, trousers with their crease,
remembering from time to time
his *komboloi* he runs the beads along
then, chin in hand again
half shuts his eyes, sets off once more
in what I'd call his reverie
outside the taverna, the bottle
of mineral water scarcely broached.

translated from the French by Helen Constantine

Waiting (1)

That was the sweetest moment
waiting for the bus, the tables
in the little café shaded
by the trees in the square, where the air
fanned gently in from the sea
and where I drank a café frappé
before I left Gythion, that had little more
than this transient pleasure to offer me
—but was this not the very stamp of it?

translated from the French by Helen Constantine

Waiting (2)

Unhesitating, tables, chairs
bestride the pavement, find
the shade of trees in the square:
bags by my feet, here I can wait,
calmly, for my bus, watching
the sky, blue between branch and leaf,
and sucking through a straw

my café frappé—till the last sibilation, sign
that I've reached the lees.

translated from the French by Helen Constantine

— MARIE ÉTIENNE (b. 1937) —

from **The Ebony Mare**

Visiting Gaston

Fortunately we have arrived at last
Gaston's house is situated
Just outside the limits of the town
Stuccoed with white low and almost buried
The blue windows are thrown wide open
The fireplace occupies the whole back wall
The living room floor is terra cotta
Then Gaston emerges from the shadows
He opens his arms wide encloses me
I can feel his long hair against my cheek

I can feel his long hair against my cheek
While we're having dinner another guest
Tells a story about Jean Vesoul
                              "He
Teaches his course half-reclining his back
Against the wall his trouser fly open
His erection entirely visible
But he never notices and no one
Dares to tell him"
                    Would we be lacking
Authenticity? What is an exposed
Sex a bloodstain on a skirt?

Letter to M.R.

You had brought me an enormous bouquet
Of flowers probably they were daisies
Some of them blue like blooms of lavender
The others mauve bordering on rose-pink
All of them cut in your mother's garden
I had arranged the bouquet on my desk

In this dream I was living in the dark
Downstairs room in which I had worked for years
When you came to see me—for you would come
To see me from time to time—you'd sit down

To see me from time to time—you'd sit down
On the side where I'd placed the bouquet
You hid yourself behind the flowers to
Which I'd given water and which I had
Tended but they withered all the same
One day there was only one left
                              You ap-
Roached you hid yourself as well as you could
Behind its stem and its petals you said:
"My mother's coming she won't understand
How or why I parted with her flower

How or why I parted with her flower
Don't be upset I'll give it back to you"
I had picked up the vase then in order to
Give it some fresh water and to bring
It into your study you were resting
Your foot all this time because you'd hurt it
When you had fallen down the stairs
                              I had
Seized this opportunity to take
Care of you despite our differences
So we could share the blue of those flowers

translated from the French by Marilyn Hacker

— GABRIELLE ALTHEN (b. 1939) —

Rooms

A cell for each one
Each man wept within his mandorla
Children and adults looking the same
Each one set in his silence
The Christ in his glory
Had departed elsewhere
Time would soon part with the air

Little fellow who is myself
Little fellow who is my brother
Have I so thoroughly left the blue of the olive-trees
Do you remember the wind's beautiful hair
As for me I say that I am one
With this prison
With the head's cellar
With the hovel of space where spirit lives
But the light that's lacking
Enjoins us to name the lack of light
Clenching this dark terrain
Little fellow pay attention
In your den in my den
In our blind men's dens
Our foreheads are that windowpane
Fitted on metaphysics
And as for me to keep me busy
One by one I pick up
Barely faded shards of stained glass
On the ground at my feet.

translated from the French by Marilyn Hacker

— EMMANUEL HOCQUARD (b. 1940) —

from The Invention of Glass

The strip is so thin
that there's only one face.
Brilliance excludes
prepositions. All
response presumes a reverse.
When the vowels
and the diphthongs are
opaque or translucent,
the consonants stay
transparent. Configurations
of color and of space
barely glimpsed. Echoes
of a tongue of
invisible signs.

"It's simply a matter of
meeting this phrase." The subject
never leaves its grammatical
glow. The little locked
words fix
objects and the quotation
declared as such
short-circuits.
"It's only a matter
of recognizing this sentence"
which we didn't know.
The debt to the already-said grows
with each new period. The
letters often open
onto strange wishes: I hope
it all happens just as
you'd imagined. But
the autobiography begins
with hypothetical
bits of sense. "This is what
you're going to hear. This is
what you're going to start
to understand." From quotations
to allusions, the narrator
is omniscient. On the map
she reorients while
he replaces the prophetic
conscience: columns of white
steam and animals gifted
with clairvoyance:
foreseeing rain, earthquakes,
and even the arbitrary
lines of weeds
there in the cracking pavement.

translated from the French by Cole Swensen and Rod Smith

Spiritual Distress

And damn the almanac-makers who leave you
stuck between debts and death
or a week with seven tomorrows. Today
here's another gent: *History's convulsions,*
monstrous metaphor of our
spiritual distress. Listen to this, distress:
in Burgos, in the Middle Ages, a baker's son
converted to Christianity, and his father,
in a fury, flung him into the oven.
Saint Mary, says the chronicle, saved the son and
the citizens of Burgos burned the father and

don't wander too far off, distress, and start to giggle
because what comes next is a riddle: my first is
a convoy of Jews sent to Auschwitz by
the Prefecture of the Gironde; my second, a procession
of bullet-bloated Algerians who float
under the Pont Mirabeau; my third the funds
of a national political party in the sixties,
and together they make the *proper name* of a great
spiritual distress which is certainly not called
Martin Heidegger and don't get annoyed, what's annoying
is that all this should merely be allusion.

translated from the French by Marilyn Hacker

Treason

Poets lack modesty in their adventures: they exploit them.
—FRIEDRICH NIETSZCHE

May they have nothing to fill their mouths
on their last journey! Months of running errands
in the marketplace—no fun at all, but, sometimes
when the sun sets the heart of the world on fire
and your voice rushes up to stop
everyone seeing it, it's as awkward
as your uneasy hormone surges
so three or four of you gang up behind

a hefty matron, shiny cloth glued to her skin
by floods of sweat and you shout at her
between the produce stalls *lady, lady, your dress
is up your ass* and take off around the fruit crates! While
red, green, ochre, the air swings her huge
peals of laughter back at you. Heartstopping:
with ten hard-saved francs you could have
the soccer ball *Made in France* smelling of leather
and penalties at nearly nine yards, great games,
great shouts, great fights until the night
of time which won't sleep, when the tall
candles give back to the stars some of the
energy we get from them, with the ten francs,
those pus-balled motherfuckers, they
went straight to some hairy-cunt whore.

translated from the French by Marilyn Hacker

— ANDRÉ VELTER (b. 1945) —

Red or Nothing

As for me, I live my life in red
—PAUL VERLAINE

I'll tell you that my mirror is red
and my lamp is red
and my mouth and my heart
red as a red secret
with no comeback, no drama
red of stone and sun mixed together

I'll tell you that my past is red
brick of blood or dusk
less brittle than it might seem in ruins
with that shudder of red dust
on the abandoned guardpost
of reddened walls.

I'll tell you that my memory is red
against the red rocks
and rusted harrows

at the four corners of the labyrinth
where fate changes from one commotion to another,
an archipelago, a seeding of red stars.

I'll tell you that my shadow is red
in blacksmith's hands
that rummage in red ash
that forge a bit of demon, a bit of angel
with no concern for what clings to the cutting edge
or the scarlet dream of an old fury.

I'll tell you that my soul is red
whittled from the fossil wood of a bauxite mine
and that it sings red
covers the world's murderous noise
mounts an attack on noble sentiments
which are in the red.

I'll tell you that my sky is red
wider than all the laundered territories
that unroll into the red valleys
and tell you that my fatigue is red,
red my migrations without start or finish
and finally that I see red.

translated from the French by Marilyn Hacker

— ABDELWAHAB MEDDEB (b. 1946) —

from **The 99 Yale Stations**

1.

At the century's sill
Hölderlin's finger
is a singing cicada

2.

In the town the bells toll
with both hands he grabs the tocsin
which does not shake his bones

3.

In the factory's breath
he hears the call to prayer
overthrowing the recumbents' stelae

4.

Arcs and columns of Andalusia
enclose the temple of the brothers
where the treasure shimmers

5.

He flies on the green carpet
the shell opens in the night
at sky's end he tracks the pearl

6.

The yellow bus flies over the gulls
he dives into the foam and washes
his mud-stained handkerchief

7.

The squirrel scurries along the cable
the leaves turn red
a passerby from Asia burns up

8.

The town is a closed pot
day gnaws at the lid's joint
his cut finger drips into the rumor

9.

The desert inside the body
no fruit to squeeze water from
thirst is a white swan with black neck

10.

Under the stone shelter with open book
memory's envelope cracks open
and the birthplace reenters day

11.

On the dream's wings the sirens sing
along the hillside the flowers of forgetting
the sea offers him a salver of figs

12.

Between the languages between the races
nomad erring among the continents
he discovers in himself the name of dusk

13.

The echo of his voice crosses the ocean
the waves carry away the bodies of the Blacks
whose laughter bellies out the sails

translated from the French by Pierre Joris

— GUY GOFFETTE (b. 1947) —

So Many Things

All winter you neglected
the strong red umbrella
let its ribs rust in the grass and mud
let the north wind crush the birdhouse

without uttering a word, you gave up
on the rose beds, the apple
that rounded off the earth.
By indigence or distraction you left,

let so many things die off
the only place to set your gaze
is on the draft slicing through your house
and you're surprised, still, surprised when

cold seizes you from summer's very arms

translated from the French by Julie Fay

Around the Flames

To walk around the flames when what is burning
isn't a burnt branch from a dead forest, an old
bouquet of roses, unimportant papers, a sky
halfway decided to dress up in cinders,

but the house of all your promises—
and which were kept for more than a day, O
fickle one, you who could never
see a hill swoon in the sunlight

without wanting its shadow side, to leap up
and touch its flank, to bring your body's
trajectory into its fall, tell me, which one
was kept that you cannot unclasp

the fiery necklace clutching your heart?

translated from the French by Marilyn Hacker

The Number

What is it that's still keeping you here
in the damp air and in the wind
scowling at the lilacs? Is it
the house where in the shadows you once touched

stone bodies and made tears gush forth?
Or the path through the brambles which your steps
let you lose in lassitude
like an old desire, a childhood abandoned

beside the pond, which continues keeping
count of the dead on its own near the sky?
—and you would still like to lean your head
on its frail shoulders before reading

the last number of your days there in the grass.

translated from the French by Marilyn Hacker

from **How Long?**

[. . .]

Everything was the heart of all forms of being. Even the silent humble rock lost in the sea.

We used to recall sublime pages for celebrating trifles. Confusion.

Intelligence of the secret, season after season, even if you dreamed of the contrary. Wisdom, though, of the secret. How to reveal everything to everyone?

At the end of the bed of the overly modest, the hen with a crop of pride often kept vigil.

Brutality, in fact, didn't really disturb him. What did upset him was crime.

He was well acquainted with the dark pebbles of boredom, those strange warm stones which could move around—and even breed.

In short, he coped. Was his puppet, inside, perhaps simply juggling better and better with his entire history? his childhood, his youth, his adulthood, now so advanced he already felt over the hill. He didn't know much, actually. But what he did know was that it was, without a doubt, still a juggling act.

Unfortunately and fortunately. Mixed. Shared.

But, sometimes, he ran for cover: "Do you think you will die of love?"

Or he got to thinking. Out loud: "The older I get, the less I believe that desire, hunger, sleep and death are all there is. That would be too simple." And the other, facing him, who was smiling.

He also thought: "And if they try to hurt you with words, however contrary or spiteful, repeat them to your saliva. And spit. Immediately."

"If I had to choose, however, I believe that what life depends upon is rather in the shape of a bird." He continued.

For there was often fire in gazes. Still. Even if all those eyes were stamping or pacing up and down—waited there, at the palace gates, without having the slightest idea about what was going on inside, or who ran the place.

And yet, he would never forget the blow of the mallet striking, in the center of the flames, the skull already nearly black.

Everything existed. Even speech.

translated from the French by Michael Tweed

Conversation with Mohammed Dib

Those white ones standing naked leaning stones
brought beyond exile preserved
erect in memory's patched daylight

Those who are dancing far off, murmur woven into echo
welcome reserved for the one who, dead, prepares himself
his face splattered with quenched desire

Those who slash in an instant a cheek red as an eventful
evening closed windows nightlight life
evoked then a handkerchief moves across the plate

Those black ones guardians of hounded tribes
who appear in smoke only after the third attack
and then sink into the ashes faded forever

Those golden ones deposed idols of a glowing childhood
time turned a heart which lost its vision
emptied the house during the farewell ovations

O all those whom love never marked with craving
who leave you crouched in a desolate place
watch you in the slow throbbing of a lie

And the only She who leaves you in a night gone stale.

translated from the French by Nora Makhoul

On the seventh day of my birth

I spoke the language
of the world I'd come from
bore witness to a shadow
which was the shadow
of another light
which no one saw

in the seventh month of my birth
my mouth took the shape of the void
I cried to tell what was true

and that which the present had taught me
of the past of the future
but no one understood

the seventh year of my birth
I dreamed what had been
on the world's lined page
I traced letter after letter
to remind myself
of what I had to forget
and of what in me was already dying

translated from the French by Marilyn Hacker

— JEAN-BAPTISTE PARA (b. 1956) —

Svetla

For days on end
I give my heart to the silence
and if I close my eyes I see
a white cypress near a spring
peacocks walking on sandy earth
a handkerchief moistened with spit
the silhouettes of saints
on the icon's gold ground
and your face standing out
against the light of your name.

When I open my eyes
the shape of it all
is still intact.

translated from the French by Olivia McCannon

Tomorrow

I'll walk along by the rapids
and my life will be lost in the roaring, pass into shadow
like a lost prey, a Colchian pheasant
that takes flight leaving a feather
and the silence where I start to be.
I'll sleep on the wet ground

and if I wake to find the world like a brandished whip,
a breaking storm, for its veins of light
will I open a hand clenched round the perfect sign
of my imperfection? Where the sky ends,
will I then reveal the empty palm
that wished to erase my name without hate
the way sand or dust is blinked from an eye?

translated from the French by Olivia McCannon

— ARIANE DREYFUS (b. 1958) —

Rosas 1998

"While in reality, they are growing older"

The dancer whose name I do not know
has sat back down.
She has not lost a piece of her body.
Who appears better will disappear better

As she no longer moves I see her breathe heavily
And her face damp

Even very slowly
Even sweetness can be gone beyond.

A male dancer and a female dancer
Take the piano in their snow

—I need.
—To come back under the lights, you already said it.

She doesn't knock, but she counts
To enter
Who knows where

And then yes, she knocks with her leg
The male dancer lifts her up under her breasts
Without breaking her wait

Another prefers throwing the empty chair
Which is still vibrating

And otherwise
Music sends time into ecstasy

Bare feet
Yes love can be crossed
from one side to the other
Feet very dirty in the light
—The work in the caresses—
You must be
the immediate dancer
We must

not let go of each other's hands growing old

translated from the French by Donna Stonecipher

— EMMANUEL MOSES (b. 1959) —

Souvenir of Liège

What else remains besides time, bare, unchangeable, for us to belabor
In unfinished discussions, interrupted by glances out of windows
On these autumnal days, reflections of reflections . . . like the gray pond that has
    so often seen
The little footbridge, and a last fisherman leaning over the parapet, some acciden-
    tal birds,
The haloes of the lamps behind the facades of the rue aux Juifs.
The rain that was announced will be spared us today but not the trembling
Of the leaves or the dirty light discharged into the city;
The silences—they too are unraveled, each word taking on the significance
Of a call of distress:
How to keep ajar the door that gave on perspectives all azure,
The majestic bay where the night collected itself?
Lizards slid against the hot stone like so many drops
Of eternity
And all it took was a seagull to burst
The inattention, the dull absence attached to the morning.
Maybe dreams will know how to save us.
Crowded platforms, trains departing, horse carriages gleaming like brand-new,
Will we never disappear in the little square of a window
For those who remain behind?
A room will make our consciences echo with the here,
With the now, with the shimmering point at the end of the breakwater
That was the entire sea.

translated from the French by Donna Stonecipher

White Siestas

At the moment I approach the shore, the white shores
under a sky of beams and rush, the refuge
of a lizard—its tongue, its drowning eyes.

The door rattles, the shutters—just barely,
under the light pressure of wind, where a whole world perishes,
a deaf pestle crushing, sun
in the ruined mortar of another world.

Cradled by the complaint or laughter of childhood
weapons are laid down outside; and liquid armfuls
in which grace cannot be contained; like water,
if not deep, refused, deserted,
I fell asleep, I sleep without finding sleep,
the sea birds, the storm clouds—

translated from the French by Ellen Hinsey

Sanctuary

At the indefinite limits
of the city which goes to ground, at that border
littered with camels fettered together, there, where the animals live
—the sky thrust into their stomachs
by turbulent handfuls of stones, of sand—
where all my life leans into another body,
the shoulder of a child dares,
without guiding anyone along the blindness of streets—

where my hands are no longer mine in the way they brush
locks, forges, the fire
that is governed by your absence.

translated from the French by Ellen Hinsey

Night II

From your face tonight
your body, taking form, here
the offerings

from your shadowed cheeks
hue of the surroundings, too,
asking for them

the pear in the basket
your wishes for meals like this
almonds.

translated from the French by Jennifer K. Dick

Night III

There's a slow country
of almonds, of your
eyes or this step nightly

traveling soundless or with so little
from here to there, lengthy
where we're going, long hair.

There's only slow country,
of your steps, of your hair,
where we're going today.

translated from the French by Jennifer K. Dick

— VALÉRIE ROUZEAU (b. 1967) —

Won't see you soon: 4

I am not wearing black just because you are no longer visible

I can think of you in blue for days on end

Can find you unusual flowers and pretty enough, heavy enough vases

It's hard to give you things, it always was

The other day I stuck my feet into your big empty boots and your dog came out for
    a walk with me

It was raining and I slopped about in them you must have kept stones in your
    pockets

And again the other day I did not particularly bring you a bouquet

translated from the French by George Szirtes

Takeaway

Axle grease sticks to your nose
Makes you squint, makes you sweat
Follows you everywhere since you were born
Filthy mug filthy job bastards
Follows you everywhere even to bed
Ruins your life

translated from the French by George Szirtes

Gather me some

Woman alone only to weed a field
The blue of which she always must be thinking
Rolls on in April without music to see the road
Less good heavens how blue it was a field
Its hot color here she is completely
For it better to cover it throw herself upon it

translated from the French by George Szirtes

Fido

Lovely green-eyed firefly close to lawn
Where dog is lying lying there
In the shade dog who's had his day shat his last shit
Doesn't move cut grass stays well and truly put
Doesn't look like a brute to take for walkies either
Ideal for the firefly to dig its peaceful hole

translated from the French by George Szirtes

⤲ LUXEMBOURG ⤲

ANISE KOLTZ (b. 1928)

from **The Fire Eater**

III

In the church's slaughterhouses
we are transformed
into vultures

We devour
the body of Christ
thrusting our necks
into his blood
with unavowed violence

— —

I am looking for a baptismal font
to hand back my name
to drown it
in its holy water

I take original
sin upon me
once again
like a force
a carapace
that makes me invulnerable

— —

None of our complaints
will be heard

God is a deaf-mute
No one has taught us
sign language

— —

The fallen angel
who looked at himself
in the water

43

drowned
in his image

— —

On the seventh day
God fell asleep

The earth is still trembling
from his snoring

— —

God
lights a fire
in the darkness
to discover
in the blue of the flames
another darkness

— —

I no longer believe in God
henceforth
He has to
believe in me

— —

Wasn't it written
that he who'd drink
the blood of Christ
and eat his flesh
would be reborn like Him

But his blood coagulated
in our mouths
his flesh spoiled
under our eyes—

We will live on
dust
and rain

Because our death
will be a death
that lasts

translated from the French by Pierre Joris

from **The Desert**

The desert counted its wrinkles;
the eagle and the falcon immediately spread the news.
— EDMOND JABÈS

it is due to the general indifference of
the grains of sand
that the desert came about
but also because the sand
knew how to remain gregarious

——

to know that all the grains of sand
of all the deserts sleep in me
does not reassure me
like them every night
I get under way
searching for a dry dream
a dream which in order to defend us
would brave the meanders of humidity

——

I went to station myself
on the line separating one desert from the other
to watch the grains of sand
getting married in secret
before crossing the border

——

when I said I had the desert in me
I was thinking less of the dryness
than of the incessant swarming of the sand
and caught in the swirl
I stopped weeping
even though I had been weeping for joy

——

each desert hides a secret
each secret hides an injustice

nobody knows who slipped it in there
but it makes everybody rejoice secretly

— —

I've read somewhere or did I dream it
that the desert was the scar a sea left
oh what anguish to think
that one day the wound could open again

— —

in my childhood my youth my life for short
I have known many a gathering of sand
the words I have spoken or written
rest there temporarily
a wind comes up and worries them

— —

I envy the anonymity of the desert's sand grains
they come and go they say hello good night
they love & know how to recognize each other

because there where one ends the other begins
in the desert the eternal return
is a question of life and death

translated from the French by Pierre Joris

✴ SWITZERLAND ✴

— ELISABETH WANDELER-DECK (b. 1939) —

from **controcantos**

8   4.16.1994

nearby the curtainless window display and I have to look
commenced is still not recalled what takes place buzz thinking
sober fluttering still falling for drink bitterness falling down night
field of vision shining knuckled under racing rap head stray thinking patter
    of hearts
unturned I give you words my word unturned draw
me out to you to dream whirled up is still not recalled
drift bewildered condition to marked one blown up in brazen beauty
disabled uncompassing of your arms dreadfill hush of your speaking
heart blasting I sit in front of the device and cry
tinny wind reading to pieces listening to looked at seen
also plastic sheets firmly established not sound proof but anyway
encompassed nearby the curtainless feeling and you have to look away
stunned indignant us a hesitation tenderly ridiculous

translated from the German by Elizabeth Oehlkers Wright

— URS ALLEMANN (b. 1948) —

For the Lyre

The hand that reaches into your breast and seizes your heart
to rip it out falls off. It's yours. You bend over
to pick it up. Then your heart falls out. We throw
ourselves to the ground into Ours, to beat, clap, sink in
the hearts hands teeth. Choke it down. As you plunge,
your head is already sliding off your shoulders and climbing upward
turning inside out like it is not imaginable
but sayable. Some think blood, too,
has flowed there. Far away weeping. Meekly
making sounds, the strewn-everywhere, the bones of
others. If by chance Orpheus arrives

I'd sing something for him, the flesh-
eating lyre, push his share of the handed-down
across to him.

translated from the German by Elizabeth Oehlkers Wright

— PIERRE VOÉLIN (b. 1949) —

from Lents passages de l'ombre

In memory of Nadezha Mandelstam

Speech and its taste of slate—drinking summer
And honey and bitter certitude

You are only a visitor in remembrance
Elsewhere the bitter sweat of the dead

You alone listen
Shelling, one by one, the words of song

Here, day pierces the eardrum of the dead

— —

These lamps go lightly in the air
—it only stands to cry out

One releases the dogs
At ease in their drool and oblivion

Far off Vosges O aging mothers
Blue-ringed eyes used-up mothers

Hail hail these unpardonable lands

— —

Night laid out like a harrow
Light on my shoulders

I taste the saliva of ivy
And the herb of chance ground by Time

Clay and marl make a tomb

translated from the French by Ellen Hinsey

from **Musicales**

Forcibly digging this black
abyss, invisibly
a hand gathers note by note
                            a song
(oceanic, fecund)

while cries, wrested sibilants
in zigzagging lines
melt into infinite space
(further! higher!)

Pouncing on infinite space
in zigzagging lines—

wrested cries, sibilants
            and the wakened abyss rolls its parallel,
continual, sea in its fingers

Rain, soft rain, at the end
—summing up all, guiding
guiding
            toward the silence
                    (The ocean-piano)

> *It is getting dark . . .* Robert Schumann, letter,
> February 7, 1854

Where did it come from? A singular
motif asserts istself, commands!

utterance
born of itself, for no one
(or for what angels in rags) oscillating
on the threshold of its disappearance,
it recalls its exhausted
voices, it turns
in circles, its lament
already nameless
                    (Disappearance)

Forever lost? No:
brought back from watery depths

saved *in extremis*
the ancient exultation
the rebirthed sun
springs slowly and leaps

Lazarus unbound, solemn
step by step mounting
rising, toward us
    (Resurrection)

At the summit
the beating of this note—
beyond sharp
like a butterfly above the chaos:
  Birth
of all the great sonorous magma,
the expulsion of noises that set off
and of sounds
   pulled, pulled
out of a disorder

for the resolution of its own
pure
possibility
    (Schöpfung)

   translated from the French by Ellen Hinsey

         — KURT AEBLI (b. 1955) —

An Old Gaping Wound
Wheedling Out
An Unmasked Smile

1.

tied up into bundles
newspapers grace the sidewalk.
the bright peopled
afternoon.
the for-weariness-upright-remaining
hand of his clock face.
the characterization *figure* applies to him.

the characterization *motionless sea* even.
His words followed by
rats.

2.

The sole to-be-taken-seriously inhabitants of the city
brought home the money, cursed and

                           sweated
and demanded of life chewing gum.

3.

A gigantic loudspeaker system exhaled vapors of
destabilization.
Police cordons drove off
the mourners.
On the esplanade of the cathedral everything went
with a few well-aimed shots according to plan.

4.

The sun a postscript, the sky
an anomaly, the ocean
genuine blood.

5.

Pure excuse was approaching the greatest significance.
Misfortune was tired of waiting for him.
The entire surroundings seemed

                              with a tone of friendship
to say to him: go on, we'll be right there.

6.

He slept overnight in his coat.
In the morning a new generation woke him.
The day began without day.
The beast that invented the noise,
the supersonic speed.
Between-the-houses stood for a time, without a house.

       translated from the German by Elizabeth Oehlkers Wright

Saturday in Sintra

The last pigeon,
the one that persists when the rest of the flock
is already scattered on the rooftops,
holed up between walls,
the lone one flying downward into the piazzas,
blinded by the sun,
perhaps merely dumber than the others, impervious
to that dull, horizontal clucking,
—while clumsily losing,
grain by grain, the food it's offered—,
the one that dashes into the void
of an imaginary venture, a threat,
the fear of a whistle,
and draws flight from it, converts the peril
into a game of looping and soaring,
the escape into a senseless race against the swift
shadow of the gull,
a shadow that truly flies and disappears;
the bird that seeks out the wind of the streets
and chimneys, that plunges into traffic and is left
a heap of gray feathers, repugnant,
on the side of manholes,
don't look at it.

translated from the Italian by Chad Davidson

Star, Meteor, Some Shooting Thing

That one coming out of a building with a full-face crash helmet,
jumping toward an afternoon of tar
and wind against his neck, impatient, and savoring
the scent of mixture and of the two-stroke engine
or perhaps of fresh-cut grass, the short kilometers

that will zip by free of care, pure images
of faces and fleeting bodies, windows
like screens or glimpsed nostalgias, forgettable
sorrows: a light accompanies him. To leave,

just to leave, to get lost, to become
star, meteor, some shooting thing.

Suburbs of nothingness, and in every house
the same blue flame, and clear signs
of frustrated hopes and oppositions
that have been utterly crushed.
Dogs on leashes, old folks, playgrounds.
"Do you know that once upon a time some forty head
of cattle used to graze here?" says one,
tapping his foot on the polyurethane surface of the small field.

This is the afternoon: a diffused dazzle,
the unexpected greeting of those you pass by.
And some knowing looks, that say thank you.
That say we are here, in spite of it all.

The watermelon, for example, that a group of Turks
kindly offered us, was delicious.

translated from the Italian by Marella Feltrin-Morris

— CHRISTIAN UETZ (b. 1963) —

AND FROM YOU the pain stars stone-souled,
so that the finish is never-ending.
You mute mortal-light,
you quivering nothingness,
what is it that wants us to keep getting in the way?
Shot-light sluiced through all pores,
so that the drowning would dissolve,
And whenerr it pleases the dream turns more real than the
                                                    room,
the elation stronger than life,
timelessness deeper than time,

and the wound more open than the world.

translated from the German by Elizabeth Oehlkers Wright

Miradouro de São Pedro de Alcântara

Left handed I cut pictures
from the red of the hibiscus:
cold light on the stone swaths of Baixa
tourists in packs
drunk dogs
in the harbor a freighter and rusty tanks.

The lovers beside me kiss with their fingers;
on the facing slope the church stands up to the heavens;
something opening for me too, cyclopean, its eye.

translated from the German by Elizabeth Oehlkers Wright

from Saisons du corps

If I had loved better
these days with their good smell of bark
these copper twilights
the mountains exposing their toothless jaws
if I had walked more upright
along trails that lead toward dawn
where faith shelters us from doubts and time

if I had known how to savor the full laugh
of the river that rocks in its fleece of leaves
my head held to the trunk's pillow
my cheek cast amidst thyme
if I hadn't fled like a coward to the back streets
and believed in the false lights of the city
in its burning waltz of noise

perhaps I wouldn't—stumbling
rake my wooden head against the walls of night

translated from the French by Ellen Hinsey

[in the mildness of the afternoon the]

in the mildness of the afternoon the
continents lie near each other like drowsy

cows the meadows of the oceans are very blue
mister magellan draws in his secret

diary the continents stretch languidly
in the mildness of the evening mister magellan's

sea maps are silhouettes of local
livestock like dreams of the spanish

queen in the mildness of the night the continents
feed in the meadows of the ebb tide

in the meadows of the flood tide mister magellan
sketches the coastlines of the cows

in the mildness of the morning the still-
empty pages of magellan's diary shimmer

far brighter than the dreams of the
queen like fresh milk from the continents

translated from the German by Donna Stonecipher

[brown dustbeetles everywhere brown]

brown dustbeetles everywhere brown
dustbeetles also in our lac de cygne

and without wings and in every
dashboard of every dream and

for every time of day brown dustbeetles
also tuesdays also in the arabian nights

unfit to fly unclassified and brown
between the instructions for use in the

dream of arabian tuesdays on both
banks in the wind-shadows unwinged

in the dust brown dustbeetles everywhere
in every hydraulics in the dream

translated from the German by Donna Stonecipher

⤜ ITALY ⤛

— RAFFAELLO BALDINI (1924–2005) —

The Knife

What is this you brought me? it doesn't cut at all.
Don't just stand there looking at me, go get me another one.
Did you find it? give it to me, come on, we're getting older here.
Damn you, this is worse than the other one,
it's even rusty. Forget it, I'll go myself.
Here, hold it, can't you? are your hands crap or what?
grab it by the ears and hold it still,
or it'll spray blood all over and make a mess.

translated from Romagnolo dialect by Marella Feltrin-Morris

Picking

Go ahead, you pick, it makes absolutely no difference to me,
they should too, I'm not just saying it,
go ahead and pick, for me any of them are just fine.
You like this one? take it then.
Or this one? you're not sure? you like both?
take them both, there's plenty.
Only one? whatever you want, think about it, no rush, this one?
me? what do you want me to say, you're the one who's got to like it,
my opinion is that I think it looks like a good one, you think so too?
so take it then.
And the rest of you, don't just stand there frozen in place,
first you're laughing, and now you're all stressed out?
pick whichever one you want, I haven't even given it a thought,
they're all the same to me, do I have to draw you a picture?
But you, you're not set anymore? I can see it in your face,
you're having second thoughts? you want to make a change?
what are you looking at? show me, you want that one?
go on, put back the other one, you know you've really got a good eye.
So now, everyone's picked?
And this one's left for me, well, just look what's inside here,
I hadn't even given it a second thought,
you know what I've got to say to all of you?
that if I'd been the one with first choice this is the one I'd have picked.

But then again, really, they're all nice.
At any rate, we're all even, one for everyone,
no bickering, you're looking at me, you're not happy?
you want this one?

translated from Romagnolo dialect by Adria Bernardi

— GIAMPIERO NERI (b. 1927) —

[seeing him again had not been pleasant.]

seeing him again had not been pleasant.
In spite of all the water under the bridge,
those names would reemerge,
the Cremonese, the Cook,
the Mountaineer, the Owl,
the Midget, and the other ones on the lists.
He had been caught at the bottom of the net,
the only one of that crowd.
He worked as guardian at a zoo,
accustomed to life's uncertainties,
and his looks hadn't changed much.
During breaks from his work,
in an almost barren field
he farmed a small number of snails,
mollusks that fear water.
You shall put them alive—he told me—
in a mixture of milk and rye,
and when they are well fed, cook them.

translated from the Italian by Marella Feltrin-Morris

Overlappings

I.

Tilting his head back, the guest imitated the call of an owl. A short note,
almost like a bark, or a cough.
He had a thinning beard, and large, yellowish eyes.

II.

Floating in the air, lighter than the air, the eagle owl's feather lingered.
Gray, lined with black streaks.

III.

Its Latin name is Bubo bubo.
From the dwarf owlet to the large eagle owl, the philosophical family proceeds.

IV.

The eagle owl or Smintheus, a mouse destroyer, is said to be rare. It lives
in deserted woods, but stumbling upon its stern stare, its
ruffled feathers, can be unsettling.

V.

Trading lumber is a common practice in the mountains. The trunks
of fir trees are chopped. Log piles for reducing to sheets and wood chips.
An eagle owl once flew into one of these warehouses, perhaps chasing a mouse.
It was found the following day, powdered with dust, stupefied.

VI.

About its sound, keok, keok, its call, teck, teck.
They proceed from their original form, without changes.
Signs from a lost world.
Sometimes at night one can hear a shrill call, an agitated sound.

VII.

About its literature.
Owls, by Sparks and Soper, and an old edition of David Copperfield with
a dedication dated November 1944.

VIII.

It alighted on the majestic branch of a plane tree.

IX.

In conversation, we would casually talk about it. The tenant
had seen it land on a branch, then idly fly away. Was it an owlet or an owl?
The apparition, unique in its kind, would never reoccur, and the
question remained hanging, like many others.

translated from the Italian by Marella Feltrin-Morris

[I believe I should have a child:]

I believe I should have a child:
who looks at me from the unmade bed and smiles
while I listen to a distant heavenly
dreamy music. . . . The door
opened onto the infinite, and an infinite
prayer. Calm words
whispered in the open wind
of a dark night. I look at you,
son, sleeping serenely,
in colorful exultation, camouflaged
in red blankets, on a white couch
a little blue hat on your head
to cover your short hair cut
like a prep school boy or a soldier.

Only me, I alone look at you,
son, not bearing any gifts for you
today on the occasion of your sixteenth
birthday. I can only manage
a few stifled virtues to soothe you
in a future that no death,
no matter how untouchable, shall brush
with its hooked horrid hand.

translated from the Italian by Peter Covino

[I licked you between dirty sheets,]

I licked you between dirty sheets,
I explored your body, submerged
refuge of my refused sex
your body was smooth, tender
a restless refuge, quick
to penetrate my body.

Now the tricks next to the long
river are not enough, ragged fishermen
possible assassins, indolent
and mutable position in the bed;

I miss you in spirit
and in primitive sweetness,
folded sex, fresh
boy like food
to eat hungrily.

translated from the Italian by Peter Covino

— MAURIZIO CUCCHI (b. 1945) —

Letter and Prayer

I will lick your face like a dog
I will dry your face with a kiss.

Dear lost Luigi
today you are more tender, defenseless brother
in my mutated thoughts.
Your skin is white, like paper,
and I write on it.
This is my greeting and the sacrifice
of the soul will be lighter.
On the blessed silence of a field
the shadow of the last word rests.
Peace be with you nevertheless,
and with those who kept quiet. We are
the body accustomed to suffering.

translated from the Italian by Peter Covino

[From the Cairo to Loreto]

From the Cairo to Loreto
a short walk, holding each other, along the boulevard
and I was in her belly.
They were hesitant and exchanged smiles
more tender than restless.
Il Duce was already hanged,
but toward Piazza Argentina
with the chaos and the crowd in turmoil
she said, "Luigi,
let's go back home."

translated from the Italian by Peter Covino

[He left throwing us]

He left throwing us
into sudden bewilderment.
In a bag at the police station
there were checks, a comb
a wrist band.

Good-bye, I say now without trembling
I have saved you, listen to me.
I leave you the best of my heart
and with the kiss of gratitude,
this overwhelming serenity.

translated from the Italian by Peter Covino

[Why do you breathe on my head?]

Why do you breathe on my head?
Maybe you are this small figure,
with the clear dress, horizontal, haloed?
But who preserved you, what brings you here,
with your enormous glory?
He who is a prisoner—you say—looks for an escape,
it's his right.

Even as I did, out there . . .

Perhaps you are mere vibrations,
you are in the vibrations of the brain . . .
But where did you put it, little soul
your beautiful mandrake?

In these walls
there's no smell of piss,
carbonic acid, and putrefaction,
as there is in your ancient ones,
and certainly I will remain halfway there,
or even farther. Incomplete.
There are no flights of filthy bats
here. Nor rats all teeth and tails.
In the white of my uniform, of this suit,
fleas do not nest.

I too would like to say: I'll go
even if I had to wear out my feet and legs all the way to the knees!

translated from the Italian by Peter Covino

At Vacation's End

At vacation's end from the train see
who still plays and bathes on the beach
their vacation isn't over yet:
will it be like this will it be like this
to leave this life?

translated from the Italian by Peter Covino

To Pasolini

What a blue sky see it's cleared
in honor of the anniversary
of your murder.
A perfect day for a game
of soccer see? Or is it that from there
nothing at all can be seen
nothing? Don't you feel what a strong wind
just kicked up? With a wind like that
the soccer ball probably escaped you
blown away like you from us that day.
It's some November with the colors of April
we're here alone with you Pasolini
with your death.

translated from the Italian by Peter Covino

Little Girl

With the satin stitch
with the cross stitch
diligent she sewed her lips
she tied the knot.

translated from the Italian by Cinzia Sartini Blum and Lara Trubowitz

The Lady of the Snow

It snowed so much, a lady loved a gentleman
  so dearly.
The snow settled on the city, the love of the lady
  settled on the gentleman.
It snowed day and night, day and night
  the lady loved the gentleman.
The city and the gentleman, semi-submerged, immobile
  endured the snow and love, waiting for spring.

translated from the Italian by Cinzia Sartini Blum and Lara Trubowitz

— PATRIZIA CAVALLI (b. 1947) —

[To simulate the burning of the heart, the humiliation]

To simulate the burning of the heart, the humiliation
of the viscera, to flee cursed
and cursing, to hoard chastity
and to cry for it, to keep my mouth
from the dangerous taste of other mouths
and push it unfulfilled to fulfill itself with the poisons of food,
in the apotheosis of dinner when the already
swollen belly continues to swell;
to touch unreachable solitude and there
at the foot of the bed, a chair
or the stairs to recite a good-bye,
so that I can expel you from my fantasy
and cover you with ordinary clouds
so that your light will not fade my path,
will not muddle my circle from which
I send you, you unintentional star,
unexpected passage who reminds me of death.

For all this I asked you for a kiss
and you, kind and innocent accomplice, didn't give it to me.

translated from the Italian by Judith Baumel

[The rain brings me back]

The rain brings me back
the dispersed pieces
of my friends, it presses down
flights too high, it slows down escapes and closes
on the side of the window, finally,
time.

translated from the Italian by Judith Baumel

[Almost always he who is content is also vulgar;]

Almost always he who is content is also vulgar;
in contentment there is a thought
that's hurried and doesn't have time to look
but moves ahead self-contained and maniacal
and bears contempt toward those who die
—Move ahead with life, come on, cheer up!

He who is fixed in grief should not frequent
the cheerful and carefree runners
but only those who walk equally slow.
If one wheel jams and the other turns
the one that turns does not stop turning
but advances as much as it can dragging the other
in a weak and crooked race
until the cart either stops or topples.

translated from the Italian by Peter Covino

— FRANCO BUFFONI (b. 1948) —

[Techniques of criminal investigation]

Techniques of criminal investigation
Are being applied, Oetzi, to your hair
By the analysts of the Bundeskriminalamt in Wiesbaden.
Following fifty centuries of peace
In the deep freeze of Similaun
They are studying the message in your genes
And analyzing the remnants of your clothes,

Four animal hides stuffed with grass
That you'd pressed to your breast in the storm.
You were dark, you had begun to suffer from
The early stages of arthrosis
In the thirty-second century before Christ
You were thirty-five years old.
I'd like to shelter you in a tent
To give you a bit of warmth
And tea and biscuits.

They say that you might have been a bandit,
And in Munich they are working
On the parasites you were carrying yourself,
And that you had retained sperm in your rectum:
You are in Münster
And the laboratories of IBM in Mainz
For organic chemistry analysis.
I see you again with a pink triangle
Behind the barbed wire.

> *translated from the Italian by Michael Palma*

[If you don't know what it means in English to maroon]

If you don't know what it means in English to maroon
Think of a runaway black slave
He's a maroon
And through one of those semantic
Conversions that are the jewel of languages
To maroon someone
Means on the contrary actively to abandon him
Especially on an island. A desert island.
The verb as is clear goes back to the eighteenth century
And the classic example which is equally clear
Cites Jan Svilt, homosexual sailor marooned.
The verb is regular.

> *translated from the Italian by Michael Palma*

from **Winter Dwellings**

Our souls should be sleeping
the way thin bodies sleep
lying between sheets like a page
hair behind the ears
ears open
fit for listening. Flesh
sharp and brittle, hollow
in the darkness of the room. Light bone.
In the same way the membrane binds
feathers to an angel's shoulder.

The ears of the sick are transparent,
the color of window panes
yet they still hear
the rolling of the beds as they are moved
by the arms of the living.

At four o'clock, on holidays
visiting time ends. Slowly
their faces turn to the walls.
In the empty hallways, an aquarium-like peace falls.
Azure lights from overhead and below,
above the doors,
on the edge of the stairs.

Nocturnal lights.
The sick sleep one
next to the other
laid on identical beds.
The only difference is the way
they bend their knees
if their knees
still bend, the difference
in the way their covers rise.
Few are able to sit up straight,
as would the bedridden at home
and each bed has large-toothed metal wheels,
springs that snap,
locking the mattress into place

or suddenly raising it.
The bed squeaks then falls quiet.

Christmas lights.
The ward is a plain of imperceptible mounds.
With silent bows, the thoughts of the dead pass each other by.

Winter lights.
In the staff room, tinfoil glimmers,
the scent of wine floats into the air.
If the living leaned their faces close to the fogged windows,
if they stuck their tongues out slightly,
the air would taste of wine.
There's a moment before dying
the night turns like a key.
Such mysterious signs the streetlights make to the dying,
how many shadows their bodies cast.

Ten o'clock. On the tablecloth, a rabbit collapsed
beside boiled potatoes, strained asparagus in casserole.
In the room, a solemn misery reigns.

The living call out to one another as if from faraway ships.

translated from the Italian by Chad Davidson

Earth

Round, frozen in its oceans, transparent
like a cell under the microscope
or horizontal with mountains planted firmly above fields
with the tongue of rivers and the stretched-out sea.

Every now and then I have an inkling of vertigo:
we're turning faster. Asleep, I cry out, "I'm falling"
and then I feel space, blackness, the stars at the nape of my neck,
fear which vomits forth a thousand spheres.

"Oh, that would be hell" you say and doze off.
So I meditate on hell. It's enough if the curtain's weight
tugs the rings along the glass . . . with precision I see:
the marching of a line of ants, the vast starry night.

I try to take hold of hell by its border
(a strip of black, emptiness, fear)

to make it whirl in the courtyard as the fir tree does in the sky
to become the insect that I've always been:
that's born and forgets itself in the air.

translated from the Italian by Jamie McKendrick

— VALERIO MAGRELLI (b. 1957) —

[I have often imagined that glances]

I have often imagined that glances
survive the act of seeing
as if they were poles,
measuring rods, lances
thrown in a battle.
Then I think that in a room
one has just left
those same lines must stay behind
sometimes suspended there and crisscrossed
untouched and overlaid like the wooden pieces
in a game of pick-up-sticks.

translated from the Italian by Dana Gioia

[I have from you this red]

> *And the crack in the teacup opens*
> *A lane to the land of the dead.*
> —W. H. AUDEN

> *—as when a crack*
> *crosses a cup.*
> —R. M. RILKE

I have from you this red
cup with which to drink to all my days
one by one
in the pale mornings, the pearls
of the long necklace of thirst.
And if it drops and breaks, I , too,
will be shattered, but compassionately
I will repair it

to continue the kisses uninterrupted.
And each time the handle
or the rim gets cracked
I will go back to glue it
until my love will have completed
the hard, slow work of mosaic.

It comes down along the white
slope of the cup
along the concave interior
and flashes, just like lightning—
the crack,
black, permanent,
the sign of a storm
still thundering
over this resonant landscape
of enamel.

translated from the Italian by Dana Gioia

[Evenings, when the light dims]

Evenings, when the light dims
and I lie hidden in bed,
I gather outlines of ideas
that flow over the silence of my limbs.
It's here I must weave
thought's tapestry,
arrange my own strands
use myself to draw my own figure.
This isn't work
but workmanship.
Of the page, then of the body.
To evoke thought's form,
measure and fit it.
I think of a tailor
who is his own fabric.

translated from the Italian by Anthony Molino

An Italian Evening

The checkered tablecloth in the white
light.
And in the evening.
      It would be enough to see
         it is evening,
see it at all the tables
of the building
half littered from dinner
or empty with only the remote control
reflected in the blank screen.

It would be enough for the fists clenched without a glass
to open—
    suddenly
they would turn over to beg
beating on the table
and on the flat bone of loneliness.

        One would see
many men,
many men with their heads bent, thick
tongues,
   silent before the screen, in the white light,
of the evening.
Her goat muzzle, spring would
put it in those hands to graze,
confident.

translated from the Italian by Gabriele Poole

Michelangelo's Pietà, Carriage

Riding back from Rome one
must pass through tunnels,
     many spells of darkness, flashes, strange
fractures of the light.
And the silences of the body in these fast trains

One can hardly recognize one's face
in the flash immortalizing it on the glass,
the magnesium eyes of years.

The fellow who for the whole trip
stares at the closed bag in front of him,
the girl with dyed hair
and pierced lip
who wants to tell her life story to a stranger.

And the other one, ugly, swollen
with medicines, his hat
pulled over his baldness, is crying
                    or perhaps has cried.

I read in the railway magazine:
                    1498, five hundred years since Michelangelo's Pietà—
and I see that restless abandonment
                    the long arms,
white, the mother looking
so much like a young girl, God's body asleep
in that rapt whiteness.

Matter
that cannot believe in itself—
just like these travelers,
in the sleep that magnifies
the evening carriages.

  translated from the Italian by Marella Feltrin-Morris

⤞ MALTA ⤝

— IMMANUEL MIFSUD (b. 1967) —

The Day of the Dead (in Bratislava)

If you were here, I'd ask you to recite
whole chapters that now are buried with dust.
Then I might have some clue as to how
I'd found my way to this unlit station.
From which no train is ever going to leave.
From which no footstep leads me away.

If you were here today, you could color in
the blank map by which I was led alone
through the streets, the blind corners I turned
so that now I've arrived at this precise spot.
I've no idea how to pull myself out of here.

My blood, the fairground where ghouls hang out.

translated from the Maltese by Maurice Riordan

The Twentieth of September

They stream out of the accordion like youngsters
with long curly hair down to their ankles.
And they go out into the wind on the open sea
and count the waves coming to rest at their feet.

They stream out of the accordion like pensioners,
their eyes dejected and bleary-red.
They walk and walk on the road to tomorrow.

They stream out like nameless notes.
And I'm like the one you can barely hear.

Like a note that has no wish to end.

translated from the Maltese by Maurice Riordan

⤐ ROMANIA ⤏

— DANIEL BĂNULESCU (b. 1960) —

You'll Shrivel Up You'll Be an Exotic Fruit

There's no need to forgive you
Because as soon as I fall asleep you'll no longer exist for me

You don't have to move or sigh
Or whimper in every last wisp of your cells
Because as soon as I fall asleep
You'll no longer exist for me

Turn over a new self to your fetching tail to your tomatoes
Be proud satisfied with your friends distinguished in society
Act as if from tomorrow on
It would take an earthquake to get you to lift your skirt
And only spaded earth would give you back part of what you've lost
Be reasonable
You've such beautiful hands that haven't yet wised up
And never will
Lips the bulldozer driver won't ever know thoughts the carpenter won't ever hear
Breasts the gravedigger won't ever lay eyes on

Who'll prepare you and wash you
Who'll place the small coin in your mouth
Who'll slip you in my pocket
Where's your soul
And where now is your sweat
The Scala patisserie window steamed over
I'll send a madman to wind you up with just one finger
Until you'll no longer bore any window

You bored me
You're just a tuft of dwarf vegetation my imagination plucked a grille
Through which my gaffes ogle you as if you were a giraffe
You're graced with dresses spice cake and flesh
But as soon as I fall asleep you'll no longer exist for me
You're no more than a gesture someone once made to me
Someone who drank all of life with me
You're the thought of my socks stuffed with my feet
Like an out-of-work man's breast crammed full of work songs

translated from the Romanian by Adam J. Sorkin and Alina Savin

Bloody Bad Shit

I've never lived as if I could taste blood, even when I got kicked in the kisser. Only swarms of mosquitoes hung around to applaud my écarté over the muddy Bahlui. And what the hell's the point of living like that? At night in the industrial zone of the city, not a soul anywhere the whole long way to the city limits. An electric hum above your head for miles and miles, potholes in the road, eyes of neon and Freon. Hunchbacked tram rails in the middle of the highway. Not a trace of Coşovei's electric snow in the industrial zone. You walk to the edge of town, and if you feel like it, you walk on and on, through the marshes and over the hill until you reach Bessarabia.

I'm standing in the gas station listening to the streetlight above my head. I swat mosquitoes on my face. If they've already bitten me, blood spurts out. No way does this mean I've come close to living as if I could taste blood. I've read two famous texts written in Iaşi about blood buzzing around a room inside a mosquito's guts. Usually it's bitter cold here. The Russians shove Siberian ice cubes against your prostate. Half the year you have to wear boots, wrapped in a warm muffler. The faint light of the bulbs sprinkles tiny needles of orange ice over the belt of the city. Iaşi is made mainly of belts. Slender, on the point of breaking apart, it hangs in a sado-maso harness of poorly lit belts. With train-station buckles. Nicolina Station, International Station, Central Station, North Station: a Monopoly city. Whores in every belt hole. Hoarfrost glittering on their silver blouses, but no mosquitoes. Blood, whirlpools of blood and cream, but no mosquitoes. Gasoline fumes, a mirage shimmering far down the road. When it's cold, not even that.

I once became mired in the marshes just past the industrial zone. I was going fishing with friends. We knew nothing about fishing, but it was summer. The day was hot. They pushed old Blanchette. With her varicose tires, nervously, she spattered them with mud. Soft and warm. Two months each year, the belts of Iaşi melt into the city's flesh. The mosquito larvae grow fragile antennas. I wanted to compare these antennas to something, but it turned out stupid. "Antenna" in itself sounds dumb. You can feel how the image gets suffocated by trash in an apartment building stairwell. "Cable" is just about as bad. Moreover, you can't say, "The mosquito larvae grow monaxial cables." Well, in truth, you can. And with toenail clippers you can cut the cables. The antennas. You can torment the mosquitoes along the banks of the Bahlui. You can create discomfort.

I told several groups of my students about the boiled rat in the washing machine, pulverized between the steel of the drum and my family's linens. "That's sickening," they told me. An incorrect image. Politically. (Not all of them would lose the color from their cheeks. But they weren't living as if they could taste blood, either. Their eyeballs, like their blood cells, are the colorless color of barely lit asphalt in fall. Their existential varix is as black as a prune. They seem extra-sensitive to cold and to the future. They float on the other half of the biscuit, by the Nicolina Market, on the opposite side of the bridge near the packing plant where meat is sold at half price, though not many people know about it, so there won't be a mass pilgrimage to the frozen relics of the animals. In fact, my students' cheeks are bright even though they rarely eat meat. With faces of a deep purple, they would sing, *I've been mistreated.* Man, they treated me like shit here in Iaşi.)

From underneath the dining hall on the Maiorescu (formerly Pushkin) campus there comes a smell of methane. On the terrace, the loud, crude Turkish beat of the *manele*. October. October in the navel. A universal navel, a boundless navel. Only a moron would say you should live as if you could taste blood and you should leap over the lips of the navel. You can dump truckloads of cannonballs into the navel, you can spit into it. Bubbles of saliva, like fish eggs without DNA. No, *with* DNA, Eugene corrects me. You spit DNA. A salmon neglecting to sacrifice himself upstream. A kick in the kisser, guts and gore, never living as if you could taste blood. I haven't any idea where the others went.

(Subject: here comes the nastiest part
Date: Fri, 06 Oct 2000 16:53:26 +0000
From: Radu Andriescu <Crazyescu@>
To: Dan Ursachi <MusaBadge@>

Badge, last night really ate shit. I danced the *manele* with the gypsies in my neighborhood at an Internet café, a huge black wolf almost bit off my balls, and I sprained my other ankle. Today I've got to attend a memorial service. Really bad shit, couldn't be worse, you can just about taste it.)

translated from the Romanian by Adam J. Sorkin and the author

— RUXANDRA CESEREANU (b. 1963) —

The Killer

She can't. The woman. Can't.
The fish of her heart no longer breathes.
Its scales seep red, stain the moonlight.
She kills her machinery of birth,
her frenzied thighs rising as high as the sky,
her nights and days ripped to rags.
Sinful but alive,

light camouflaged under her skin like ground glass,
she stays in the tunnel.
A girl sleeps an arsenic sleep
in the emergency room.
Killer, I lick the oily heart's honeycomb from my lips!
Your face strobed by sleep's flicker,
you flee through the garden, smeared with rain,
and strike against the buoy.
Old tigress, you who kill behind bars, you've fled.
You know He can see you from aloft—
God the Plush, God the Slasher.
Like a mad nun, you wander,
your head pungent with blood,
deposits of blood you can smell
all the way from the kingdom of heaven.
The believers adore you with their eyes, tongues lolling,
drooling Pavlovian dogs.
Devoid of grace, you yourself are a topsy-turvy chapel.
You descend upon them like a spider at sunset.
On your bosom, black lilies.
Your teeth, white as tombstones,
purify altars and famed steeples.
The hooves of the murdered stampede over my body,
dripping musk, crippling me.
Killer, from your throat a dying city rattles its death rattle.
The silence grinds out luminescence in lambent silence.
I should sip champagne. Cross myself.

*translated from the Romanian by Adam J. Sorkin and Claudia Litvinchievici
with the author*

— MIHAIL GĂLĂȚANU (b. 1963) —

At the Virgin's Breast

I. My First Love

My first love was the icons.
When I was a small child, I'd bring my lips close to the Virgin Mary, for I was just
    like Jesus.
The obscurity of the background seemed so obvious to me.
Now, I don't know why, it doesn't seem that way.

My heart was so placid and clear, it flowed.
At that time I was afraid, ashamed to speak about my love.
I'm really saying, you discover such simple things much too late, sometimes not
    till old age.
But you're heading toward them.
That's why my first love was the icons
and my small lips sucked at Mary's nipples where
she holds the child to her breast.
To be in love with the Virgin wasn't sacrilege
but on the contrary adoration,
which you'll never feel later.

Oh, and how I bit my new teeth into the Virgin's teat!
She only beamed at me!
Her milk splashed my face.
The Virgin's breast was so heavy with milk.

II. Noli Me Tangere

The icon in front of the altar was tall, nearly a meter and a half,
and I measured my height against it.
The Virgin Mary made me a sign from there,
overjoyed because I was able to get closer and closer to her,
as if behind the glass.

She let me caress her all over.
She pressed her cheek to mine.
Later, scholars challenged me in endless debates
about profanation, sin, the Virgin Mary's breasts.
Noli me tangere, they kept saying that this portion of her All-Holy body
screamed at me.

"Why do you go on interrogating me?" I protested. "Devils, pharisees, betrayers,
why do you doubt my love and put it up for sale?"

I couldn't lend an ear to their rubbish. I said, "The Holy Virgin's breast, you
    damn fools,
is nothing other than
the altar screen on which our world is propped.
And, before all things, my world."

III. Why I Never Found My Mate

My first love, it's a fact,
was the icons

which were too high to touch and kiss. I groped my way toward them.
I aspired to grow as tall as the breast of the Giant
Virgin and to lap up the light
that poured down the painting from above, as in a church.

Sex is a mystical substitute—I understood this later. As things stand,
Saint Virgin Mary was my beloved, too.
Now I understand whom Jesus loved his entire lifetime
and why there was no room for any other woman in his life.

He was the baby pledged to his Beloved. He cuddled
only with His Trinity. Only with the Holy Ghost did he unite.

Oh, yeah, yeah, this is why it's hard for you to find your mate, my mother
would tell me. Too many icons luring you to pray
are budding their thighs in your mind.

translated from the Romanian by Adam J. Sorkin and the author

— SIMONA POPESCU (b. 1965) —

Madi's Laugh

Madi was the nickname of Mariana Marin (1956–2003)

"It's like I'm some kind of old poet,
just a few people visit me," she says from the other end of the line
with her wounded voice
interrupted by a kind of snort as though she was laughing
like she always did—always!—when
there was nothing to laugh at.

Then she said something about
"this postmodernism bullshit," but I didn't understand exactly if
she wanted to say that postmodernism was bullshit or if it was bullshit
because idiots talk about it
who don't know anything and talk all the same . . .
And then she told me about a girl, a niece of hers she said her parents left her
with her and this girl turned and said:
            "Now, TRANSFORM!"
I told her that *on TV* there was a cartoon—she didn't know—where all kinds of
things say
        "I WILL TRANSFORM!" or something
    and they change shape like this:
    wwwwwwooooaaaap! and bam, See ya!

I didn't know at the time that
Madi would die in two months
the day after we met with Richard W.
and she asked me how I was and I said: "You know, I'm teaching this kind of
seminar about contemporary poetry at the university and
it's awful,
to see them.
You're better off, Madi,
that you don't see them,
that you don't see."
"Hey"—she said—"I write.
Like I care if they don't care. Not my problem."
That's what I loved about her!
That's what I loved about her!

Too bad you never heard her laugh . . .
Basically, it's too bad you never heard her laugh
(sarcastic and tender at the same time
like she was sorry
like she was scared of something
her own courage, maybe, ALL OF IT).
And then, not three days later,
a little, hardworking machine with Bobcat written on it (Bob cat!)
shoveled earth down over her.

translated from the Romanian by Sean Cotter

— SAVIANA STĂNESCU (b. 1967) —

The Infanta Augustina

they took augustina to the fair
with gaily colored spikes they hung her
in the corner of a wooden booth and put
a red circle between her breasts step right up
ladies and gentlemen and try your luck
five points if you shoot the horse ten for the knight
fifteen for the castle gate and one hundred
that's right one hundred points—THE GRAAAND PRIZE
for a bullet in infanta's chest
show your stuff champ ready the rifle steady

against your shoulder take aim fire count how many
eyes wink half-open between augustina's
breasts BINGO that's a hit her legs flail about
her head her arms oh mama
look at the queen jitterbug
this plush teddy bear for the little guy
in the man-size cap hey big shot you're next come on
who wants to take a pop you get
one hundred points for the infanta
it's not difficult to hit her all you've gotta do
is squeeze the trigger when
she screams *nooo* with women this always
means *yessss*

> *translated from the Romanian by Adam J. Sorkin, Aura Sibişan, and the author*

The Infanta Margherita

noble gentlemen come hear my sad tale
blond margherita has been put under lock and key
shut tight in a music box its walls lined
with finest silk they nailed her foot
to the gold velvet floor
round and round she turns crying *mar-ghe-ri-ta*
people laugh how cute how cute
she longed to run away but they drove another nail
through her hand then chained her to the ceiling
she yearned to move freely but they crucified her
on a metal arch no longer can she dance round and round
mar-ghe-ri-ta still how cute how cute
now she goes *pop* when you open the top
such a silly a clown with fake tresses
and a smile smeared across her face the blond buffoon
springs up just-like-that from her brocaded hoopskirt
swaying like an idiot you'll find it hard
to believe that this eyesore a scarecrow in a box
once upon a time had a name
mar-ghe-ri-ta

> *translated from the Romanian by Adam J. Sorkin, Aura Sibişan, and the author*

The Barren Woman

the barren woman imagines she's giving birth
she twists in the sheets and heaves herself about
she sprawls spraddling her legs against the wall
she thrusts and convulses
runs rivers of sweat
and calls me by name
she even gives birth to me
only she feels how the unseen crown of my head
bursts out through her sex unreceptive to seed
only she hears me gasp and squall
she gnaws my umbilical cord of shadow
and she fondles my head and body
with eager hands

the barren woman licks her faceless whelp
her skinless heartless cub
only she strokes me and knows me
and suckles me on her nut-like pap
I nurse without a sound
and then let slip the delicate nipple and fall asleep
baring my gums and teeth of mist

translated from the Romanian by Adam J. Sorkin and Radu Andriescu

11 May 1998

every so often I'll watch the balls rolling across the green velvet (there's a metaphysical something in the play of spheres—I once occupied myself with the game I even achieved a certain popularity because I could make a couple of shots considered impossible—we agreed to call them "tangents"—though it's true I'd often goof up the mickey-mouse shots which meant I wasn't really a good player) I sipped from my glass and from my cigarette I spoke a few words and gave the impression I was listening to a few words   you were cold I took off my black sweater and you put it on I envied it fair and square as a lucky rival   miss zöld glanced in boredom at her watch tossed her long black hair wavy and lustrous glanced again so shameless and exciting that her clothes evaporated   my friend ogoniochika her head shaved to zero sweetened the evening with a moldavian accent (I'd find it very agreeable to curl up inside her uterus)   a poet who had no name would now bring vodka would next go out for cigarettes   I wondered how tuone udaina felt speaking dalmatian to himself in a summer garden I sniffed you secretly as if my prey   as if a flower as if

the light   what good to pick you what good to let you be   your laughter teased
my indecision   your delicate shadow loomed enormous against the dutch dikes

translated from the Romanian by Adam J. Sorkin and Bogdan Ştefănescu

— IOANA NICOLAIE (b. 1974) —

Suspended

Loneliness is when
you hear the whine of motors
in the sole dining room
that's yours for now
            with curtains of club moss
                and your life in the split waistcoats
                    of the balconies
in jackets with clasps made of pins
and liver reminding you of hepatitis
with green seeds

it's when your hair
is half cut
or much too wet and falls straight
            at a touch

it's when you scrub the tub
and feel its warmth
near the steep back
near the barleycorns in that lifeless place
you can't retrace your steps
there it is
but you can't reach it
the mists of such happenstance
so flimsy and attenuated

loneliness is a washing machine
it's the tiny shy square buttons of the interphone
it's this sky like the enamel of a pot

it's the arched midpoint of the silence
that I always bear with me
like bells after mass
in a small mountain town.

translated from the Romanian by Adam J. Sorkin and Irma Giannetti

As Big as China

and we perched on the damp stone benches
old newspapers under our asses
one of us said hey I really want to make myself
a necklace of cigarette butts

that was sometime in '95
because after we emptied the second bottle
we balanced it on the first
and the bottle didn't fall

then a girl with a violin showed up
she knew just one tune
and she played it for us twice

boredom as big as china someone said
let's polish them and hang them around our necks someone said

translated from the Romanian by Adam J. Sorkin with Radu Andriescu

Tenderly Caressed Sucked Licked and Spanked

I don't think I've ever been on better terms with myself
or ever written better
than when I was fifteen every day I used to commit
several pages of pornographic writing before going to bed
only, only for personal use

I don't know if you can imagine what went on in those little tales
but I can tell you that in their every word
I was tenderly caressed sucked licked and spanked
by dozens of women men children animals
who all thanked me for existing
there was no love between us only what
I'd call perfect
communication

translated from the Romanian by Adam J. Sorkin with Radu Andriescu

MOLDOVA

— EMILIAN GALAICU-PĂUN (b. 1964) —

Pietà (Ivy on the Cross)

ivy on the cross: vegetal blood
through arms spread wide
powerless, paralyzed
look at their veins, bulging,
bluish green: wooden crosses
the ancient aristocracy of cemeteries

ivy on the cross: passionate, sainted
Magdalene winding around the foot
of the stiff crucifix: from the cross
Jesus, nailed fast, stares transfixed by
her lithe body in which God
discovers Himself—*Aletheia!*—in the process
of photosynthesis: more air

for the cemetery (only six feet lies
underground—the rest rises in the open air
from the grass on the graves as high as
heaven: nothing but cemetery)

in spring: pious widows
keep coming to whitewash the arms
of the cross, which is bleeding (every March
the cemetery caretaker,
deeply religious, prunes
the green fingers like young branches
of both arms of the cross,
as he believes sacred and proper:
that each cross remain
a cross crucified in and of itself)

ivy on the cross: it doesn't want to know
about the caretaker, it doesn't want to know anything
Magdalene-ivy taking
each cross of fresh wood
for the Savior in the flesh

crucified upon Himself, ivy-
Magdalene winding around His arms
year after year—until one day they fall
to the earth's lap: *difficult is*

the descent of the cross from the cross.

translated from the Romanian by Adam J. Sorkin and Stefania Hirtopanu

— ALEXANDRU VAKULOVSKI (b. 1978) —

Amputated Homeland

in this town everyone is
unhappy on this earth
there is quiet before an
explosion yes my love I'm leaving
I am leaving across the earth
of my homeland
there everyone lives out the pleasure
of not knowing
the pleasure of losing
of not being run over by
a car of raising
unhappy children of
eating and not barfing
(*sorry,* vomiting) not once
I am leaving my love
my homeland is where
I am
love love love
you made me happy
you made me forget everything
I will never forget that
not once
I'm leaving

translated from the Romanian by Sean Cotter

Bessarabia go home

yes, that's better
the last time we saw
each other you were sad that I was leaving
but you still left first
I waved to you
when the bus took off
I pulled the posters of Jim
off the wall
I packed
and thought of you
nibbles on your ear
scratches on your back
I drank and promised you
that I wouldn't smoke grass
I promised that everything
would be great how great it would be
if I could take care of you
you said
yes and we went down
the stairs and on the wall I
saw *Bessarabia go home*
and I swore and punched the wall
and I said
I'll be back

> *translated from the Romanian by Sean Cotter*

⤐ GREECE ⟊

— YIORGOS CHOULIARAS (b. 1951) —

Occupied City

The headlights of the military vehicles
stain the white walls of the firing squads

I am pushed by photographers' flashes
deeper into the darkness of history

In the light of the kneeling black dresses
in the damp embrace of the earth
as bruised bodies are being washed

A bar of soap slides in its furrow, rolls over;
upon it one day
surely the regime will slip

translated from the Greek by David Mason and the author

Refugees

On the back
of the photograph I write to remember
not where and when but who

I am not in the picture

They left us nothing
to take along
Only this photograph

If you turn it over you will see me

I am asked, Are you in the picture?
I don't know what to tell you

translated from the Greek by David Mason and the author

Borges in Crete

We led him exactly to the point
where he imagined he had started.
The stones were fiercely hot in the ruins

as the sun now penetrated everywhere
an enduringly uncovered past.
Here is where the labyrinth must have been,
he told himself lost in thoughts
no longer broken by the light.
We looked without seeing.
Here it must have been totally dark
just like now, I can see it,
he was saying while the cicadas noisily
sharpened the horns of the bull.
We were probably talking among ourselves
when with his hand tightly—just like then
had they been able to see him—
on the thread which no one even now
could see, if it existed,
he must have found his way to the exit.
Because we lost sight of him
for a moment, blinded as we were
by the sun in the mythical mirror
helping into flight the real
reflection of a world of illusion.

translated from the Greek by David Mason and the author

Pencil in the Bread

bread sweet bread, bitter bread, of society and of the
confined, bread of my mother and my father, bread of
the earth, a dried-up slice, with klarina or a
saxophone only, bread of exile and of your homeland,
bread of the hungry and the insatiable, bread of the
fool and the unjust, syllabic bread, holy bread, of the
dead and of the courageous, raisin-bread, chleba, nan,
bread shared four ways, consecrated bread, true bread,
bread of fairy tales, white and black, moist bread and
dry, wedding bread, unleavened, bread of the cook,
hungry bread, of my sister, bread of angels, quotidian,
bread from wheat and from corn, rice bread, musical
notes of sliced bread, bread of food, bread with
butter, bread and olives, bread and salt, bread of
words, bread of good and bad poets, and those who make
their bread from words, ironic bread, bread of love and

of the spasms of sharp little teeth in double-bedded
sleep, greedy bread, moldy in the basket, bread of
winter, bread full of summer, lips inflamed by bread,
ah, betrayed bread, daily bread, of the useless baker
of the charlatan, bread

translated from the Greek by David Mason and the author

— LIANA SAKELLIOU (b. 1956) —

The Lion, the Sleeping Woman, and the Island

The Lion:
    Nothing has sunk
    into your skin. Your profile
    hasn't changed. No expression.
    You haven't stepped toward the setting sun,
    only taken its color.
    I could have grabbed you,
    warmed you inside the curves of my legs.
    But you look like a veil
    closing in on itself in sleep,
    helpless, fragile and lost.
    For me, you should know, you're a drab
    piece of landscape, a dead name.
    Let the salt cover me
    so I won't have to see you.

The Sleeping Woman:
    Your words are incoherent to me.
    Uncontained, in the middle of the sea,
    you are wild with loneliness.
    Are you guarding the sea?
    Is this your power?
    Naked. Stark naked.
    And always restless. Why?
    The tides stumble over your feet
    and fishermen let out their nets.
    Where are you looking? We are all here, on this island.
    Listen! Can you hear? People are calling
    from the shoreline, "Welcome!"
    What do you see? What are you waiting for?
    Love me.

The Island:
>They have surrounded me, put me under siege with rocks
>that now have voices.
>It's terrifying to be living among symbols.
>I'm their island. They
>set my boundaries.
>The sun rises from the Lion,
>sets on the Sleeping Woman,
>stops midday at the Clock.
>I'm the Clock, the one who still believes
>in postcards, who rows through enchantment
>striking poses,
>opening only in the expanse of my territorial waters.
>Houses are built, houses decay,
>churches cringe at my personal history.
>But I won't stop exploring their dark rendezvous.
>I keep, as best I can, my distance.
>But the young men turn their prows toward the Lion,
>their breath, like the sirocco, touching his mane.
>And the young women stroll on Saturdays along the harbor,
>seeing only the Sleeping Woman,
>the sun setting on her breasts, her stomach, her gently folded legs,
>safely removed from the Lion's insistent stare.

translated from the Greek by Don Schofield and Harita Meenee

Variations

Seaspray collects
along the corners of the statues' eyes
in all the central ports of the islands;
I cling to objects I can know by touch,
objects that leave their glass boxes and come to me,
each offering, with a wink, its own interpretation.
They become ideas and quietly stroke my cheek.
With smooth, clean fingers
I construct with their help my paper appearance
as if from a child's book of cutouts.

I love the seaspray and the blind statues.
I am not the sea, you are not a local sculptor.
We are touches flowing through a land of fragments.

Dissolved by whatever it touches,
light becomes the skin
of another life. Our hearts enlarge
so we can demand a veil of mist
over the mirror of our earthbound selves.

translated from the Greek by Don Schofield and Harita Meenee

— HARIS VLAVIANOS (b. 1957) —

De Imagine Mundi

For John Ashbery

"How beautiful, how unexpectedly sweet life would be
if we were not obliged to live it . . ."

Yet once things were different.
The messages brought by the seasons
were part of an absolute truth;
the looks, the gestures, the trivial talk
meant something,
the chance indications
these two with their secret conceit confirm
that love is something more
than a game of longing.

A clear sky
or a handsome man
poring over a manuscript
(metaphors concocted to contain us)
can't preserve your face in my memory

can't color the charted area
with the precision this recollection's shadow
demands.

I ask for more
much more.
A living context that's able to accept me,
a density of light that can reveal
imagination's true possibilities
a specific language whose subtlety's
                              command

can give to that dazzle the depth of your
                              beauty.

What power can check the gallop
of the disfigured dream vanishing beyond the horizon
what desire can interpret this decisive
                              gesture
that nothing can interpret?

The day comes to its end.
We have to remain here.
In this silvery haze
    the soul embeds itself.

translated from the Greek by David Connolly

Hotel Athena

> *O bright Apollo,*
> *τιν' άνδρα, τιν'ήρωα, τινα θεόν,*
> *What god, man or hero*
> *Shall I place a tin wreath upon!*
> —EZRA POUND, *HUGH SELWYN MAUBERLEY,* III

We cannot return to this land
because the land is no longer ours.
They've gone,
leaving behind but a few fragments
of a ravaged, exhausted beauty.
And poetry
no matter how many loud-roaring seas it invents,
how many suitors it wipes out,
lacks the power to reconcile
a dying hero with his invented past.

The petrified head of Argos
or a Phemius with a hawk's bill
would be a fine epilogue
to our purposeless, weary wanderings;
a memorable metamorphosis
which Daphne from the taverna next door
would recite for our pleasure,
in her soft, leafy voice.

(written in English)

Gloriana

"Don't love me, but if you love me don't take your arms away."
—RITA HAYWORTH IN *THE LADY FROM SHANGHAI*

Life—and how wonderful it is—
follows our tracks
and slowly disappears
in the depth of our dreams.

Of our dreams.
There's always a way
to talk of these
as if their secret meaning
had been revealed only to you,
though that *only* expresses
quite succinctly
just how little it has.

At first everything seems easy
—almost unavoidable.
On a beach, say,
holding Thomas Hardy's poems
whispering meaningfully in her ear:
"I have lived with Shades so long,"
and later in the hotel room
after the last embarrassing assurances:
"How gentle that candle . . .
It bids farewell to night
wiping away its tears."

Is there any point now in admitting the compact?
In saying or writing
"a love is perhaps but
an exchange of vocabulary,"
when the void that is our due
is already mirrored in the splintered light of
                                    our eyes?

The turning of the page.
The starry darkness of the book
and the agony of the transparent man
in a translated world.

"Words do not fear words;
they fear the poem."
The end is always the beginning
of a new magnificent denial.

translated from the Greek by David Connolly

— MARIGO ALEXOPOULOU (b. 1976) —

Chinese Woman's Spirit

You are white,
losing blood and life.
You stop a taxi.
The driver looks through his mirror.
You are not there.
You leave a sword on the back seat
as payment.
You become holy water,
a yellow airplane,
a toy train.
You take off the mask,
your white dream.
You serve breakfast to Kung Jiang
with your long, aged fingers.
You write love letters
in Minoan script
and leave them on the kitchen table.

translated from the Greek by Roula Konsolaki

Manuscripts of Autumn

As Kalamata spreads out
I show you the brightest path.
In the meantime, father is waiting
quiet and thoughtful
to console me.
"The visitor didn't come," he tells me,
"but you should always remember

the wooden ladder I helped you climb
as a child and the perforated autumn light."

I pack my things hastily.
I feel repressed in here.
The walls have memory.
Silence is electrified.

The moment I go
I want to kiss you.
Stop crying.
Every time you dream you can't be
robbed of your flowerbed,
deprived of the joy of return.

All right, you say to yourself,
after all, I owe nothing to nobody.
I only owe an apology
to memory
and to Ms. Polydouri
while browsing the manuscripts of autumn.

translated from the Greek by Roula Konsolaki

Small Prayer

to Yiannis Ritsos

I asked you to share
bread
and salt with me.
So on Sundays I wouldn't be afraid
of saltiness anymore.

However you sang alone
obscure and unintelligible
tunes.

I only heard you saying
the body,
the body
(where the soul resides).

translated from the Greek by Roula Konsolaki

One Night with Seferis

I saw Seferis in my sleep
holding me in his arms (in my single bed).
His face gave me strength.
He was plump and quiet.
I feared that my father would wake up
and catch me in the act,
sleeping with him.
I whispered to him the first line from one of his poems:
"I'm smoking incessantly since morning."
I complained to him about my surname
which is long and ugly.
He only said:
"He loves you a lot, you've been loved a lot."

translated from the Greek by Roula Konsolaki

⤚ CYPRUS ⤛

— STEPHANOS STEPHANIDES (b. 1949) —

Ars Poetica: Sacred or Daemonic

à tel prix appaiser
Ma chaleur Cyprienne,
—PIERRE DE RONSARD (1524–85), ÉLÉGIE XIX

Do not be deluded
I have a split tongue
Moving between reluctant whispers
An inaudible pulse articulating peace
You know you will never find
In the lull of your dead muses
And the platonic lambda
How to reach pure sound?

No matter if the signs are Greek or Turkish
I lose my way
Even when there is only one way to go
The police sniff and tell me
My hallucination is out of order
And their dogs label me "under control"
I slip away looking for relief
In everlasting summer or everlasting death
And when I find you
I strip you naked
In reckless desire for your disease
(or was that only in my dream?)
I do not know if it's your malady I want
Or if I am diseased by your desire
I negotiate the pullulating mirage
And my body sizzles in my Cyprian heat
And rolls in flames into the blue of the sea
Embers evaporate in the clarity of the moon
And the tempest of the stars
Weaves halos fudging stories
Of roaming phantoms in an overlay of cities
With statues of your damaged fantasy
Who lost their heads and genitals

In impetuous recklessness
Or in the world's tormented ideology
And I pound your words
Chasing poetry of merely mind or merely sexuality
Tow pure white butterflies
Paying off this lack in broken stone

So don't believe me
For different daemons speak within me
All looking for their missing parts

(written in English)

— LYSANDROS PITHARAS (1960–1992) —

Green Line

I can't see this green line.
Textures are more useful,
like the crevice this finger traces around your masks
and the damp breath of those still alive
and the theater of sighs,
as we post our condemnation to various presidents,
the acrid envelope's lip.

And sometimes our little towns are quiet
and only flags flutter as tributes to the silence,

And I poke my tongue
into the hole of my history
and wriggle my toes in the damp sand, beyond the cafeteria,
and observe that I can't see this green line, I just can't see it.

I can only see gold,
and the eyes of my people blacker than embers,
and the strong smell of their lovemaking,
and secrets which they say nestle in their breasts,
standing like monoliths looking toward the sea,
saying nothing
as if they are chanting.

(written in English)

Kiss My Corpse

Kiss my corpse. Kiss it, so that azaleas bloom on your lips.
Grimly a guitar plays
A mother goes insane
   A father falls to his knees.
I leave you a life, with the smell of powdered baby
I leave you a life, with dripping blood
From the broken bottle that cut through the vein.

Kiss my corpse. Kiss it, so that, between the cradle and the grave
A crazy celebration begins
With the pleasure of memory my flesh changes color
                             And shrinks
Because I've recorded my death with my own camera
And I can show you, naked, in slow motion
                        With fearful fame
                        With fame, I can be vile.

Kiss my corpse. Kiss it, so that echoes of blood pass through you
Inherit the peace, as divine revolt is over.
Come on, kiss it, and learn
Why broken poets are always the first to run to their death.

translated from the Turkish by the author with Stephanos Stephanides

I Worshipped Too Many Gods

1.

I worshipped too many gods, but
After the long winters in the North I know now
Sun, you are the most real!

   Ganged up with the Sea, in this
Arid paradise, what have you done
To the lost pieces of porcelain childhoods?

I'm back, and have little time, so tell me.

2.

The land, which gives seven, and takes nine
I'm back—against the proverbs
It's arthritis accumulating in my joints

I'm asking you about those who hide in oblivion
And what hides buried inside you
And others dumped in the bottom of the well

Crossing over the limits of conditions
Overturning the towers of light onto thorny Mesaoria plains
And with the feeling of guilt

I'm back, and have little time, so tell me.

translated from the Turkish by the author with Stephanos Stephanides

⤐ TURKEY ⤙

— ENİS BATUR (b. 1952) —

F Minor—D-940

Of these two pianos one must surely be
the other's misgiving. Play it at night
before bed, it's blood, play it first thing in the morning,
one is the other's phantom. Naked, wet,
woman, how did it ever happen
that a man struck up these sounds:
of the two pianos, at least one feels broken.

translated from the Turkish by Saliha Paker and Mel Kenne

Dear Bartleby

You loved *Wakefield,* my young friend, and there's more
to it as well, if I'm not reading too much
into what you've written, you're overly affected
by my odd tale. "I was surprised,"
you're saying somewhere, but in truth it's you
who surprised me with your astonishing remark:
you plainly think I write what I live,
the lives woven into my books you see
as nectar gathered from my own days.
No! Don't be downhearted, the stale life you think
you lead is a hurricane next to the undeviating
flow of my hours. Friend, I never had a life.
And in view of the perfectly empty years
of the past, I never will: my body
is a boat adrift on a calm lake surrounded
by mountains: everything, yes everything
begins and ends on the precarious stage
at the bottom of my mind. If I stopped
I'd go crazy, but I can't stop:
without letters tumbling down to my fingertips,
I'd have cracked up in nothing flat.

translated from the Turkish by Clifford Endres and Selhan Savcıgil-Endres

Face-to-Face Conversation IX

I've always wanted to be one less than myself, he said: my fate decreed that I be one more. Didn't I pass this way before, didn't I leave a notch, now rubbed off, just here, on this big, white silent stone, on the top floor of that house I'd met a dark-skinned woman: aged, tired, complacent, she'd come from far away, settled in your midst, she called out to me one morning, using my full name even, knowing who I was, she declared to me with heartfelt sorrow that my day, my time, was up, I died, he said dryly, and after a few days turned to ashes, if I've suddenly come back it's because I forgot something: maybe a smell, a color, I don't remember so well now, maybe a word less or more.

translated from the Turkish by Saliha Paker and Mel Kenne

— HAYDAR ERGÜLEN (b. 1956) —

Pomegranate

Winter is too vast let's go to the pomegranate
the surface of the day grew cold, to the pomegranates
pomegranate will have something to tell us
a thousand warm words strew from the summer
my tongue dry, from here let's go to the pomegranate
pomegranate has a house, very crowded
I wish we lived there too
the house too big
every room a distance, children closed boxes
the back yard a chaos. When we split grapes
how we were vineyard friends, it seems,
the thief is robbing the garden
from its leaves
the vineyard
stripped naked
if the roughneck enters the pomegranate garden
sadness, fall on words prior to the skin,
before the tongue feels cold feels sad, the skin
must bloom and disperse us, going to the pomegranate
the house like pomegranate a garden inside a garden
woman, garden to love, the mad a creeping ivy woman
holding to your love, now, let's go to the pomegranate

say, we coaxed this love from the hand of pomegrenade, let's.

translated from the Turkish by Murat Nemet-Nejat

311
series 2 *(turkish red)**

builders of the idea of turkish red
poets dervishes and wandering lovers sitting
at a drinking table based on the
refinement of ancient times
> *turkish red*

child sultans
looking at the reds in Seçuki tiles crying
> *turkish red*

the manner of eating oysters & serving them
the entering to the salon & the use of napkins
the liveries of the servants at the table & their *from-the-right-and-the-lefts*
entering the restaurant & picking a table
athenian banquet tables and Euphrates nights
as I was thinking of these thoughts
> *turkish red*

thinking of an Azerbaijan girl
with her crescent and star earrings
I am building the
tie between
the lights of the bridge
> and its shimmering
> reflections in the water

seeing the water as a necklace the bridge
 as a star-crescent body
> (*

> _____ = turk

 bridge

like a bridge, departing from myself
like a Turk, red, I am crying *turkish red*

> *translated from the Turkish by Murat Nemet-Nejat*

---

* Müldür was married to a Belgian painter and spent several years in Belgium. Different color titles of the poems in *The Book of Series* refer to the names of specific colors in her then husband's paint box. Words in italics in the translations of "series 2 turkish red" and "series 2 blauwviolet" mean that the words appear in the same language, English and German, in the originals.

548
series 2 *(blauwviolet)*

thinking of you I always find the equation of the straight line
which passes around cape hope creating an 8 degree
angle with the polar axis, *blauwviolet.*
an eagle is migrating under two dancing butterflies.
under wet mao grass someone is *I* laying a pair of
pearl earrings. to the annals of martyrdom a *t*
tear of ice is falling. window swallows
and city swallows losing their direction
are migrating toward the north and my heart *i*
is always broken thinking of you, *blauwviolet.*
as if in a *rooom* dedicated to *youu* in my heart
you are kindling some grass thrown in one corner and
my eyes like secret bamboo chests are
bowing to their secrets. as an earthen pot's
breaking because of what it holds and protects
is illogical, I am going to a deer hunt
chasing myself or
we are going. I am saying good-bye to my kin
and we are going on a long river trip until
blauwviolet waters cover our thrones . . .

translated from the Turkish by Murat Nemet-Nejat

— MUSTAFA ZİYALAN (b. 1959) —

Days

One.
First,
first.

without anything else—
being.

Seven.
heaven.
enlightenment
in the twilight mascara
of your eyes.

Eight.
according to you, a zero tightening its belt.
according to me, two zeroes kissing.

Ten.
a stick and a hoop rolling in the nocturnal meadows.

Eleven.
Sleeping back to back.

Thirteen.
I love differently, please lie a different way.
don't wrinkle your nose—talk to me.

Fourteen.
No thirteen.
Are you dozing off or just keeping quiet?

translated from the Turkish by Murat Nemet-Nejat

— SAMİ BAYDAR (b. 1962) —

Gigi

Gigi, the angel of invisible meetings
we did so well making angels listen to music
kids are now embarrassed, of their big ears
angels are sleeping in the meadows Gigi
bored, they are weighing bird seeds
but not selling them to birds Gigi,
I am getting by in dust and shit,
who is attempting to remind birds
that they eat seeds,
who is laboring in the meadows Gigi,
tailors for fairy tales?

I'll croak like an idiot Gigi
like an idiot hiding my love from you
I'll seal you inside a wall Gigi
you'll be invisible but people will see you
they are onto what I saw Gigi
your wish, a broken doll in the garden,

wishing me to trip and fall
don't reveal the places I've been Gigi

translated from the Turkish by Murat Nemet-Nejat

Here It's Coming

nothing can make us roll down the wall
neither our being kids
nor navy suits
not even our curly hair
if one must talk of an equation.

As for our shadow, as if lost in the wall
with the candle expired in your lantern
one night after feeding the kids
and putting them to sleep
opening the door, if,
standing before us,
basket on your back, with two signs on your chest
which today I would kid you about,
that was not the shadow.

A rose, if you saw a pillow before you,
a sheep, a sheep if you lay down on a grave stone.

The ambassador of our belly, the rose
we are saluting it with a hand
here it comes
we see those kneeling and saluting
kneeling and saluting.

translated from the Turkish by Murat Nemet-Nejat

— SEYHAN ERÖZÇELİK (b. 1962) —

from **Rosestrikes**

Rosethroat

Magpie in my larynx,
marten in my heart . . .
females jump

i jump
right & left,
screaming
screaming . . .

but now I'm hoarse.
Rosedusts escaped to my throat.
A thorn pricked my heel . . .
At my most delicate spot

Magpie in my larynx,
marten in my heart . . .

I looked at the moon, hit at the heel
This pain has no relief.
No one likes the moonstruck . . .

if it's getting light.
That is, if it's getting light.

Now my larynx a magpie,
marten my heart,

rose petals pricked my veins.

While the marten's squinting
petals swim in my blood.

The marten's pumping blood to its thighs,
to my eyes.

And my heartflesh dry like a rose.

It's *beautiful rose.*

Windrose

Twisted
round,
destroyrose.

Twisted
round,
back
squeezer.

Marten worships rose
sitting on my face,

Mattress turned
upside down.

Fortunerose

Fortune rains on salt marshes,

This is the condition of the rose. we sit up,
leaving behind coffee cups
to their own.

Leave tea leaves to their rose formation.

Through reeds the marshes refract fractions of the moon.

translated from the Turkish by Murat Nemet-Nejat

— KÜÇÜK İSKENDER (b. 1964) —

from souljam

sixty-seven

i will hate the spider crawl-
ing on me. on me, i can't kill it

sixty-eight

carnation crack in ice.

sixty-nine

what if summer's thaw started at this critical juncture?

seventy

oh, left left your divine body like a broken sculpture
in my hands!

violence is the foreign tongue of the body
fragmentary improvisations of yearning

seventy-one

verses of adventure:
which color is blowing the dancing young man,
feet and body naked,
i can not tell.

seventy-two

could you understand, the curse of a course, to be read only by a compass?

seventy-three

spring wrote me no letters of utopias, winter did.

seventy-four

your loveliness is *where*
is missing,

where is *missing*
is the air!

seventy-five

post *naked lunch*
panislamic
femininity

seventy-six

penelope's explosive reweaving
mystic riffs of absence

seventy-seven

my soul is a jelly fish, without a womb

light descends in the gutted out space of the dome.

translated from the Turkish by Murat Nemet-Nejat

— DİDEM MADAK (b. 1970) —

Sir, I Want to Write Poems with Flowers

Sir, you get angry that I write poems with flowers,
you don't know. I hide my scattered body
behind flower curtains.
I sit in the dark, don't turn on the lights.
The wound clock is ringing, ringing until unsprung.
I recall an aching love.
This is the unnecessary sheen of a knife.
I'm the illegal rain kept for years in the clouds.
Once it rains, it'll cost you.

Sir, I'm a basement girl
whose only boss is loneliness
For now I'm solid like plastic vases
but I'm worried. In a while
in your twelve E shoes you'll step
on kids in the garden.
This is not nice, sir.

"Day is night" I'm saying,
casting bread crumbs to birds.
They'll eat glass shards
in my dream, in a bowl of water,
in technicolor lego blocks.
I'm trying to tell you, you won't listen,
no, I don't think
I can wait till the morning.
One should tell one's dream immediately.

My soul was 14, sir,
it got older in the cold of a marble table.
Prosthetic legs were attached to my soul, delicate and white.
I walked in the city squeaking.
They even whistled at the prosthetic legs.
Meanwhile, an unarmed force in me
made of flowers was besieged,
on the screen *the rustling of organza* was playing.
I tried to slip away, couldn't.
Due to that, sir, writing flower poems
from the angle of my soul I find useful.
Whatever, I remember
all the movies I see,
taking shelter in the endless night of movies.
At *Sophie's Choice* I cried a lot.
If they make a movie called *kissing tetras*
I'll cry there too.
Does one forget the spinning wheel inside,
besides, I'm used to remembering.
"I'm a magpie, sir."

Sir, there are no more armadas
or sailboats.
I'll burn a large quantity of paper.

A cormorant dove into water,
lost for a while,
even if it reemerges, having swallowed the whole world,
death isn't too large a word, sir.
I know I smell bitter like chrysanthemums.
But do you know the loveliness
of a lonesome love which makes scrambled eggs with sausages
at the stove and eats it?
A rose will tell a rose, if I see it,
but I'm lying
roses aren't much for talking these days, sir.

translated from the Turkish by Murat Nemet-Nejat

⊁ BULGARIA ⊁

— EDVIN SUGAREV (b. 1953) —

Liminal Moments

the light languishes
fades

as if someone scraped
ancient church frescoes with a rough stone
as if a shroud was draped over the colors
or a crazy monk dipped his brush into black ink
and the shadows grew denser
more visible and solid than the real things

dusk falls
the warmed earth is scented
with walnuts and wine
and the bats
in slanting flights
glance off
the secret little lakes

translated from the Bulgarian by Ludmilla G. Popova-Wightman

— LYUBOMIR NIKOLOV (b. 1954) —

Apples

The apples have fallen and rot in the yard.
And you aren't here.
Otherwise, everything else goes on like before.
The cricket creaks in the dry grass.
The windowpane is shattered.
The stone has fallen by the bed.
Shards of glass cover the pillow.

translated from the Bulgarian by Miroslav Nikolov

[I'm the master of the empty house.]

I'm the master of the empty house.

I enter the bedrooms, lie on the beds,
Caress the heavy dressers full of linen,
I smell the perfumes
And bury my beard in the white sheets.
Having removed the mirror from the wall
I wander about the house
Watching how the mirrors from the other rooms peer into it:
The pink vases, the blue duck in the bathtub.
I swig Barbados rum straight from the bottle.
I open the windows.
Slowly, one by one, I set fire to the curtains.
Come. You'll easily recognize
The red house, up there on the hill in Highland.

It's ablaze.

translated from the Bulgarian by Miroslav Nikolov

— BOIKO LAMBOVSKI (b. 1960) —

The Clay Man

Hey, Doctor,
what shall we do with
the clay man?

He doesn't want to study.
"My eyes," he says,
"crumble from the letters."

His eyes look like
frightened drops.

Unfit for a soldier.
Wearily the military committee
found dove disease
in his brain.

No good for a clown—
he trembles
badly,

trembling to the right
trembling to the left
his smile

Hey, Doctor, what
shall we do with the clay
man?

The doctor raised his hand to his forehead.
Earth after drought—that's what his forehead is.

The doctor doesn't believe
in God's mastery.

The strong one doesn't believe the weak.

The fish doesn't believe that the net's hugging it.

The healthy one doesn't believe
the sick.

The tree doesn't believe
in the saw's kiss.

The living one doesn't believe the dead.

He doesn't believe in the doctor,
the clay man.

translated from the Bulgarian by Kristin Dimitrova

— MIRELA IVANOVA (b. 1962) —

Apologetic Telegram

for Georgi Rupchev

You remember of course: I was drunk
and kept begging you to kiss away my tears.
I wanted to stay with you that night,
but I was afraid you might cure me of all my guilt
without whose pretend-sweet burden I can't live.
I weave my guilt into a rope ladder
by which, soundlessly, I get to God,
or at least to my corner of heaven . . .

I didn't stay. Stupidly, inexplicably, I put on my mac
and made endless excuses.

You remember of course: we're different.
Guilt before you is the most perfect step
to the top, where we'll meet again.
I kiss you soberly and clumsily
but all the more ardently.
     Mirela

translated from the Bulgarian by Ewald Osers

— KRISTIN DIMITROVA (b. 1963) —

A Visit to the Clockmaker

I crossed the street
to enter a secret shop
where hundreds of hands grind time.
Charted small faces leave aside their arguments
about missing moments & start
ticking reproachfully, peep
out of three walls with shelves. Two alarm clocks
ponderously hurdle the minutes.
A grandfather clock with a pendulum necktie
shows me the way.
A sunbeam
inscribes on the counter
its own vision of accuracy.
Down there, the clockmaker
is tinkering with the open intestines
of a disbatteried body.
His door rang its bell.
"A new timepiece?"
I dislike giving false hope
so I said "A new chain, please."
Then thought, One who will manage to slice
          time into amazingly thin straps
          and thus make good use of his life
          will be the happiest of us all.
The clockmaker raised his gaze
& would not agree.

translated from the Bulgarian by Gregory O'Donoghue

The Ritual

Listen to what that man said
while waiting at the counter

He who came to know everything
is always dressed in black
I don't drink I commemorate myself
every second you know
such and such number of cells
burst into our brains
every minute dead men
every day funerals
rain and mud drunk gravediggers
I am not a priest but I ought
to be a priest of myself
to wail upon my own death
to be gravedigger and graveyard
fortinbras of my own body
I don't drink any more
I commemorate myself

after all we owe ourselves the ritual

translated from the Bulgarian by Biliana Kourtasheva

The Love Rabbit

I won't be long, she said,
and left the door ajar.
It was a special evening for us,
a rabbit stew was slowly cooking on the hob,
she'd chopped some onions and garlic
and carrots into little disks.
She didn't take a coat
and didn't put on any lipstick. I didn't ask
where she was going.
She's like that.
She's never had any sense of time,
she's always late; that's all
she said that evening:

I won't be long;
she didn't even close the door.
Six years later
I meet her in the street (not ours)
and she suddenly seems worried, like someone who remembers
she forgot to unplug the iron,
or something . . .
Did you turn the stove off, she asks.
Not yet, I answer,
these rabbits can be very tough.

translated from the Bulgarian by Kalina Filipova

⊁ MACEDONIA ⊁

— KATA KULAVKOVA (b. 1951) —

Bronchitis (a psychopoem)

I accept the diagnosis.
The body has a number of familiar reactions
to known illnesses.
The symptoms are provoked in dreams:

Naked in person, I seek a cure.
I seek black cat, beard, mud, wool,
a dirty story and disfiguration
with dirty hands, just so that you get the picture.

This is chronic fear.
I breathe for two.
I burn for three.

You have seen through me from the inside:
navel and roe, psychoclitoric places
the divans of the flesh where passion might reap
. . . negatives . . .
Quietly, you've outworked yourself
it's a conspiracy. A mole.
Interestingly enough,
you're becoming less of a stranger to me.
My pores are yours.
You can be domesticated, you're resilient
and resistant. *Mot juste.*

The therapy should be changed.
Alter the place of living,
fly away to the high clear skies
and undertake something with a future,
I know, but I've got better things to do.

Don't be embarrassed.
You've got a whole paddock for your endeavors.
I won't tell anyone you're here.
They are only human.

translated from the Macedonian by Ilija Čašule and Thomas Shapcott

What's Slouching

What's slouching like stagnant air
through these Balkan corridors?
Eroded erudites,
plague-ridden radicals,
communists, nationalists,
bloodthirsty ecologists
with milk teeth,
descending from the national parks
with conserved views,
reserved
for outbursts of tribal passion,
Freudian complexes of minimal difference,
for random reservists
and condoms of all different colors too.

Whatever is slouching
will never reach Bethlehem or Jerusalem
nor Mecca or Medina
but hurrying and scurrying
down different European corridors
in red crescent or red cross ambulances
will enter a wilderness of mirrors,

in Versailles,
where terrible tailors
cut out new corridors
and a well-turned verse
is reversed to a stammer.

translated from the Macedonian by Graham W. Reid, Peggy Reid, and the author

Decent Girl

I took my perspective of the future to a thrift store
but nobody would buy it. The net is prickly
and there are no more heroes. Sorrow is purely physical pain.
If there's no water, let the eye-fluid hanging on the glasses drop.
If you wear no glasses, pretend you are Chinese
(one eye looking eastward and one looking westward
equals *écriture féminine* in a male society).
The fashion of the Orientals
comes back in a package of diet food.
And bless me while I'm still a decent girl.
Tomorrow or the next day I'll lose my sinful ways,
I'll wear embroidered blouses from the Ethnographic Museum
of Macedonia, and someone will have to pay for them.
To survive, we'd best turn the lector's apartment
into a gallery. We shall exhibit
varicose veins, dried umbilici, retinas
and broken hearts in direct proportion
to South American soap operas
(tell me why you left me and married my sister),
and sorrow is purely physical pain
cured in my country by surgical operation.
How I recognize it by the pain in my index finger,
crucial in the expansion of mobile phone networks.
I don't know why my uncle didn't beat me in a sack.
At this age it's best if somebody else
cuts your umbilical cord,
and I am not afraid of Virginia Woolf,
I fear Lidija Dimkovska. Have you heard of her?
A woman not wholly christened,
whose friends have all taken the vow,
the bodiless woman and all those she's loved remain unmarried.
That almost completely non-woman of yours
(likely sponsored by Soros to become tender?)
almost to the negation of Medea, of Judea, of her.
No, I am not afraid of the numbers 1, 4, 7 in the eye clinic,
or of the mortgages on religious holidays,
what I'm afraid of is the existing attitude of God,

the God who does not exist, and I'm afraid of his great eyes.
Alas, what a multitude of words! Dictionaries are a lucrative job.
You sit at home and play: Something beginning with . . . !
From now on I shall speak in onomatopoeia,
Or better, in metaonomatopoeia.
Be that as it may, it was nice meeting you, Father.
Were I not a woman you could've taken my confession.
But I don't mind this either.
We're having tea, biting each other's nails
and licking our lips. Chirp chirp! Metachirp metachirp!

translated from the Macedonian by Ljubica Arsovska and Peggy Reid

✴ ALBANIA ✴

— VISAR ZHITI (b. 1952) —

Hunger Strike

Even within prison
There is a prison.
They throw you into it,
For example, if you do not work.

Lying on the floorboards
Of your coffin cell, you have not eaten today,
Nor yesterday, nor the day before yesterday, nor three days ago,
Nor since the Second World War,
Nor will you eat tomorrow, nor the day after tomorrow,
Nor when you are dead.

"Go ahead and die!" said the guard on the first day,
On the second he squeaked like a torn boot,
On the third he fell silent.
The stains on the wall trembled on his face.
On the fourth day, he said: "Eat!"
"What's wrong," he said on the fifth.
Then came the sixth day. In fact
Nothing happened. The seventh day hid
Behind the ninth. The first year of Christ
Before the November national holiday.
The death of the tyrant was delayed.
He was as stubborn as an ass.
The men from the command came
        to your cell,
All with their heads bowed, reflecting
In the dish of cold soup.
The dish was the eye of the cyclops.
The mice were eating the bread, scampering about,
Musical notes on the scores of . . . doctrine.
The walls
Dance back and forth,
A cry runs barefoot
Down the corridor.
The cockroaches take fright. Look how they scuttle

Skull-less, out of the seams of memory.
Patches of light from somewhere
Lay in the room
Like vomit from a sick day.

translated from the Albanian by Robert Elsie

— MIMOZA AHMETI (b. 1963) —

Extinction

You were once blue-colored. You have grown dark.
Do you not know what this means?
Remember how my ray
Shot into your sky like an arrow.
—Remember.
The satisfaction of security has darkened you.
Now with your hands in your pockets you make fun of the others,
But why does your face
No longer bear that lordly smile of tranquility?

As a warning on those April evenings
You interrupted my every word with a leaden silence.
Blue-colored, you blue egoist,
Slowly you went out in my hands.

translated from the Albanian by Robert Elsie

— GAZMEND KRASNIQI (b. 1963) —

Adam

1.

The body—symbol of a thought which veils,
The thought itself—symbol of something else which veils,

And yet, he does not know if he is on the road to freedom of fleeing from it.

2.

He still has no faith or pious words, heaven or hell,
His only riches—thoughts, feelings,

While the scales of causes remain unseen, and things imbibe their energy.

3.

He values thought because he does what he thinks: he feels like a worm,
But is convinced that he is on the path to sanctity,

Indeed, he even sees sanctity in the worm.

4.

Time is for him but a way of thinking
When he endeavors to rise to the words "I am right,"

When he sees that God needs nothing at all.

translated from the Albanian by Robert Elsie

— LULJETA LLESHANAKU (b. 1968) —

Fresco

Now there is no gravity. Freedom is meaningless.
I weigh no more than a hair
on a starched collar.
Lips meet in the ellipsis at the end of a drowning
confession; on the sand, a crab closes its claws hermetically
and moves one step forward and two steps to the right.
It was long ago when I first broke into a shudder
at the touch of your fingers;
no more shyness, no more healing, no more death.
Now I am light as an Indian feather, and can easily reach the moon
a moon clean as an angel's sex
on the frescoes of the church.
Sometimes I can even see asteroids dying like drones
in ecstasy for their love, their queen.

translated from the Albanian by Ukzenel Buçpapa and Henri Israeli

Walls

And if a wall, long and thick,
A high wall
Should rise in front of you . . .
What would you do?

I would close my eyes, I would crouch
And rest my check against it,
I would find peace in its cool serenity.

And if this wall were death . . .

translated from the Albanian by Robert Elsie

⚔ KOSOVO ⚔

— EQREM BASHA (b. 1948) —

The nightingale sings

Who is that bird singing on a branch alone
And where is its flock
Which is the plaintive song
And which is the season

> That bird has a voice adept
> At singing on a solitary branch
> No friends no family
> It has come to earth on its own
> With a flute in its beak and anguish
> Which is neither a wound
> Nor a song

What is that mourning so near which belongs to us
Sing to us nightingale sing

translated from the Albanian by Robert Elsie

— FLORA BROVINA (b. 1949) —

The Year 1981

The stench and clank of metal spread,
The music of the streets has taken refuge in the suburbs,
The little girl has scraped her knee, off with you now and don't cry,
Wide-eyed he emerges from the crowd,
Entering the race,
The unseen arena, toreador and bull,
Olé olé olé,
The weight of the tank leaves tracks in the asphalt,
Olé olé olé,
He rushes forth
And grasps it
By the head,
Covering it
With a red cloth,
The machine, now blinded by the eagle,

Is dazed
And disoriented,
What black beauty,
Empty flowerpots
Cascade down from balconies,
Rakatak, rakatak,
Rakatak, rakatak,
Flowerpots hurtling through the air
Know nothing of the curfew,
Rakatak, rakatak,
You in the midst
Plant artificial flowers,
The policeman screams and takes down your address
While guarding the shattered flowerpots
And tank tracks in the asphalt.

translated from the Albanian by Robert Elsie

— ABDULLAH KONUSHEVCI (b. 1958) —

Heavy Burden, Your Fragile Body

With my gnawed liver,
With my lashed lungs,
With my fingers stained and tarred from nicotine,
I am of no use to anyone.

I cannot believe
That you would be foolish enough
To bestow your love on me.

I don't know what to do
With my insomnia,
With those shadows of fallen friends.

Heavy burden,
Your fragile body.

translated from the Albanian by Robert Elsie

⤜ SERBIA ⤛

— RADMILA LAZIĆ (b. 1949) —

Anthropomorphic Wardrobe

There's no more room. We are full.
Everything we stored, layer by layer
Folded, packed in as if bandaging wounds.
Belongings we hung by a hook,
Belongings we lined up on hangers,
Winter wishes, summer dreams,
Suns, snowy peaks,
What's yours—what's mine, sighs and sobs—
Now shifted every which way.

Forgotten. Taken down in a hurry.
Thrown in the corner: Turned inside out.
What is indispensable and is less so
Thrown on top of one another.
Once made to measure, then grown short,
Grown too tight, faded or shiny—it's all here.

Adam's little broken rib.
The plucked angel's wing.
Venus's fur and love-stain.
Rings. Combs. Ghosts. Moths.
No one can find anything here.
Where is it? Turn it upside down! Rummage!
Lost, then found again.
Rejected, then cherished again.
Cobwebs sway. The mouse gnaws.
The butterfly spreads its wings.

Torn in the eye. The sea on its last breath.
Night-day. Loves-doesn't love.
Throw it-keep it. Give-take.
This to the dry cleaners. This to the devil.
This to the Salvation Army. And this—not in your life!

The creases of lust. Washed-out heart.
Weepy muslin. Ariadne's thread.
Adjectival lace. Aorist.

Sentence-rags. Flake of words. Peek out
Of drawers, dangle. Expired. Eternal.
Trickle. Ooze. Shed tears. Drip pleasures.
The snivel of time passing. Used-up life.

translated from the Serbian by Charles Simic

— NOVICA TADIĆ (b. 1949) —

Antipsalm

Disfigure me, Lord. Take pity on me.
Cover me with bumps. Reward me with boils.
In the fount of tears open a spring of pus mixed with blood.
Twist my mouth upside down. Give me a hump. Make me crooked.
Let moles burrow through my flesh. Let blood
circle my body. Let it be thus.
May all that breathes steal breath from me,
all that drinks quench its thirst in my cup.
Turn all vermin upon me.
Let my enemies gather around me
and rejoice, honoring You.

Disfigure me, Lord. Take pity on me.
Tie every guilt around my ankles.
Make me deaf with noise and delirium. Uphold me
above every tragedy.
Overpower me with dread and insomnia. Tear me up.
Open the seven seals, let out the seven beasts.
Let each one graze my monstrous brain.
Set upon me every evil, every suffering,
every misery. Every time you threaten
point your finger at me. Thus, thus, my Lord.
Let my enemies gather around me
and rejoice, honoring You.

translated from the Serbian by Charles Simic

Far Away from Forest Sounds

Far away from forest sounds and angry cries,
far away from crowds of highlanders rolling
across the squares, across the Belgrade sidewalks.

In semidarkness I go from chamber to chamber.
I wipe the dust off a sturdy table with my palms.
I thread over the Bukhara carpet or soak the color in my eye.

Warm color lives in Algerian Berbers' drapery, too.
I'm quiet, unhurried. A spider in a hidden corner of the house,
an oyster with a speck of sand in its slimy womb.

I'm music to one's ears, stalactite in the darkness of the cave
or a brush that glides over the white canvas
like wet lips over the skin of a woman still asleep.

While the red sun lazily sets over the savanna,
its blood drips on the leaves just as here in spring
ice breaks and slowly flows down the Danube.

translated from the Serbian by Tomislav Kuzmanović

— ZVONKO KARANOVIĆ (b. 1959) —

Melancholy

It is almost painless
like loneliness
like the smell of blond, just-washed hair
caught accidentally while passing
water flowers keep on dying
until one
lives to see the morning
and then they disappear
I'll tell you once
about the wreaths of dried up flowers
we left
on every birch tree
lost in the fog
on a muddy road somewhere in the country

about the girl whose hands shiver in the rain
for seven long years
I was looking for my sister
and found her one afternoon
behind the first row of books
on plants
her voice was metal
she swallowed coins
and joints
with chocolate
we never met
she slept in the walnut shell
and said that conversations are
nothing but long good-byes
she used to enter my room often
and touch my hair until
she turned into dust
into hands that shiver
in the rain

translated from the Serbian by Tomislav Kuzmanović

— DRAGAN JOVANOVIĆ DANILOV (b. 1960) —

On a Sunday Afternoon, a Soul is a Fascinating Fascist

On a Sunday afternoon, a soul is a fascinating fascist.
The Golem has slurped up my gondolas of cobwebs
and silk, and flung the oars into the dolphin's mouth.
Decorated firs, far in the hills, are lonesome.
The windows are frozen mirrors under which
reindeer come to me. It's cold in the rooms where
I'm nobody's son. In an empty parking lot
little girls play hopscotch. Their tiny thighs are
virgin snow. To write sentences just like that, granny
across the way waters her potted
geraniums, just like the door squeals in its
hinges, just like the lightning bug's belly shines, like that.
Izabela, I've spent that perfume you bought me
last winter. No longer smells of anything this day
that poisons me with babies' tears. There are as many

children's tears as there are innocent skulls underground.
Under the Kremlin. If only I could fall asleep on
a cart full of hay. Fall silent on your lips
with a seven-mile scream. I keep my gods
in my shoes. Shoes are the karma of the archangels who
have not yet learned to walk.

translated from the Serbian by Tomislav Kuzmanović

— MARIJA KNEŽEVIĆ (b. 1963) —

On-Site Investigation V

CAREFUL BEYOND MEASURE, we who take everything into account,
the owners of the archive of useful advice, we, our own parents,
overlooked the shame in the sour smell of the clothes—the grounds for

slowed reaction time.

Despite constant warnings from the gliding lines of trees. Attentive
readers of other people's eyes. Born for good deeds, we still
believed that at least this path was given to us to stay

young, children of the night, favorites of the moon.

And we waved at those coming toward us and at those
overtaking us; determined to share happiness of this discovery,
we could not care less if someone thought: Look! Two hopeless creatures!

Two forgotten windmills! If someone asked quietly,
Why is it so full tonight? What is it telling us?
Would we understand the sign? And when did you and I,

experienced characters from works of classic literature,
become dependent on matters of the soul?

That was the first time I suspected that everything had already been decided,
that we had been promised to the accident, in the fast car, with the same
    questions,
the driver and the passenger of so little help to one another.

translated from the Serbian by Tomislav Kuzmanović

Fortress

I built a fortress, called it Patmos
or Armageddon, so that in it, I could be happy
or depressed, closer to the beginning and closer
to the ruin, an apprentice and a master, rejected
as only the lustful and the humble
can be. What illness is this, what
choices have I? Lovers are like
the unborn: they don't care about visible borders,
their warm eyes ask if the kings will return,
if they will leave
blessed ignorance or pure happiness behind.
Revelation spills over into the roar of the distant
space. The feeling of abandonment benumbs.
The fear of idleness speaks in my voice.
I follow this fine order, concord of the torrid
heat and snow-covered valley, an echo of a waterfall
and rippling of the wheat. What was bare
is now lush and lonely.

After each death the Milky Way grows a drop
bigger. The ground around the Fortress has been plowed,
the bridge erected and, in the distance, a wrapped-up figure,
like a needle, weaves into the horizon.

translated from the Serbian by Tomislav Kuzmanović

Snow in Your Shoes

One does not build a house collecting cutlery
even though a few extra spoons
come in handy sometimes.

One does not build a house from new curtains
even though different views
from time to time
should be shielded by new cloth.

For a home to be a home, among other things
you need a lot of things
you would gladly renounce
in advance.

Listen to what Eskimos say:
to build a good igloo,
for years you have to carry
snow in you shoes.

And a safety pin, forgotten
in your coat collar,
near the jugular.

translated from the Serbian by Novica Petrović

⤬ MONTENEGRO ⤬

— BALŠA BRKOVIĆ (b. 1966) —

The Babylon Song

It is more and more difficult to write a letter.

The irretrievable clearness of words is lost.
Every poem used to be full of
uncanny meaning:
on the one side there were the woman and night,
and on the other light and I.

Now it is different:
Penelope's weave of my civilization
is undone overnight, it ebbs easily.

If all words have been spoken,
everything, it then seems, has already happened.
And that would be terrible:
as if the World were a great Theater
in which for a long time there has been not
a single writer, or director, or musician.

The whole of space, the Stage, the Planet
is inhabited by actors
(gone wild without all the Others,
without the Manuscript of the Creator)
an entire ocean of actors
infinitely repeating
scraps of the same roles.
There is simply no one to tell them
What to say, or where to go.

If all the words have already been in His wrath,
then we have forever been—tired.

Still, the limits of the unutterable are wider and wider.
And it is more and more difficult to eat the darkness of the last Nothing
and spew the light that changes everything into Being,
into the certainty of Language.

Oh, sweet demons of erudition!
When God spilled the languages over Babylon
perhaps He only
gave us sturdier material:
after all, one does not get to the Creator's throne
by piling bricks.

translated from the Montenegrin by Ulvija Tanović

— ALEKSANDAR BEČANOVIĆ (b. 1971) —

Pessoa: On Four Addresses

So, I drew the line. With a sharp stroke.
As always, whiteness waited. I could
feel my legs going relentlessly numb: the night
was making its way through the branches of nearby trees,
bringing frost. I stretch and get up: everything
needs to go quiet, everything needs to become so distant,
for the *persona* to feel relieved. When I abandon
my writing, long-lasting peace enters the room.
Things seem familiar, then.
I'm no longer in the room: my handwriting is
a short line of strokes. The heart's architecture
resembles the architecture of a city: few paths
lead inside, many lead out.
After all, streetlights in Lisbon are cold.
The subject is a puny clerk, a dying instance, a necessity
character: he leaves written marks behind, then.
Then I can even imagine you: somewhere downtown,
near the intersection where the cars are noisier than
usual, with a careful move of your hand you drop a well-
sealed letter into a yellow mailbox.

translated from the Montenegrin by Tomislav Kuzmanović

Great Preparations

Unquestionable are the holes in the ozone layer.
Tomorrow's day, too, is, to a good extent, unquestionable.
The printing of this poem, weekly results
of matches of the *Primera Division,* a handful of small
and large events—they're for sure unquestionable. At least as much
as the smell of coffee and the color of my jacket.
Profane things possess a special certainty,
the kind we usually don't pay attention to.
Here I have always especially respected a number
of side-certainties. It is unquestionable that little Georgie
had skillfully grappled with English.
Rotation of Earth is, probably, unquestionable.
And then, many place-names, our names
and driving along dusty roads. We need to talk
only of unquestionable things. Things not praised
by poets. Fear of happiness is certain,
death—most certain. Lonely people know this
—at receptions, in cold hotel rooms
and automobiles. Contemporaries of Martin Heidegger.

translated from the Montenegrin by Evald Flisar

⊀ BOSNIA AND HERZEGOVINA ⊁

— MILE STOJIĆ (b. 1955) —

A House on Ice

We knew also those who never loved anybody
They say they used to make up inventions, machines
which will, allegedly, make the steps of future generations easier

We used to meet strange people who light their hearts
through fiddle bows of violins on town squares
returning home late, happy and empty

We also saw false prophets who claimed
that they heard God's voice every evening. And magicians
who are tied, thrown into the sea and then they swim out again
dry and happy

We did not look down upon flimsy whores either,
friends of the night,
watching them in the morning full of sperm and alcohol
on intersections, with thumbs up and souls as simple
as two plus two

But we have not met the people like us yet
who were building a house on the ice. When we woke up
it was not there anymore

We will never understand what it was like, how long it lasted
where exactly it was

Where were the walls, the ceilings,
where was the door. And although we know that it is
not there anymore
we still get worm

By the lights of its windows
by the warmth of its doorstep

translated from the Bosnian by Miljenko Kovačićek

Paper Tea

It's not something you die of—
waiting for evening to fall,
huddled around yourself
like family in a dining room.
Real people die of something else!
On the shores, in the fields,
in the jungle—
                            of water,
Of thunder, of tiger.

And you—you'd end your life
by a tiger's skin flashing
in the darkness!
                            Nicely and quietly;
no bleeding, no screaming . . .
The way it's done in the books . . .
as on the wing of the Snow Queen . . .

But wait a while. Summer evening
will start to fall over town,
over things, over us.
We shall drown sorrowfully,
flooded with sleep.

You'll wake up, dust on your desk,
Yet the better ones will die
of something else: on the shores,
in the fields, in the jungle—
of water, of thunder, of tiger . . .

translated from the Bosnian by Amela Simić

War

War
and nothing is going on—
I go into town to beg for cigarettes

I've always known your scent
but you're never been closer—
sometimes when it's cold in the morning you
put my underwear on by mistake

in ten years we haven't been together as much
as we have these five months—
now you've got my sweater on all day

your joy
at the packets of humanitarian aid
makes me happy and sad at the same time

and I ask myself: where on earth do
you find us coffee every night?

There isn't a single pane of glass left in our windows
and there's just no way to get rid
of the lagging flies

translated from the Bosnian by Ammiel Alcalay

— MILJENKO JERGOVIĆ (b. 1966) —

Feldwebel* Zorn's Motorcycle

Feldwebel Zorn told me in the winter of forty-four that this mess
Was coming to an end, the whole World knew it but the Germans, he was leaving
    and was not coming back
With any luck, next month he would board the ship freighting glass
And if he survived in the hold without water, food, and light, he'd drink rum with
    fishermen in Havana
And he would be called Francisco García Goethe, fine, I said, you know that your
    words
Are going to the grave with me, I know you don't need my advice, so farewell

---

* *Feldwebel* is German for "staff sergeant."

You misunderstood me, Šulc, I'm not a boy who needs to confide, nor am I a fool
   to brag
I need someone to leave my Zündapp with, and you know your way around ma-
   chines and you understand this little male
Weakness, this that I'm leaving the world behind, but I can't leave my motorcycle,
   so if there's any luck
And we all save our skins, I'll be glad to come back to Sarajevo and get it, with a
   bottle of rum for you
And a straw hat for your Missus, fine, I told Feldwebel Zorn, I'll wait for you—
   Francisco
Forty years have passed, I've never heard of him, he's not among the criminals of war
He's not among Castro's compañeros with beards, he's not in letters or postcards
Just the Zündapp, in the corner of my shed, among the wardrobes, bicycles, and
   automobile tires
Grease keeps it from rust, moths, flies, and ants have died in it, this sticky trap
In which there's no salvation, either for them, or for me

translated from the Bosnian by Tomislav Kuzmanović

— SENADIN MUSABEGOVIĆ (b. 1970) —

Dawn at Auschwitz

This morning
things have finally,
through the shriek of the officer's whistle
which penetrates the cracked barracks boards,
whispered their names to us.

As I open my eyes
two mice scurry into their hole;
frightened by our pasted faces
they twitch their legs and huddle together,
in the warmth of their bodies
on our smells to feed.

Images that slip by through the morning haze
the gray dog's paws whose tracks in the snow
resemble the dark eye sockets with their gaze turned up to the sky,
in which white infinity freezes;
and the electrified barbed wire which stirred by my movements
touches the lines of the sky and the snow,
in the sounds of the doomsday harp;

and the officer's shining badge from which
the eagle with spread-out wings
plucks out pieces of my flesh
enter me
like darkness enters
a child's eyes.

The crematorium smoke softens the harshness of the landscape,
creating in it the contours of a female body
which speaks to me alluringly of the gentleness of the heavens.

Here death has no spasm,
no twitch.
Everything is the same.
The sunrise and the sunset are the same,
like the line of the horizon
streaked with rays on the snow
in which I will be laid by my mother's hands that used to touch me
in my dream.

Only order and firmness exist.

translated from the Bosnian by Ulvija Tanović

✛ CROATIA ✛

— BRANKO MALEŠ (b. 1949) —

Crystal

the hills are of iron combs
whose tunics are wedge-shaped tongues
your ore—you broken mop!
clay has split like a ruin

cracks are eating a candle
in the dark ice of esophagus
Bees are piled up
photonic honeycomb is—a leather word

where darkness gathers
on a sooty meadow!
villagers comb swords of that
which are listened to as herbal readings

in the morning soapsuds
a face is flying
everything happens like on a white sailing boat
and foam has risen—like lace of curls

a rope of pike hisses like frost
a nail of silver cracks floor by floor
an owl and a jar are fuming by the creek
the creek—a stake of winter

tradesmen whose slanted eyes
loudly speak of tense skin
carry young algebra in saddlebags
and ears of a carpet

oh, you are such a shiny silo
like a salmon
a colossus of letters!
like an intruder—oil spills on porcelain

translated from the Croatian by Miljenko Kovačićek

Journey

just as we pass we pass
and if we meet we meet

in the morning I milk the cows and spill the milk into the sun
god, that's why the eclipse passed across my face
like a pencil like a birch like a blind man's cane

and I don't speak from my mouth because all of me speaks, just like when
the sea cuts into itself, it hurts in your mirror, giorgione, when all
art moves south, a plain glade will stay behind like
a blueprint of eternity, because I build my voice from snow, don't let
the earth see you there, I will, for sure, art equals
solitude, go ahead, take a bath in your eyes, through what will I then
glance at the bottom like through clear water, and then you play
a little because the water runs, HERE COMES THE NIGHT, LET'S
    GO THERE
I'd like to take one innocent sip of that darkness
your snail coils into its home verse and carries me, but
the wind unwinds that picture again, like in the spring when
I start learning foreign languages so that I don't go out, so what if
I walked in to humiliate myself under the white skin of the wall, what drives
on saliva, dark happiness itself, when the sun splashes you in the morning
and you wake up: make a note of that window and close it shut, not that one,
that's my poem, a dog barked, goggled its eyes, you
can leave you can leave, as the stainless steel NN hails
the roses on the state lawn, make them wake up for everyone
just make them come down after they've slept enough, but I enter my hand
like the plane, and see: words are fireflies that
glowingly fly and if they pause, they just go out

translated from the Croatian by Tomislav Kuzmanović

Eyes, Ears, Mirrors

forty green dragons are greeting my blunt arrival
I am going just like that. I spread like the wing of a Peloponnesian crane,
deep eye for literature, split surface, every comma,
eggplant, green pepper, south, gorgonzola is strabismal and persistent;
crystals of workers' children and semantics that cannot be stopped:
I say to myself that history is really the only omnipresent
alternative, with which the green old folks of the dragon, hip-hop,
spill all over the melancholic surface of the innocent, pale,
syphilitic Ljubljanica, full of the seas and of the coasts by which
shy ships of cocaine & Laški golding land.
the river only moans, with dry lips and slow jerks:
where is that ugly statue of history at all?
I used to have it in my left pocket, but it fell out:
I used to have it in my eye, in my ear, in my rotten Converse sneaker,
full of Balkan sweat and cheap European antiperspirants:
where is that wild and endemic high-heeled shoe Europe at all?
in the north, west, east, south and in between.
wherever I am alone: I refract in the mirrors,
in the multicolored silence of my own musical memory
which does not let me speak. Just as it does not let any foreigner.

translated from the Croatian by Miljenko Kovačiček

Radio

night, agave, gulls, kontador.
in its burning hot puddle, slowly, toward the bottom,
the wax ascends to its symbols.
if I really listen to the radio now,
if it's really nighttime now
the stampede of slow death
in every telex of your sleeping breath,
then I really move
a small, black, burning obelisk
on deserted beach from east to west and back again.
in the morning, on the green shores,

fishermen will swallow your shoulders under their wet raincoats.
your volga profile
that heavy fog moves for hours
toward its own rotting remains.
I flick cigarette
ash into my shoes.
that will make me walk more easily tomorrow.
six months ago, in winter,
while insects behind the wallpaper
built a pontoon of trains and roses
I listened to the radio
in the single-bed hotel room.
at that time over moscow
the cranes were already on the way to forget you.
palme got killed several days after that
during the first minutes of the green megahertz
when your uniform
was already a heated space suit
with the etched constellation
of melancholic sex.

translated from the the Croatian by Mario Suško

— KREŠIMIR BAGIĆ (b. 1962) —

a house

it is all right, I do not
need a doctor, I read
the newspapers, between two strong
puffs, two injections
of immunity, I build a house
I make up a personal paradigm;
I decline ranges of bones,
oases of muscles, inner
organs, brain.
in order to deceive, I bleed a little.
guests are in the house, the house
is tumbling, it is burning. smoke is
its beginning and its end.
the scent of burning is the scent of blood

and the scent of printer's color,
calling, the vocative.
Between two strong puffs, two
"chapters of a common
history," the plan of my body
is carefully coded.
everything is all right. I do not
need a doctor.

translated from the Croatian by Miljenko Kovačiček

— DAMIR ŠODAN (b. 1964) —

Durruti 1936

Hooligan-hero, anarchist leader,
son of a railway worker, a guerrilla
with the eyes of a child and the face of a savage
proletarian propagandist, Buenaventura Durruti
insisted most of all on clarity of expression.

When he had the floor everybody understood.
Emma Goldman said that she found him *a veritable beehive
of activity.* And he was allegedly always in a good mood.

Durruti's Column
was built on self-sacrifice and libertarian spirit.
His funeral magnificently draped all of Barcelona in black
and red. A glorious crowd of half a million
poured down Via Layetana just like that.

Even the Russian consul
was deeply moved
at the sight of that crowd with fists in the air
who swore in that anarchist
who believed that only generals rule by force
and that discipline always comes
like a spout of enlightenment
exclusively from within.

translated from the Croatian by the author

I Like It When You Come Around with Your Friends

I like it when you come around with your friends after soccer
And I cook some apple pie and cheesecake

Afterward we drink wine and schnapps from the refrigerator
And we talk loudly, without being wonky.

The radio is on
And the neon light above the sink.

We talk about hate and war criminals,
about possible options for our future
and about everything that suggests
there is no life in this country.

It is summer and all of the windows are open.
The people some floors below us
Can clearly hear our voices.
Sitting at the dining table, they may
get an objective impression of the situation
And see what all of this is turning into.

translated from the Croatian by Andrew Wachtel

— BORIS A. NOVAK (b. 1954) —

Uni-verse

The light and its night: shapes and their shades, waves and shores—their graves,
and the moon not only full but fulfilled: and a field—a handful of distance,
and the wind—a forefinger of the air, and a bird—a wedding ring of nothing:

and a traveler and his traveling toward the end of steps, into the root
of an endless circle: a voice, and yet a silence of everything,
the silence, and yet a praise to everything: wondering blossoms among petal
    of senses:

touch is the nearest neighbor of the untouchable: a secret weaving of birth: a native
death: a mystery of word, a word of mystery: universe, a unison of unheard star
    chimes,
universe, an unspeakable rhyme of rhymes, universe, one and only cosmic verse . . .

translated from the Slovenian by the author

— ALEŠ DEBELJAK (b. 1961) —

Cast Vote

That crystal morning, snow over snow:
in capital cities they might be ashamed of it.
That conference of birds, and light upon water,
the parliament of dreams that knows no fear
of getting old, and she, alone this winter
morning, her face that sees itself within
a flower etched by ice along the glass,
her reflection thawing and piercing
the window: is she really so strange?
Outside, her shadow sputters again
like a match refusing gravity and singe.
In the vast expanse of frost and worry,
not even a minute to think, she was the one
with the courage to disobey silence, disobey
orders, she could not be voted down and said:
Look, in the shallows of this common river
the Black Sea claims as its own,
fish still wriggle out of a boy's hands, tracing

a nearly perfect arc, and with them everything
that flows, everything that falls, rushes
without reason as one's childhood rushes by—
look: we are not a wall but a shutter
some far-off god is opening halfway.

translated from the Slovenian by Andrew Zawacki and the author

Every Breath You Take

And then the voice says: Shut down your reason, spread your
wings and soar across the sky. Animals rise in the blood out
of molten rock, a sea of burning floods me, I ride on an
unknown animal, furred and warm. It licks my cheek. There
is a tangle of strange creatures, fiddles played by melancholy
donkeys, schools of transparent fish. Nostalgia. In this rock,
in this wind, dolphins with flashing eyes, pulsing flocks of
birds.

Wax of the human, sweet and salty and bitter, oozes from all
pores, eyes are flooded with milk-acid of stars. Montes veneres,
soft swelling olive trees, sweet buds of candied cherries.

Let me sink into you, grace of the gaze, scream of seagull,
wind, warm wind that whips out of tiny stones, warm sway
of an ass's back, fast cold olive trees, sea in its depths and
in its colors washing over head and heart—an end to lamentation,
an end to weeping: every breath you take now is a
hymn.

translated from the Slovenian by Theo Dorgan

May

I saw it, how it was born after an April shower.
When time paused, it stepped from the thicket and
through the door and spoke to me in a forgotten language,
with the voice of fleeing rain that floats
up from the pillows of hermit crabs' dreams,
that loosens the steps of a timid deer.

Then I saw the sea begin to breathe and the rind of the earth
begin to grow warm and rise like dough.
Now the morning rinses the windows and facades of the houses,
caresses the smooth skin of the trees, the cold brow of the stones.
The morning awakens the seraphim and brings the streets to life
and touches the young girls in their swinging skirts,
their trembling thighs and sexy eyes, their fragrant
skin, their wanton laughs that echo and hover
in the evening when the cut grass carries its abundant gifts
and the night calls of crickets melt into the darkness
and Li Po visits me and kisses me
with moonshine from a sleeping age.

translated from the Slovenian by Erica Johnson Debeljak

— ALEŠ ŠTEGER (b. 1971) —

The Returning of What Is to Come

For my grandfather

Surrendered to the expanse of forehead, to the grace which
Melts my body, I speak of fingers of
Earth; of fingernails of grain, which kept safe
My childhood: great waves of air, the sea

Which filled its attic with clouds.
Your mouth of copper, of metal, on which
Gentleness died, so that buried in your
Hands it might be born again as peace oscillating; as

Gestures, which build eyes out of ashes and light. Your
Mouth in the image of a women's fairy tale and a man's
Ear. Your mouth: signpost of death, imbedded in dreams.
Your mouth, which taught me while I was in your arms to listen

To how the golden flowering grain keeps silent, as it crumbles in my
Veins. How the rain keeps silent, raising temples of water on
Shoulders of air. How the torch keeps silent in wind's forests,
How your silence keeps silent, teaching me a dialect

Wherein between wheat and the mouths of clouds I melt into the sky.

translated from the Slovenian by Tom Ložar

✈ HUNGARY ✈

— IMRE ORAVECZ (b. 1943) —

Soldiers' Graves

Ever since I can remember,
they had always been there,
in our garden, next to the cemetery,
they were lined up in the potato field,
packed in side by side,

they formed a long, narrow island on the flats,
the waves of plantings lapping against them,

at first I thought
children were lying under the mounds,
they were so short, so tiny,

they were no special trouble,
we simply detoured around them
and were glad
that we had that much less to hoe,

only in the spring they were a bit in the way,
we had to be careful then
that we didn't plow into them,
or let the horse trample them,

in summer we sickled the grass from their borders,
but we didn't take it home for the cattle,
we threw it into the hedgerow,

once every year, on All Souls' Day, we'd weed them thoroughly,
put them in order,
and place lighted candles on them,
as if they were relatives,
but only one on each,
because they cost money,

sometimes I tried to relate them to the bloodthirsty beasts in Soviet films,

but it didn't work,
I couldn't take offense at them,
my friend Miki always came to mind,
whose father hadn't come home from the war

and might be buried like this somewhere in Russia,
or even worse than this,

then as the years slipped by,
they sank deeper and deeper
and got smaller and smaller,
the wooden crosses rotted and got lost, along with the foreign names,

I began to mix up the old acquaintances,
Kurt for Hans,
Hermann for Jürgen,
Otto for Reiner,
until finally I completely forgot
who was who, when he was born,
and how old he was when he fell,

we paid less and less attention to them,
we realized we couldn't look after them forever,
we couldn't hold back decay,

sometimes we were thoughtless enough
to sit on them,
or step on them,
although we still kept them in mind,

in fifty-six, when we swapped the garden for a building plot,
they were still there,
but when the vacated field was annexed to the cemetery,
and, so to speak, they took their rightful places,
they were mercilessly churned up, even leveled,
a new funeral home was built,
a little open area was wanted in front of it,
and that's where it was,

since then they've been unmarked,
but those resting below are no longer alone,
in the meantime they've acquired many companions,
a whole villageful of civilians moved in,
and it got so crowded
that the cemetery had to be enlarged once again.

translated from the Hungarian by Bruce Berlind and Mária Kőrösy

The Hole

The sheep with the trepanned head stood on the other side of the fence,

in the shade,
facing us,
its head hanging,
motionless,
silent,
an arm's length away,

in its head was a huge funnel-shaped hole
which we could see down into,

the hole consisted of mildew-colored concentric rings
that narrowed to a single point,

in the point something throbbed,

the whole thing was like a bird's-eye view of an exposed surface mine,
only the busy engines and trucks were missing
from the circular berm,

we would have liked to reach in through the pickets
and poke in it with a stick,
but we didn't dare,

we just stood there holding our breath,
and looked at it, stupefied.

translated from the Hungarian by Bruce Berlind and Mária Kőrösy

— ÁKOS SZILAGYI (b. 1950) —

O!

O! happy days
rolling out of those little clockwork gears
fading away from the face of the clock,
happy days, rambunctious watermelons,
the burlap sack slung over time's shoulder
is bulging—let's go!
happy days, the sun's shining
right through my five fingers,
o you voracious dumbbell happy days,

pressing my ear against your swagging belly
nights I listen to your happy, burbling guts

translated from the Hungarian by Jascha Kessler

You Think

Think I'll forget, think I'll forgive you,
my bred-in-the-bone murderer?
Think I just slid from under your heel
as it came down monstrous on me,
think I'll let you stroll with your sweetie now
down the tender aisle of grape leaves?
As I lie spinning on my lacquered back
an inch away from your town's gigantic shoes?
You actually think I'll just fade away
like a drizzle if you look at the sky?
Still don't know me, my little June bug?

translated from the Hungarian by Jascha Kessler

— BÉLA BODOR (b. 1954) —

What to Expect

3 billion kilos
of humanity was killed
in WW II

In Hungary
800,670 kilos
of humanity/year die
while 380,000 kilos
of kids are born.

My father died in 1979
70 kilos, say

In 1985 my child
weighed in at 3.6 kilos

We feed it

translated from the Hungarian by Jascha Kessler

The Lake at Dawn

Vast water: the silence of dawn.
Celestial blue: silence, dawn's
vast water. Vast, celestial, blue
silence, dawn's vast water.

Velvety swells. Silent,
rippling tremors, silence,
vast water, celestial blue,
velvety rippling trem-

ors, hazy, thickening swells,
vast water, blue, rippling, vel-
vety stirrings, celestial,

blue silence, swelling, vel-
vety stirrings, rip-
pling, dawn blue, celestial.

translated from the Hungarian by Jascha Kessler

A Banal Poem. Subject: Love

Those we loved, they're dead.
Faces behind hands, shy.
Shawls dropped, modestly awry.
Those we love, they're married.

Those we loved are busy in the kitchen.
Darkling hair heavy as a cross of flowers,
yet weightless. On you their gaze lowers.
Those we loved are bearing children.

(I wait for you in silence, without pain.
My back to the border, on a clattering train.
You caress your hands with mine.)

(You put my lips to yours. Kiss your lips with mine.
Remonstrations asleep, songs asleep too.
Those we loved, they're dead too.)

translated from the Hungarian by Jascha Kessler

In Praise of the Sea

to my mother

At the edge you stop,
like that, easily,
though in your head
you let the pen run on,

tracing its airy arcs,
its peaceful, lighthearted
jogging run over
the undulating endless

smooth white blank
page of paper,
you let it run as though
running over the sea,

your feet touching
the tops of the waves,
treading their troughs,
arcing over their crests,

the pen, your pen it is,
half-dreaming, half-falling,
and yet still:
almost awake.

At the edge you stop,
infinite waters before you
infinite watery surface,
and you glance at it,

contemplating the waves,
their life rising, falling,
resurging, panting, dashing up,
and crashing down again,

and up above! the gulls
screeching in the air,
albatrosses, and
all those other birds,

flying and floating by
as you gaze at them,

envying their easy flow
over their own pages;

and watch your pen
run on, on yours,
your laughter as they
run, racing up

from out of nothing,
your words, the waters,
their deepest deeps,
the repeating rhythms,

perhaps, of the waves
falling again, and new again,
the crashing tops of the waves,
and the longing,

the longing to utter
at last, to be able at last
to utter, to tear
out of yourself

rend from yourself that
What is this? Infinite waters . . .
and a still sea.
The light voice!

The sea cannot be uttered,
whether heavily, or
lightly, the prankish
pen runs nowhere.

But the birds! They know
why they are wheeling
overhead, and they know
who called them here,

and who it is
will gently see
to them when their
loveliness is gone.

translated from the Hungarian by Jascha Kessler

Snow Covers the Garden

snow covers the garden, the night is gray
we see mere nothings as in a mirror
calm have I always sought, and not terror
it's not the Blessèd Virgin's Lenten way

silence waste and peace to be found nowhere
the snow sifts down, the trees stand bare and still
the signs we leave are signs of signs that will
say we are or were all the signs once there

the city looms a yellowed dome of light
shreds of a tattered sky go slipping past
what gleams above the snowy garden's night

wings of silence, ever heavier wings
heavy portents that we too fall at last
though I sought in calm just what dying brings

translated from the Hungarian by Jascha Kessler

⚜ SLOVAKIA ⚜

— MILA HAUGOVÁ (b. 1942) —

To Withstand Evil

Alpha lives on. She sleeps less.
She hardly dreams. She loves much more.
She blooms in the wastefulness of autumn.
Her sight weakens.
She suffers a silent, deaf mating.
She is afraid.
A man in a circle of evil. Around his neck, blood.
Alpha conceals herself from him, the household serpent hides away.
Can one withstand evil only with evil?

Alpha steps out over the world precipice.
Her brow is furrowed. Her hands are devoted
to movement; she dresses wounds, buries
the dead, comforts abandoned children,
cultivates healing herbs in her garden,
plucks fruit, waters the parched earth,
wanders beneath the trees at night,

intercedes with the long dead.
Far from her the man is lost in a labyrinth of faces.
It's Sunday. Alpha draws breath, her hands
folded in her lap like thousands of women before.
She does not pray. What she sees and knows
is too much for God. She has to bear it alone.
She holds on to loneliness, the word, morning—

*translated from the Slovak by James Sutherland-Smith and
Viera Sutherland-Smith*

Alpha Centauri

Or it could also be different.
Only the entangled voice, flexible bodies, stems,
a gentle bestiary instead of animals
until after you've recognized the signs. Snow on the face.

Lakes in the sea. You remember only the last line.
Just now you will catch the stone spiral in a trap for light:
we have made love before being born. In the March snow
a moonstone. The boy angel holds the whole sky with his soul.
We'll be lost together in loss. I'm nothing of what
I am part. I pretend that there's no shadow beyond my body.
Only a silent diamond under your hand. A double-winged knife, foothills
into which I move unaware. Crags, hot backs, defiles.
A fertile mythology: the transparency of the routes of birds.
A bird falls beneath my feet. It widens the rift in both directions.
Double-mouth. Unvoiced speech. You wish to close
what should remain open. Unknown languages wander through us,
fitting tightly to the limits of escaping rays.
Lord, how it blazes. The animals crouched within us guard
the last warmth.

> *translated from the Slovak by James Sutherland-Smith and*
> *Viera Sutherland-Smith*

— DANA PODRACKÁ (b. 1954) —

A Diary

. . . this hand is colder because of its distance from you.

You: I do not know if he survived.

Me: Someone lifted the tablecloth covering a dead woman's body, but the corpse wasn't there. Instead, there was a puppet made of bread. No one there stood up, no one touched the crust, as if they all knew that in every one of us someone or something has died, at least once.

You: Any story of a man and a woman cannot avoid including death. That is a rule.

Me: Have you ever killed anyone? What did you feel?

You: Nothing. It was like I was in a dream. I was young, I had a weapon. I survived, but years later:

Peter: I was in Istria. I was taking photographs. It wasn't in some bombed-out cemetery. I was in a field full of bombed-out pumpkins.

You: Years later, I dragged a boy from the wreckage of a crashed car, about twelve years of age. One of his eyes is reduced to a pulp. I take him in my arms, and for the first time, I feel death. The dream is returning. I want to save him so badly. The ambulance is coming, it's here, but then it goes away and the motorway is empty: no cars, no people, just me alone. To this day I do not know if the boy's alive.

Peter: When Christ walked to Golgotha, the thing he was carrying wasn't yet a cross. Just two pieces of wood tied with a rope. It only became a cross when they nailed him to it.

Mila: A daughter, someone's daughter is lying on a sheet, face down, so young, hair beautiful like a fall of water, silent . . .

Dream: Someone died. Maybe it was you. We dragged around the town at midnight, drinking from a bottle that we shared. Then someone tore off all her clothes, when the dawn came, and started running and shouting through the streets.

Mila: She lies there, not speaking. At night when I am writing, trying to choose quiet words, I am afraid that even they will hurt her.

Me: My daughter, although she is now grown up, wants to be fed from my breasts. This hand is colder.

Mila: We must find out if he is alive.

Me: Does the intensity we create perish with us? Are we too becoming pure energy? Energy doesn't have consciousness, or does it?

Mila: You must find out if he's alive. But what if it is all a dream?

You: I want to live, standing on that empty motorway.

Me: There is, I know, an eternity in love. But who amongst us is capable of love? This hand is warmer because of its closeness to you.

translated from the Slovak by Robert Welch

— JOZEF URBAN (1964–1999) —

I Blow My Nose Inartistically

We who don't blow our nose nicely
offend polite company
and the routines of decent society

For not blowing our nose nicely
it is necessary to cancel us
from the list of folk who live decently
and to change good manners into laws

to exile us somewhere to an island
and there we'll blow our nose like Robinsons

For not blowing our nose nicely
we must be deprived of our inventions
of making babies
planting birch trees
and our railway track systems
and be left there on an island
so we won't blow our nose in discussions
and slobber over company
who've come to gorge upon each other, nicely,
utterly to the limits of decency.

translated from the Slovak by James Sutherland-Smith

— IVAN KOLENIČ (b. 1965) —

Skin Is a Wrapping of Bones

Every day one verse.
Every morning one powerless lampoon
from sadness and icy grass, oxygen
in the roots of summer—how they sprout
from your bitten tongue. You keep
it red, well-hidden and perfectly
protected behind sharp teeth
which recollect blood. So what
I say is, "Skin is a wrapping for bones,
for veins, for the army of hurts . . ."
(you can do nothing about it) even if
you shelter your silky remembrance
in a glass jar of preserves.
So, not one stupidity—in the ashtray
my hair smolders, in the dark
someone horribly strange comes close to me.
Here endeth the blues—should I say more?

translated from the Slovak by Stefania Allen and James Sutherland-Smith

from Epigraffiti

Admitting one's mortality is granting God's right to eternity.

Anxiety is what remains repressed when inhaling and exhaling.

The magic of fiction lies in deluding reason that it is fiction.

Hope is the last to die—only after us.

Human action is the modification of possibility into irreparability.

Even the buzz of a mosquito is a communication.

Human stupidity is an expression of humanness itself.

A secret of communication. Given the difficulty of expressing oneself, every lie is holy.

The most natural form of openness to the world is naïveté.

Even murderers may have an opinion on murder—provided they be philosophers.

His phantoms hired him as their confessor.

From the point of view of this or that otherness, we all look the same.

Dialectic is the intellectual form of the unbalanced mind.

Knowledge—a narrow, twisting hallway, lit by a fuse.

Humanity is and is not to be blamed for its lack of humanity.

Life is an act of chance; death, one of inevitability.

An indirect proof of God's existence is God's indifference to human fate.

Evil does not manifest a lack of good, but a desire to know good.

Through death nothing ends, nor does anything begin.

translated from the Slovak by Madelaine Hron

How to Endure the Sun if Not Tiptoeing

It all unfolds naturally, depending
on who you follow—

even beyond the very first door
you can still arrive with ease
in front of a mirror,
that will send you out to the unknown

or you may come to feel the ticklish
weight of an atom just stilled,
just observed
at the imagined intersection
of a planetary latitude and longitude
you have long searched for.

From that glimpse alone you'll find yourself
turned into a crossbreed
of numberless handshakes
suddenly at the top of a mountain designed
solely for this expedition
that will positively not come to a close
before you bring
the charged egg
back into the airy nest from which
you exalted it.

Offspring fully sunk in their swings
can still feel safe
about their weightlessness

which comes under scrutiny
with every fresh moment of awe-inspiring
dizziness.

They rise on nothing
but a few crumbs, grains
shared with shaken pigeons
who keep nodding yes to everything
they have never been asked

by them, the philosophers.

translated by Martin Solotruk and Marc Woodworth

⇥ CZECH REPUBLIC ⇤

— IVANA BOZDECHOVÁ (b. 1960) —

Everyday Occurrence

Suddenly he stood at my table
without knocking
with a white rose wrapped in paper
and a question in his eyes.

The afternoon had drizzled into dusk
and the café was smoke-filled with people.
Carefully we picked our silences
until at last we know
that even together we cannot
cure the world.

So don't be afraid of happiness
or of the smile of Prague Castle
above the weary river.

All that is left today
is the rattle of the departing streetcar
because the rose looks forward to getting home.
Do come again.
Maybe something's beginning.

translated from the Czech by Ewald Osers

— SYLVA FISCHEROVÁ (b. 1963) —

The Only Place

I always stroked
my face with a violin bow
and my breast with the bow,
I ate the horsehair
and became the empty space
inside the violin; I lie there
with a dead child that cries. I don't cry. I could be

something like amber, but
immaterial, or air
    deep under the mountain
    where that aged Chinese
    caught sight of five suns; but next day
    there was only one.

Amber, I said, but only
its gold translucency,
the color of the sea that in the morning
cries
under one sun
and one violin. The dead child
cries; it knows there's
only one sea. There
        we found ourselves:
naked, on a long
solitary beach,
      the only place
      where we shall ever belong.

translated from the Czech by Jarmila Milner and Ian Milner

The Language of the Fountains

I was holding a mirror in my hands for you,
and the ends of your shaved beard
floated in the soapy water,
little, everyday deaths.
The epochs stuck together like veneer to wood,
tight and precise, with a breath between
by which a monster changes
    into a genius,
and the cafeteria's windows to mirrors,
in front of which the dumb goblins learn to speak,
to score
    a defeat.
A defeat of a nation.
And of all dead languages.
The era of quotation marks has begun:
a double mockery of the ideas
    inflated inside them.

But the salt statues still stand by the Dead Sea,
there's still Jerusalem, Athens, Rome,
still someone living in Prague who speaks Yiddish—
and memory, sister to self, sister of sin,
and guide to the saved
    leads us back
    to our own destruction.

Here the cafeteria's a church for smokers!
Defeat's a beer. A bloody sausage
    and birthday cake.
Cowardice
    a bridge into time,
and whoever knows a thing about time
will tell of even a God—
will answer God,
    a hole inside him
    the colorless nooses of history
    fall into.
And the rich and powerful fit nice and tight . . .
Who will tell of the dead children
    on the trembling sands of history?
Who will see—will hear
    the language of the fountains, sweet, predictable
        as a throw of dice?
Who will speak of the dead children
    on the trembling sands of history . . .

    translated from the Czech by the author and Stuart Friebert

Eggs, Newspaper, and Coffee

Eggs, newspaper, and coffee
are the first lie of the world,
saying that it's
        in order.

What order, while the whoredoms
of Jezebel, your mother,
and her witchcrafts are many?
said Jehu to King Horam
and shot him
        between his shoulders.

What order, when every morning
the ark's built up,
and the animals outrun
           one another,
wheedle money, bribe Noah:
    Brother, let me in!

Noah's taken in,
the ark rocks on pity, on grief,
a swift stream, the Okeanos of weeping,
spits it into the pan of eggs
    in the middle of the morning.
How the animals shout! How fried they are!
    Buy! Buy the news from the ark!
           they squeak from the pan,

and above them, implacable as Jehu, an angel cries:
What order?
The news of your heart's
black as night,
ugly as a Medusa!

On the waves of a compassionate coffee,
Noah sails the ship on
past shop shutters slowly lifting up,
around mumbling flowers
opening and closing their
shining petals,
breathing out pity
which papers
    the world

        translated from the Czech by the author and Stuart Friebert

Door

The door had always been closing, by itself, for ages and ages, in slow haste.

Now it won't move.

In front of it a woman is guiltily picking up a large undershirt which had fallen off the line at night. The wind perhaps. Sometime at night.

Both would like to know when, when exactly it happened, both would like to be in that moment.

translated from the Czech by Zuzana Gábrišová

At the Claws

play the dahlias, for my wife here with the birthday, the one sitting in the coat,
    I can't remember
how it goes, how it all went, dahlias, don't know the rest, you'll know them, you
    are here every day, from the pub you see it all, the whole of Vítkovice, life, even
    the gardens

translated from the Czech by Zuzana Gábrišová

[We do what? We are involved in space,]

We do what? We are involved in space,
are silent, we let the dead sleep on.
We cut down trees, fence off compost,
pry open traps in which mice have come to grief.
Evenings, we take our dinner out to the garden,
bring brushwood back into the room.
We return it yellowed to the bonfire,
its sweet smoke billowing through our wardrobes.
In the twilight we look out at the wall
and speak so as not to wake the dead.
Amidst the furniture we make love
with bodies, which are not the opposite of space.

translated from the Czech by Justin Quinn

from Lake Poems

There's been a stone pushed in my mouth
Since I met the crow
Stripped off her feathers
By the deep spring
Only unclear words I heard
When ascending to watch the rising bark of the Sun
I stole seeds from her beak
Thus I must be punished
I'll do it by myself

(written in English)

[Yes, I live inside the piano,]

Yes, I live inside the piano,
but there is no need for you
to come and visit me.

translated from the Czech by Alexandra Büchler

Nowhere

Covered by purple leaves
I'll leave my roots under water.

You will open the windows, and from a distance
hear the blows from the time when
they killed carp by the vats in winter.

You will immerse yourself in reading, pondering things
so as not to think about yourself.

You will feel good inside those voices
with two sentences left
the first made of my rib,
the second of yours.

translated from the Czech by Alexandra Büchler

⊰ POLAND ⊱

— PIOTR SOMMER (b. 1948) —

A Certain Tree in Powązki Cemetery

All memory we owe to objects
which adopt us for life and
tame us with touch, smell
and rustle. That's why it's so hard
for them to part with us: they guide us
till the end, through the world,
till the end they use us, surprised
by our coolness and the ingratitude
of that famous spinner Mnemosyne.

translated from the Polish by Halina Janod and John Ashbery

Space

(after Wang Wei)

We live secluded under the smoke of steelworks.
The area to the east and south is Warsaw.
The sun is burning out and shining through the dust.
The river is invisible, our house was built by little ants.
It's freezing and almost dark, white figures return to their homes.
The buses can hardly move—
at home dogs have had a hard day.

Today, just as before, there are redundant people.
Yet each of them can do a lot and each can bear a lot.

translated from the Polish by Halina Janod, Ed Adams, and Edward Carey

Don't Sleep, Take Notes

At four in the morning
the milkwoman was knocking
in plain clothes, threatening
she wouldn't leave us anything,
at most remove the empties,
if I didn't produce the receipt.

It was somewhere in my jacket,
but in any case I knew
what the outcome would be:
she'd take away yesterday's curds,
she'd take the cheese and eggs,
she'd take our flat away,
she'd take away the child.

If I don't produce the receipt,
if I don't find the receipt,
the milkwoman will cut our throats.

translated from the Polish by Halina Janod and D. J. Enright

— BOZENA KEFF (b. 1950) —

What's in my pocket

Sunblock, four business cards
for various cab companies (my last time driving across the square
mirrored in the skyscraper wall the red lava of sunset
like a tiger lunging,
but no one sees it probably, and I
think about the gloom of that apartment in Praga
where I'm no longer loved), three cards for outpatient clinics,
a punch-card for the pool (girls I've never seen before
doing handstands on the bottom, later they squeal and hiccup from
laughing; and I with them), a pen,
a little mechanical pencil, an eraser, an old movie ticket
("It's as if the sky were protecting us from what's behind," he says
as they're trying to make love on the edge of the desert; the reddish
earth, the blue vault of the sky. "But what *is* behind?"
she asks. "Nothing," he answers. "Just
darkness. Absolute night."), more, Nerventablets, the painkiller Saridon
(oh the blessed moment when that rusted jaw flies open and you
sink back softly into your body), some scrap of paper,
yes, the address, the Turk, 21 years old, life sentence,
would like someone to write to him. Likes movies. Right, movies,
but what tone should I use? What am I supposed to write,
how, about what, does one write letters like these? Should I write,
"The prospect of your life horrifies me. My regrets,"

or instead describe mine, but from what angle—
I haven't, I simply haven't a clue.

translated from the Polish by W. Martin

Dream of the Meaning of Dreams

Image:

A strip of purple sky lined with a remainder of sunlight, between the end of the day and the onset of night. Purple turns brown, the light dies out.

Voice (without gender or character):

—This image in a dream indicates the approach of solitude.

Image:

A valley as it must have been thousands of years ago, overgrown with high shrubs and grasses. Where is it? I see smoke, someone has put out a fire.

Voice (without gender or character):

—This image in a dream signifies a lost memory.

Image:

My friend K. is sitting on a chair, not speaking, for some tormenting reason I can't understand the expression on her face.

Voice: I wait, but it doesn't speak.

translated from the Polish by Alissa Valles

— ANDRZEJ SOSNOWSKI (b. 1959) —

Five Fathoms Down

I

Imagine it is thus
A monotonous movement

Days sink in their standing
Hours die in their sleep

Mirrors approach through mist
And the watersong tarnishes

We speak through airlocks
Broken are bridges and rails

Broken

Our positions burned

2

In the evenings birds flitter in
Thin leaves of soot on the air
And it's the same in the blood's infrared
The same in night vision
The head tossed back the mouth
Open for the shot
And ever the cricket's signal
To someone who must arrive any minute
Like the rasp of a drum with a broken snare

3

This will be one moment
And nothing will happen

And you're having fun up there
I'm driving the blood from my bright head

And when you descend deeper
I draw hearts on the mirror

I smile like it's no biggie
At the little ship on the surface

4

Clean yourself out
And lose your way

For the path is in losing
For the trace is in losing
For in losing us

A gray angel
And lightness beyond comprehension

So that what is dead will leave us
And something else cut us to the quick

This is how the dead fell from us
And left us with no living thing

     translated from the Polish by Benjamin Paloff

Errata

But of course the soul is the fifth wheel, to be
lost, not spared. Because the first violins
keep whipping up the chariots, gigs drawn
by hippocampi, deer, panthers, pigeons,
or some other phantasmagoric cemetery.
My dealer doesn't even want to hear about it.
New engine. Monotonous, the lap of life.

It'll just bedazzle you, *next year's* quota.
Man feels torn apart by models.
And when we transcribe ourselves this way,
for 102 voices, the wheels don't touch the ground,
our hair "soars to the Alps." Where the street
lets out, the duchess was dozing in her d'Aumont,
I drove up by *solitaire,* my rivals rolled up in a coach.

The arena shrinks. At the end, paradoxically,
a child under a lone spotlight rides in circles
on a unicycle. It's a marvelous picture,
a *Lehmhaus.* Music, the titles draw us aside.
They'd like to have a word. It should be: inventory.

translated from the Polish by Benjamin Paloff

— MARCIN ŚWIETLICKI (b. 1961) —

Preface

"I shall name him Abel," said the stranger
—a man to be later called, with such terrible
difficulty, father; he said it to a
slim, in some places totally unslim,
woman whom we'll later call
mother. "WE shall name him so," stressed the mother,
and he grimaced—it's him who had decided,
she should have only approved.

That evening, when they did it and chose the name,
might be set in some exceptionally
nice-looking place as well as some pleasant
time; we, nonetheless, will be malicious:
the spring of 1961, Poland.

In the garden a stupid apple tree was coming to life,
not recalling that last year it brought forth
nothing. A grass snake slithered over its trunk.

Their eyes were opened, exactly, to the end;
the trousers hung carefully folded
on the chair, on another hung the dress;
both were naked and ashamed.
The grass snake crept across the garden, eating dust and sand;
behind the wall the father's father coughed and swore
in a foreign tongue of curse; and the radio crackled,
crackled and boomed like a flaming sword.

In the night fields and night courtyards
a nonexistent elder brother whirled and sneered.
Spring. In the depots, dead buses.
Old lemonade bottles of that unusual shape,
that charming way to open them. Moon.
A nice militiaman. Moon. And the magazine
You and I lying on the table in the lamplight
—opened, not by chance, on its first page.

We'll be observing the advance of darkness.

translated from the Polish by Elżbieta Wójcik-Leese

Song of the Ill

I slept through all the carnival, delirious.
I couldn't bear the drums, pipes, burning puppets.
Today the carnival's over,
postmodernism begins.
I fiddle with the radio. This archetypal
scan of the wavelength can be performed
ad infinitum. Inside me
I have a little God, I tend

this scrap,
scab.

translated from the Polish by Elżbieta Wójcik-Leese

Foodstone

I give you meadows entrust you with rivers
may the waters spill from their channels anew
each night: "when you will go to him
and he will go to you" I give you

every last river the Wisznia the Sołotwa
the Lubaczówka nor begrudge you a flower
since I became a flower retrieved
from sleep: "when you will go to him

and he will go to you" I abandon
you for my very own fire that in
the hand becomes an even greater fire
everything grows larger in my hands

and rounder in my mouth for the stone
has been growing fuller since I became
a stone more nourishing retrieved from the bed
of the river retrieved from the deepest sleep

translated from the Polish by Bill Johnston

In the hallway of the regional hospital

their days filled with fear at every thing
that needs to be painted over in the color
of the sun and their nighttime full of fear
at a kiss since death has been drawing close

"what will become of us when the hour is fixed
for disconnection or connection to the once-more
undependable apparatus in the regional hospital where
all but the nurses proves undependable"

their night full of fear at every thing that must be
painted in time in the color of the sun and roll
roll alongside it in a wheelchair
for the sun's an invalid as it rises and sets

gripping each year the selfsame handrails in darkened
hallways

translated from the Polish by Bill Johnston

[Frost ropes in the ditch: nothing could break through,]

Frost ropes in the ditch: nothing could break through,
slip through (though maybe underground, in water
full of bare sky); the brook swelled,
the field half froze, and sharp wind now blasts dust
from furrows vanished somewhere under the ice.
Day—a bundle of gossamer
planted on the sky; a colonized,
subjugated life. Bled dry by the cold, as light
as the rind of lichen on the stones; to live, whistles
the wind,
to live, otherwise than the leaves . . . and may death be
like snow that keeps the earth
from freezing over entirely

translated from the Polish by W. Martin

Winter Elegy

how quick: the quiet avarice in whitening;
blackening, vanishing into furrows in the road a crow flock crumbles.
How clear my breath is on the pane. Fractured with violet, fields
wide, gaping. Parched ponds as docile
as if touched by gentle hands,
not bandages of frost.
The hills grow cold over the crowns of apples and alders,
in the window a light is lit in the distance. Sparks of warmth wander
into the ashes of dusk,
unthinking I break off a hunk of bread:

and we, how quick, into furrows of time, into mute
and like stones

translated from the Polish by W. Martin

Early Spring

The ice monocle on the pond
cracked.
After days of lead and torpor, finally!—

a fitting for the shadows.
Sewing them up for everything: for the stumps
of rosebushes in the garden, eyelashes,
garages. A drawing out, a cutting,
of the cloth flapping in the sun's
draft.
A putting-on of white slipcovers
on blocks of houses,
on people.

A floating down the hills
of heavy rafts of snow

translated from the Polish by W. Martin

— KRZYSZTOF KOEHLER (b. 1963) —

[A new language: the language]

A new language: the language
of the mosquito at the ear.
The language of dogs
savaging blackness.
The language of engines at night;
the language of cold blades.

A new language. The language
of song beneath blackness
and stars. The language
of moths, the language of crickets
and the lamentation
of a never-cooling earth.

The language of life.
The voice of duty and accord.
Nothing more, nothing
less. The prayer
of a water well amid
advancing deserts.

translated from the Polish by Bill Johnston

[Two columns of smoke]

Two columns of smoke
and an open field.
Vivid colors of leaves:
infinity
touches us here.

Space that opens
to the edge of the woods.
The gaze penetrates no further,
but beyond is
precisely that
which changes colors,
seasons,

and gives
a meaning to
sky and plain.

There mushrooms
are born and beneath
shade-filled branches
animals slink past.

And right there
is the limit. The staying
of the landscape,
the form in which
fate is manifest.

Woods beyond woods.
Space beyond space.
We are reaching the essence.

translated from the Polish by Bill Johnston

— MARCIN SENDECKI (b. 1967) —

Good Later

"Uh huh," says the streetcar, or it seems to say.
Where did the clock with a tune come from, I can't hear
a thing. Wrong: tremors should be caught, fixed, fitted in.
How far we've come, my dear Statistics: vanilla sugar,

three waters and pudding *responds to the deep needs*
of the reader, invites him to an exchange, embodies
a philosophy of dialogue. Is there "incomprehensible"
poetry? Of course there is! Incomprehensible poetry

is egocentric poetry, based on adoration of self,
poetry that gets off on itself – narcissistic poetry.
It's poetry that doesn't want to share anything
with the person reading it, it only wants

to dazzle the reader, shock, imprison him—floor him
with cascades of metaphors and other smart moves.
It's essentially laboratory poetry, created for
the admiring eyes of others in the field, in the lab,

laboring over their own fireboxes filled with words
nobody cares about sugar, bottled water on sale, pudding
not. The other day I found a leaflet in a track suit pocket:
"Come again? To load up on beer, you had to get cheese?"

translated from the Polish by Alissa Valles

[A little coat, white up till now,]

A little coat, white up till now,
disappears with the voice that was on the point.
You didn't see the voice, you were looking down,
as if you should at least see blood and stone.

A little coat, up till now, finally
falls apart and is used for rags. The street
is short, deserted. The next one.
One more street. This is where the city ends.

translated from the Polish by Alissa Valles

— EWA SONNENBERG (b. 1967) —

Internal Manifesto I

My self is someone else blown up to life size
made wherever and in whatever way a fluke of someone's whim
I owe nothing to anybody I choose my own mother and father
they are my friends and lovers they feed me with their own milk and sweat

I owe no debt to beauty kindness reason
I've won fortune's lottery they pay me eternity for my enemies

I don't have to drink to speak the gut-colored truth
I don't curtsy after each word my verse: sour fodder
for the folk raised on TV and fun fairs
my tongue sails the open sea I don't need
excuses from friends family soul doctors I will write by myself:
I could have played Chopin politely in a corner away from the scent
of raw meat never eating it never calling it "the border of borders"

It's good to be on the edge
one can do everything

translated from the Polish by Katarzyna Jakubiak

Uncertainty

I'll plead for you with someone you don't know
he lends me a path toward childhood meadows
and a key sharp as a needle used for piercing dreams
just don't heal over I beg you never to do that
leave a raw opening to the poem's other side
the sky cries so sweetly singing on its knees

I'll follow your childish loss in a paper
crown I'll face reality bewitched
into a cackle have mercy just stop the wars
fought by no one but you
and stop the victories always misunderstood
your screams won't cover silence

My funny little poem I'll warm you in my hands
we'll tell life we're sorry for writing not living
your naive and tender efforts to spy on naked words
flattered my ego and animated objects
watching you hurt your feet against the hard ground
I loved you more than any human being

translated from the Polish by Katarzyna Jakubiak

Notable Essay: Music

for German Ritz

Music is a German girl
and the devil is a German.
Angels are of Slavonic origin.

Reflections on angels
have a calming effect.
It's good to have some angel watching over you.

Reflections on nationality
can get people
all worked up.

Right away you get
the problem of betrayal
and fuck off you dirty traitor.

Why do I suffer so,
music asks us,
to which we answer: Because you're so beautiful.

But in fact we don't respect her
and let her scrape away
on that violin of hers.

Let her sail
around the room
like a fly.

Angels are musicians:
the devil writes for them,
and the Lord listens

(though
he's
an Arab from Mesopotamia).

translated from the Polish by Alissa Valles

Calypso

The sea's color is green.
The white sand is stained with blood.
An old woman dies at the diner, underfed,
underprepared. The telephone only takes phone cards.

Some people are hard to recognize, even
on the street. Already April, and here, imagine it,
snow. Contradictions, contradictions. Eh,
it's better late than at all, better at all.

So we can't live more now? Even when we're by ourselves
we invoke metaphors of the heart.
Imagine a situation where it never occurs to you
to think of any other situation.

translated from the Polish by W. Martin

— DARIUSZ SUSKA (b. 1968) —

Light

light, no more than that, a bus stands still
and doesn't move on; at a graveyard wall
sight, blinded by whiteness, jumps ahead
over January's deaths, crows lying dead,

and runs on, over a pub, where the view
sky pours out is the perspective of a few
low houses, paint scraped off their face
and a muddy glacier in the market place

light, nothing else will come your way,
the eye within the eye will store away
images of odd benches, scrap-iron heaps
snow-packed holes on sidewalks, streets

translated from the Polish by Alissa Valles

Death is the top player in our playground

Death is the top player in our playground,
not Suchy, who can keep a ball in the air,
or Chybowski, who is master of matches.
Death is our top player, Imiolczyk himself
with all his best tricks didn't come near
though once he put his head through glass
and the glass doors burst like ocean spray
and blood from his knees and his nose lay
clotted under the stairs. Death was the one
to beat Gruby on a bike, the first to switch
to a board. Death rules, is what I'm saying,
it builds us; builds, while we are decaying

translated from the Polish by Alissa Valles

— ARTUR SZLOSAREK (b. 1968) —

Imagination

Useless for anyone's happiness, my imagination
Struggles wildly with the redhead seen this morning on the train:
With the flame in her footstep, strands of golden fleece.
Eagerly it confirms this wonder: her fingernails' tint.

Useless for anyone's happiness, my imagination,
In love with quotations, wants to counterfeit stimuli. Disgusted
By explanations, it's not of this world. Thus it nests
Painfully in the throat of one who dreams with shame
About calling the first bones of the word as witness.

translated from the Polish by Jennifer Grotz

Temptation

And if the devil himself paid me a visit and said,
"Love me, and you will be granted salvation," what would I
Say in return? That love is the best solution?

Three Magi meet and gossip at tea.

The first has arrived on an icy train from the East.
The second confides he has been putting a baby into jars.
The third would gladly celebrate the waitress's body.

There is no mystery. It's December 24th. There are trees walking.

And if the devil himself paid them a visit and said,
"Follow me, and you will not go astray," what might they
Say in return? That everyone is left to their own devices?

Would they reveal themselves as the gifts they had not brought?

translated from the Polish by Anna Skucińska and Jennifer Grotz

⤚ BELARUS ⤙

— VICTAR SHALKEVICH (b. 1959) —

[I want to tell you what speaks to me most—]

I want to tell you what speaks to me most—

My little neighbor, the son of village drunkards,
a bright young boy,
by the gas-lamp—for we have no electricity—he
writes each evening a verse about freedom.
He is no Raznai and no Baradulin and certainly he is
no Dudarai,
but I tell you, we will hear of him one day!

With these optimistic words I want to end
the difficult evening
in our immeasurable Belarus.

translated from the Belarusian by Ilya Kaminsky and Kathryn Farris

— MIKHAS BAJARYN (b. 1970) —

[creating a homer is less complicated than you might imagine]

creating a homer is less complicated than you might imagine
all you need is exquisite taste and some patience
a pair of scissors there are still countries almost unknown
otherwise there are words with vague meanings enough beautiful names and
besides
abundance of archives and forgotten poets
at least a week at max half a century will be needed to montage and live
and to form a circle of incurably blind madmen
that everybody would take for a school on rhode or khias island
it would be good to keep it all a secret but especially the slogan
homer gets only the best and then everything will work out.

translated from the Belarusian by Valzhyna Mort

Commedia

Which circle
of Dante's Hell
is meant for the drunkards

who the day before were mixing
sweet wine with beer
and missed their chance to repent before death?

In this very circle
we woke up in the morning,
though formally speaking

we were in Poland
the city of Wroclaw
Hotel Wodnik.

The spring sun soothed our pain a little
but didn't evoke any desire
to talk in tercets.

Morning coffee transferred us to Limbo—
as pagan bastards
(i.e., virtuous pagans),

or maybe even unbaptized infants?
(you should have seen the infantile physiognomy
of a poet sitting in front of me!)

We kept ascending
the Dante's ladder
and here we were in the Hotel Purgatory:

Finnish sauna, swimming pool,
TV set, pool table
and everything is free of charge.

Who knows how far into Heaven
we would have gone
if not for the checkout time?

The receptionist's name was Peter;
but we didn't pay attention to his badge
when giving him our keys

and getting into a taxi.

translated from the Belarusian by Valzhyna Mort

— VIKTAR ŽYBUL (b. 1978) —

[I don't want to be the navel of the Earth.]

I don't want to be the navel of the Earth.
earth has navels galore, it doesn't need me.
I want to be the sky's navel.
An air pocket, a black hole's
the role for me.
There is more freedom
and more liberty
there.

Be it known:
I
and my navels
and my navels' navels
observe you from
on high.
no one can hide himself
from this diligent scanning.
No, you do not see me dissolving in clouds—
it is clouds dissolving in me!

And now
each person who tries
to reach for the sky,
reaches for me,
and my navels,
and the navels of my navels.
He reaches me,
but I don't feel him touch me.

What?
Don't you believe in my

all-navelish naveldom,
in my
supernavelism of
supernavelmost navelity,
in my
archinavel navelescence?

Then go, ask the man who reached
for the sky and broke his finger.

translated from the Belarusian by Vera Rich

— VALZHYNA MORT (b. 1981) —

Belarusian I

Even our mothers have no idea how we were born
how we parted their legs and crawled out into the world
the way you crawl from the ruins after a bombing
we couldn't tell which of us was a girl or a boy
and we gorged on dirt thinking it was bread
and our future a gymnast on a thin
thread of the horizon was performing there
at the highest pitch
bitch

we grew up in a country where
first your door is stroked with chalk
and then at dark a chariot arrives
and no one sees you anymore
but riding in those cars were neither
armed men nor
a wanderer with a scythe
this is how love loved to visit us
and snatch us veiled

completely free only in public toilets
where for a little change nobody cared what we were doing
we fought the summer heat the winter snow
and when we discovered we ourselves were the language
and our tongues were removed we started talking with our eyes
and when our eyes were poked out we talked with our hands
and when our hands were cut off we conversed with our toes

and when we were shot in the legs we nodded our head for yes
and shook our heads for no and when they ate our heads alive
we crawled back into the bellies of our sleeping mothers
as if into bomb shelters
to be born again

and there on the horizon the gymnast of our future
was leaping through the fiery hoop
of the sun
screwed

translated from the Belarusian by Valzhyna Mort and Franz Wright

Belarusian II

Outside your borders,
they built a huge orphanage,
and you left us there, belarus,
maybe we were born without legs?
maybe we worshipped the wrong gods?
maybe we brought you misfortune?
maybe we are deathly sick?
maybe you are not able to feed us?
but can't we just beg for food?!
maybe you never really wanted us,
but at first we also
didn't know how to love you.

your language is so small
that it can't even speak yet,
but you, belarus, are hysterical,
you are certain
that midwives mixed up the bundles.
what if you're feeding somebody else's baby?!
letting another's language suck your own milk?!
a bluish language lying on the windowsill—
is it a language or last year's hoarfrost?
is it hoarfrost or an icon's shadow?
is it a shadow or just nothing?

it's not a language.
it doesn't have any system.
it is like death—sudden and unscrupulous.

like death you can never die from,
like death that brings the dead to life.

language that makes you burn newly borns
language that makes a brother kill a brother
language that nobody can hide from
language that delivers men-freaks
delivers women-beggars
delivers headless beasts
delivers toads with human voices

this language does not exist!
it doesn't have any system!
it's impossible to talk to it—
it strikes you in the face at once!
even on holidays
you won't decorate the city with it
it can't be doctored up neither with fireworks
nor with neon light

oh, come one, let this system kiss my
a c c o r d i o n
and my accordion
when it stretches its bellows
my accordion looks
like mountain picks
it eats from my hands
it licks them and like a kid
won't get off my lap
but time will come and it will
show its ta ra ta ta

translated from the Belarusian by Valzhyna Mort and Franz Wright

[Maybe you too sometimes fantasize]

Maybe you too sometimes fantasize
that god resembles your most difficult teacher
the one who never gave the highest mark
one day he invites your parents to school
and who knows what he is telling them there
perhaps that any further effort is now futile
because you're never going to graduate from life

with honors
maybe something different
something completely and utterly different
but when this talk is done
your parents never come back
maybe they're ashamed now
a boy from the neighborhood tells you they're dead
he says look even the Beatles die
never mind your parents
besides who knew them except you
all their songs were written by other people

but you refuse to believe him can't get any sleep
you cry at home
you cry among people you know and people you don't know
on the street
because your parents have left and are ashamed
to return to you again

translated from the Belarusian by Valzhyna Mort and Franz Wright

⤅ UKRAINE ⤇

— OLEH LYSHEHA (b. 1949) —

Song 551

Before it's too late—knock your head against the ice.
Before it's too late
Break through, look.
You will see a miraculous world.
It's quite another thing with a carp—
It tends to plunge,
Escaping to the lowest depths,
Born to be caught, sooner or later.
But you are human aren't you?—NO one will catch you.
Carp—they're a different sort—
For centuries the dark
Treacherous shoals have been sinking.
When did our century begin rushing to catch them?
Look—its fin caresses
Their fins, it follows them,
Slips away. You're alone?
But you are human, aren't you?
Don't worry, you'll break through.
Before it's too late—knock your head against the ice.
O miraculous, wide and snowy world!

translated from the Ukrainian by James Brasfield

Song 352

When you need to warm yourself,
When you are hungry to share a word,
When you crave a bread crumb,
Don't go to the tall trees—
You'll not be understood there, though
Their architecture achieves cosmic perfection,
Transparent smoke winds from their chimneys.
Don't go near those skyscrapers—
From the one-thousandth floor
They might toss snowy embers on your head.
If you need warmth

It's better to go to the snowbound garden.
In the farthest corner you'll find
The lonely hut of the horseradish.
Yes, it's here, the poor hut of a horseradish.
Is there a light on inside?—Yes, he's always at home.
Knock at the door of a horseradish.
Knock on the door of his hut.
Knock, he will let you in.

translated from the Ukrainian by James Brasfield

— NATALKA BILOTSERKIVETS (b. 1954) —

Hotel Central

for anyone

in one of the cities where at an uncertain time
capricious fate acknowledges us
where in the evening you can hear jazz in the restaurants
in the morning—bells from the gothic arches
water lilies bloom in the canals there
people drink coffee there and later on beer
and the bicycles of radiant schoolgirls fly
in their sweet way in flocks

their backpacks bright and light
their legs long their hips slim
my God we once were like them too
ten twenty thirty years ago
but cast aside your itinerant pity
there's a Hotel Central in every city—
for those just like you who are no one for no one

here you'll unpack your ordinary things
remove the contacts from your eyes
wash your flesh get your drink
push the button on the pay TV—
there's everything you'd want; and how you'd want it too;
shut your eyes enter and take
nocturnal music knows no bounds
in the chambers of your Hotel Central

at three AM God like Bosch will come
to Hotel Central from the heavenly halls
with insects playing clarinets
with mosquitoes drinking submissive blood
with frogs and snails;
with fish, too; and all your love
is just caviar in the repositories of hell

just the struggle of a puny and a miserable slave
spread all over the walls,
of a human being—with a smiting Spirit
he sculpts and bends your body
then throws it into a tub of dung
removing it with his two fingers
shaking it looking and listening

like the first look of tender compassion
like the first touch of a somber "I love you"
like the burst of sun in the folds of a curtain—
Hotel Central meets the new dawn

and every day is like your last chance
and every night as though for the last time
and over the lily-flowered canals the bicycles
of anxious schoolgirls fly

translated from the Ukrainian by Michael M. Naydan

— YURKO POZAYAK (b. 1957) —

Alcohaiku

Today for the second time I
Cross Khreshchatyk Boulevard
And there's no one to drink with . . .

Ah weightless bubble
In golden champagne . . .
The life of an aristocrat.

Five stars of cognac
The astrologer recalled—
I cry and laugh.

When the chestnuts bloom
And fall,
I'm always at Café François.

And when the cicada
Chirrs in the grass—
You're a ruble short . . .

It seems just recently
We sat down for a drink,
And outside it's already autumn.

The phone began to ring,
I don't pick up the receiver—
A half bottle's still left.

Ah, how the bird sings,
Ah, how she sings!
I order another shot.

Yesterday I overdid it,
Falling down dead drunk—
Or maybe this is love?

I hugged a tree.
Ah, who'll take me home
Today?!

The crow caws and caws.
For the life of me I can't understand—
Have I really had too much to drink?

How comically everyone below
Is taking on airs—
I dashed from the balcony . . .

Always that awful dream—
Champagne and hooch
Plus vermouth and warm beer.

translated from the Ukrainian by Michael M. Naydan

Jamaica the Cossack

oh how many groovy wonders all over my horse my brother
even when ravens empty my eyes I'd wish to see

more

on this side bahama-mama

haitian palms on the other

and a view of freetown towers out of my bungalow

it shames me to the point of my trousers losing their color
what the hell for the sake of which subterranean fauna
we were sold out in the battle by the sea mowers-corsairs
when father wanted to seize that unearthly freetown

it offers thirteen churches and endless war against cupid
also thirteen abysses with plenty of gold and silver
girls are quite like vines growing behind the fences
they are dying for love but have to wear black gowns

at present I suck moonshine together with dick the pirate
I tell him awaken jackass I tell him repent a loser
as if when you are from europe you are no longer a human
you fucked up and ditched yourself for thirty rotten escudos

but dick is a weird fellow he parries and strokes his parrot
pats me on the back and throws his hands in the air
his facial grins and frowns are by heaven as rare
as any he might belie in false compare.

he boasts to me of a slave girl with skin the color of cocoa
buy her my gray-winged eagle it's tough without a mistress
no need to seed out a garden he chuckles and drools all over
garden grows on her body

melons pine apples tobacco

you'll make an army of young ones he says of cossack's sons
but my neck as well as my soul won't be bound by bonds

I don't hear his ramblings and I couldn't care less
my horse my unfaithful horse my doubting apostle

at night I'll go through the reed

cut a penny whistle

sit near the ocean

already missing

translated from the Ukrainian by Valzhyna Mort

— OKSANA ZABUZHKO (b. 1960) —

A Definition of Poetry

I know I will die a difficult death—
Like anyone who loves the precise music of her own body,
Who knows how to force it through the gaps in fear
As through the needle's eye,
Who dances a lifetime with the body—every move
Of shoulders, back, and thighs
Shimmering with mystery, like a Sanskrit word,
Muscles playing under the skin
Like fish in a nocturnal pool.
Thank you, Lord, for giving us bodies.
When I die, tell the roofers
To take down the rafters and ceiling
(They say my great-grandfather, a sorcerer, finally got out this way).
When my body softens with moisture,
The bloated soul, dark and bulging,
Will strain
Like a blue vein in a boiled egg white,
And the body will ripple with spasms,
Like the blanket a sick man wrestles off
Because it's hot,
And the soul will rise to break through
The press of flesh, curse of gravity—
The Cosmos
Above the black well of the room
Will suck on its galactic tube,
Heaven breaking in a blistering starfall,
And draw the soul up, trembling like a sheet of paper—
My young soul—
The color of wet grass—

To freedom—then
"Stop!" it screams, escaping,
On the dazzling borderline
Between two worlds—
Stop, wait.
My God. At last.
Look, here's where poetry comes from.

Fingers twitching for the ballpoint,
Growing cold, becoming not mine.

translated from the Ukrainian by Michael M. Naydan and Askold Melnyczuk

Letter from the Summer House

Dear _____,
The land's rusty again.
Acid rain: our blackened cucumber vines
Jut from the earth like scorched wire.
And I'm not sure about the orchard this year.
It needs a good cleaning up,
But I'm scared of those trees. When I walk
Among them, it feels like I'm going to step
On some carcass rotting in the tall grass,
Something crawling with worms, something smiling
Sickly in the hot sun.
And I get nervous over the sounds:
The day before yesterday, in the thicket, meowing,
The monotonous creaking of a tree,
The suppressed cackling of geese—all constantly
Straining for the same note. Do you remember
The dry elm, the one lightning turned
Into a giant charred bone last summer?
Sometimes I think it lords
Over the whole garden, infecting everything with rabid madness.
How do mad trees act?
Maybe they run amok like derailed streetcars. Anyway,
I keep an ax by the bed, just in case.
At least the butterflies are mating: we'll have
Caterpillars soon. Oh yes, the neighbor's daughter
Gave birth—a boy, a bit overdue. He had hair and teeth

Already, and could be a mutant,
Because yesterday, only nine days old, he shouted,
"Turn off the sky!" and hasn't said a word since.
Otherwise, he's a healthy baby.
So, there it is. If you can get away
For the weekend, bring me something to read,
Preferably in a language I don't know.
The ones I call mine are exhausted.

Kisses, love, O.

translated from the Ukrainian by Douglas Burnet Smith

— VIKTOR NEBORAK (b. 1961) —

What He Does . . .

what he does
with his life
transforms it into a body

he slips into it
and compares it to pictures in magazines

he stares at it in the mirror

he feeds it
surrounds food with music flowers
and kisses

he feels queasy

he zooms with it at night on the highway
slams on the brake but can't stop

the rear view lacks perspective

he doesn't know what else to do with this body
get it drunk shoot up drugs
paint it up and throw it in bed
change it while break dancing
pump it up with muscles take pictures
naked in a crowd surround it with things
gold gems

the body laughs
the body moans
the body vomits
the body sits on the toilet
the aging body roams the world
the stupid body gets sentences to 14 years
in prison

the unlucky soldier's body
falls silent in a mass grave

translated from the Ukrainian by Virlana Tkacz and Wanda Phipps

Flying Head

It lifts up, like a head,
a head chopped off a derelict.
It speaks, and then again
and again, its otherworldly words:
I AM THE FLYING HEAD!
Its all-seeing flying baroque-eye
streaks across the sky above the crowded square.
Blood thickens in the sky, the cut is ragged,
its shadow's heavy and deep:
I AM THE FLYING HEAD!
An invisible ax is in the city,
they dragged the headless bodies off the scaffold,
so gaping fools can drink blood cheap.
Scrape that rusty smear off the forehead
A PHANTOM—A FLYING HEAD!
You devour television melodramas?
You're watching monsters under glass!
The wrecking ball from Fellini's *Orchestra*
will break through your wall head first—
I AM THE FLYING HEAD!
Remember, there's nowhere to hide!
The crowd scrambles to hide in the square!
The dark pavement is ritually washed,
and in the Renaissance heavens the beast slouches
A MASK—A FLYING HEAD
I AM THE FLYING HEAD
I AM THE HE AD FLY

ING HEAD AM I
ING HEAD FLY I
FLY I LY I

translated from the Ukrainian by Virlana Tkacz and Wanda Phipps

— ANDRIY BONDAR (b. 1974) —

the men of my country

the men of my country
give up their seats on the subway
to the handicapped the aged
and to the passengers with children
but mostly they go on sitting
since these categories of citizens
have a pronounced tendency to die out
or travel by subway less and less often

the men of my country
they are saints under a heel
with trained insect jaws
with which they gnaw their way
to deserved fatherhood
and later having untied their hands
savor children's flesh
using proscribed methods
of raising the younger generation

the men of my country
are not mutants or perverts
they are products of secondary processing
of amino acids
this is all that remains of the nation
which loves and honors its heroes
youths so roly-poly or with pit bull jaws
their love for motherhood
has outgrown all discernible limits
and become a signature style

the men of my country
wonderful specimens for an entomologist
for they are fragile like exotic butterflies

pinned to a piece of cardboard
they acknowledge the value
of every move every sound
for life is an unending crime
that has no justification

the men of my country
blow their noses simply into their hands
for the hand is the most useful organ
for such an important deed
they usually don't have any other
important deeds to consider

the men of my country
make no effort
efforts ruin the liver
and their mouths smell bad
and have they really been born
to exert efforts

the men of my country
prematurely descend into the grave
and become weightless angels
and ideal raw material
for metaphysical speculations
and superfluous argument in favor of the existence
of god or what's his name

translated from the Ukrainian by Vitaly Chernetsky

— SERHIY ZHADAN (b. 1974) —

Alcohol

The green river water
slows in warm bends
fish zeppelins
scatter the plankton
and tired bird catchers
attempt to catch
every word.

Hold on to
the brightly colored rags and scotch tape

that bind the slashed wrists
of these heroic times.
One day you will turn off this radio,
you'll get used to her,
to her breathing
and, dressed in your T-shirt,
she'll bring you water in the middle of the night.
On the terrace the leftover cups of tea
are filling up with rainwater
and cigarette butts,
you and I share a cold
you and I share long conversations
you don't notice the morning rain
you go to sleep late
and you wake up late
I write poems about how I love
this woman and I invent
newer and newer words
to avoid
telling her.

translated from the Ukrainian by Virlana Tkacz and Wanda Phipps

⋊⟨ RUSSIA ⟩⋉

— ELENA SHVARTS (b. 1948) —

Remembrance of Strange Hospitality

Once I had a taste
Of a girlfriend's milk,
My sister's milk—
Not to quench my thirst
But to satisfy my soul.
Into a cup she squeezed
Milk from her left breast
And in that simple vessel
It gently frothed, rejoiced.
There was something birdlike in its odor,
Whiffs of sheep and wolf, and something older
Than the Milky Way, it was
Somehow warm and dense.
A daughter in the wilderness
Once let her aged father drink
From her breasts and thus became
His mother. By this act of grace
Her whiteness drove away the dark,
A cradle substituted for a tomb.
From the duct next to your heart
You offered me a drink—
I'm not a vampire, am I?—Horror.
It frothed and tinkled, warm
And sweet, soft, everlasting,
Crowding time back into a corner.

translated from the Russian by Michael Molnar and Catriona Kelly

— REGINA DERIEVA (b. 1949) —

Theory of Recruiting

Sons of bitches
were born
with hearts of stone,
cherishing this stone

all their life.
Children of
sons of bitches
were born
with hearts of grenade,
in order to
blow to pieces
everything,
and to leave as a message for their descendants—
entrails
(still smoking entrails)
of sons of bitches.

translated from the Russian by Kevin Carey

[From a land of institutes to a land of prostitutes.]

From a land of institutes to a land of prostitutes.
Dull with fatigue, so-and-so isn't kidding.
Fetters have formed a habitat. Bond.
Even the gaunt think world's end is too gaunt.
Even the dark think world's end is too dark.
So what is there to wait for, besides waiting?
Besides God descending on this horrow.
Besides Thy Kingdom! Thy Power and Glory!

translated from the Russian by Valzhyna Mort

Dark thoughts

I'm almost like that dark hallway
with a few framed photos
and lamps on the walls.
So many visitors have walked through me,
dark and light,
depending on the illumination.

translated from the Russian by Valzhyna Mort

Female Figure

In a long wide veil
she stands, turning her face
away: that looks like a poplar
beside her;
looks deceive; there is no poplar there.
But she herself would gladly become one,
as the old legends have it,
if she could only stop hearing:
"What can you see there?"
"What can I see there, you madmen?
The ocean, can you not guess?
The ocean, and nothing more. Or is this not enough
that I should be grieving forever, and you
    pestering me with your questions?"

translated from the Russian by Catriona Kelly

[Dip us in fire or water,]

Dip us in fire or water,
bending our sheet out of shape—
it won't change our nature, nor
will the structure of our mouths ever change

Disassemble and piece us together
at random, part by part, bit by bit—
We'll stay standing just as we were
leaning backwards at a slight tilt

Even if they could
cut this body into ten even pieces
I am sure I in turn would be able
to spit out a length of black blood

and regenerate, just like a snake regenerates,
bending into a bow.
               And again
I will arch this cold body:

Free
we are free
we are free
And free we will be to the end.

translated from the Russian by Matvei Yankelevich

— SERGEY GANDLEVSKY (b. 1952) —

To My Mother

Far past the dusty, locust-filled steppes,
Where gray wolves roam in the wild,
Perhaps Baskachi still exists—
Just six scattered shacks with gardens to the Volga.

That summer was uncommonly foul, raining
Day after day. The boats were drenched
In their slips. Why this, emerging
From the rest of memory, as through a spyglass?

Ten years later, as a migrant laborer
(Mere clownish scum to the settled class),
I worked in the salty, locust-filled steppes
At the logical conclusion of Volga summits.

Why has a pastoral childhood in a blue T-shirt
Come to my hardened memory?
How much water, my God, has flowed by
Since the original age of communal apartments!

It means we're dying, and it's almost over.
And the Volga runs into the Caspian Sea.
All sorts of people stand on the bank of the river.
This is the Volga flowing to the Caspian Sea.

Everything that's happened to us will happen again.
In the middle of the night I might close my eyes—
I'll be one year old, and you'll be twenty-five.
Fireworks of blue pigeons burst up in azure skies.

I'll find you in an apartment now blurred by tears
Where the first TV stood, preemie of progress,
Where a reproduction of old holy Iness
Would gaze at us from behind a shower of hair.

I'll find you mending some clothes.
The needle, under a slanting ray, will gleam.
Remember how cheaply we lived, us four
In this small village with a Tatar name?

The magic crystal of the TV's bulbous eye
Fills up with blue. The Volga appears.
"You're really not tired, Ma? Well, neither am I.
So let's keep going. We're almost there."

translated from the Russian by Philip Metres

— EVGENII BUNIMOVICH (b. 1954) —

Excuse and Explanation

I'm not a poet*
is there really such a thing as a living poet

I'm a school teacher
I teach math
computer science
as well as ethics and the psychology of family life

on top of this I return home each day
to my wife

as a romantically inclined pilot once said
love is not when two people look at one another
but when they both look in the same direction

this is about us

for ten years now my wife and I
have been looking in the same direction

at the television

for eight years now our son looks that way too

I'm not a poet
is there a hole in the watertight round-the-clock alibi
set forth above

---

* This line plays on an entry in Vladimir Mayakovsky's autobiography *I Myself*, where Mayakovsky states, "I'm a poet. That's why I'm interesting. And that's what I'm writing about. I'll write about all the rest only as it settles down in verbal form."

the combination of misunderstanding and happenstance
that leads now and then to the appearance of my poems
in the periodical press
compels me to confess

I write poetry when it becomes unavoidable
while I monitor in-class exams
in spite of all the public school reforms
individual pupils continue to cheat

to prevent this

I'm forced to sit with my neck craned
wide-eyed and vigilant
unblinking gaze fastened on a space just above the floor

this pose leads inevitably
to the composition of verse

anyone who's interested can verify this

my poems are short
because in-class exams rarely last longer than 45 minutes

I'm not a poet

and perhaps
that's why I'm interesting

translated from the Russian by Patrick Henry

— IRINA RATUSHINSKAYA (b. 1954) —

[I will live and survive and be asked:]

I will live and survive and be asked:
How they slammed my head against a trestle,
How I had to freeze at nights,
How my hair started to turn gray . . .
But I'll smile. And I'll crack some joke
And brush away the encroaching shadow.
And I will render homage to the dry September
That became my second birth.
And I'll be asked: "Doesn't it hurt you to remember?"
Not being deceived by my outward flippancy.
But the former names will detonate in my memory—

Magnificent as an old cannon.
And I will tell of the best people in all the earth,
The most tender, but also the most invincible,
How they said farewell, how they went to be tortured,
How they waited for letters from their loved ones.
And I'll be asked: what helped us to live
When there were neither letters nor any news—only walls,
And the cold of the cell, and the blather of official lies,
And the sickening promises made in exchange for betrayal.
And I will tell of the first beauty
I saw in captivity.
A frost-covered window! No peepholes, nor walls,
Nor cell bars, nor the long-endured pain—
Only a blue radiance on a tiny pane of glass,
A lacy winding pattern—none more beautiful could be dreamt!
The more clearly you looked, the more powerfully blossomed
Those brigand forests, campfires and birds!
And how many times there was bitter cold weather
And how many windows sparkled after that one—
But never was it repeated,
That upheaval of rainbow ice!
And anyway, what good would it be to me now,
And what would be the pretext for that festival?
Such a gift can only be received once,
And once is probably enough.

translated from the Russian by David McDuff

— TATYANA SHCHERBINA (b. 1954) —

About Limits

The cicadas, the cicadas are singing, Rameses.
The hemlock, Socrates, pour me my just amount.
Let the others apply to their Central Committees.
No, my brother Reason, I'm the soul, and I can't.

The buildings, my idol! Look at the buildings!
Are we really insects, with our shriveled wings
who throw down our bodies on the bunks of the hive
and drape our rags on the chairs they provide us with?

Discover her, Columbus, discover her anew.
Your descendants have grown tired of their own shadow.
What way lies open now to the stumbling Jew?
What road will tell that tired remnant where he must go?

My friend, my mutant, pliable, unstiffened,
my crazy colleague, it will come to an end.
There's a limit to vomiting and diarrhea.
So here they are, have a good look. We've made it, my dear.

translated from the Russian by Derek Walcott

— ALEXEI PARSHCHIKOV (b. 1955) —

Estuary

Knee-deep in mud. For centuries, we have stood where the bogwaters suck.
In the grasp of the inanimate,

there are no straight lines. A sack race is good for a laugh.
And like the Lord's own trumpets, funnels multiply in the muck.

Once again, darling, yours is a resinous, intimate whisper.
Once again, I'll bring you pelts and sprigs of heather.

But it's all a whim of the estuary, spidering thin borders.
By dawn, it looks like a golden wand. At night, a wooden recorder.

The dragonflies and branches emanate a velvet current
into skies and loam. This isn't a road. It's a crossroad.

In the dead water, a bulging stretcher,
you will find no bridge, no cross, no forking path, no star.

Only a stone that looks like a cloud (both resemble
countless other points of the universe so familiar as to make one tremble).

Only the dislocation of a landscape, sagging like a deflated ball.
Only a hole in the ground, or the lack of a hole.

translated from the Russian by Wayne Chambliss

Parting makes simple sense

Parting makes simple sense,
there's no special sense in it.
The air will be to blame,
the garden full of birds whistling.
The smoke and the strip of water
there by the mossy forest.
Even that the sunset cut
across the rows of pines.
It will turn everything into ashes
with the quiet oncoming of night,
so that in tormenting dreams
the eye should fall for
the thousandth time
to the keyhole of the world

translated from the Russian by Richard McKane

Four Poems

I think it will be winter when he comes.
From the unbearable whiteness of the road
a dot will emerge, so black that eyes will blur,
and it will be approaching for a long, long time,
making his absence commensurate with his coming,
and for a long, long time it will remain a dot.
A speck of dust? A burning in the eye? And snow,
there will be nothing else but snow,
and for a long, long while there will be nothing,
he will acquire size and three dimensions,
he will keep coming closer, closer . . .
This is the limit, he cannot get closer. But he keeps approaching,
now too vast to measure . . .

—

If there is something to desire,
there will be something to regret.

If there is something to regret,
there will be something to recall.
If there is something to recall,
there was nothing to regret.
If there was nothing to regret,
there was nothing to desire.

——

Let us touch each other
while we still have hands,
palms, forearms, elbows . . .
Let us love each other for misery,
torture each other, torment,
disfigure, maim,
to remember better,
to part with less pain.

——

We are rich: we have nothing to lose.
We are old: we have nowhere to rush.
We shall fluff the pillows of the past,
poke the embers of the days to come,
talk about what means the most,
as the indolent daylight fades.
We shall lay to rest our undying dead:
I shall bury you, you will bury me.

translated from the Russian by Steven Seymour

— DMITRY GOLYNKO (b. 1969) —

Passing the Church of the French Consulate

Suddenly someone entered—and, through the din of voices,
said: —Here is my bride.
—ALEXANDER BLOK

1.

O Jesu, darling, damn my nativity in the Year of Bull.
A glossolaliac I sibilated your mass,
Garden-snaked into your fate, faded into it like an otter,
Counterfeited a demon—& that's what the dames named me.

2.

I stole gooseberries, crowfoots in the municipal gardens of Tartu,
tried on the pike skeleton of the mahogany cathedral
in place of my vertebral column—the card I got, got topped,
the Mammy of God placed into my hands a vial—it shattered

3.

into seven pieces: in its firmament are reflected
the gavel of the judge Semina, the despondent cawing of a "canary,"
a wood demon's miter, the ditty about the sacraments of the grave,
the crown of Stakenschneider's palazzo in a beautiful maiden's skullcap,

4.

simmering Lesbian gardens, the Olympian torso
horseshoed, tonsuring with hoof clippers the brazenfanged serpent . . .
And all this is past. Like a yuletide needle my discourse
knits, for the sake of the past, the caparison of a prayer:

5.

....
....
....
....

6.

Sear, O blacktail maiden, me-without-a-droplet-of-lamb's-blood,
set loose in a bulbous crib or a hot-air balloon,
with a cord of flax wrap length- and widthwise my nappies
to the pitiful salvos of pianoforte or popguns.

7.

I'll have neither the ire—[caesura]—nor the dark force, nor the gesture
at the decline of life to wank off the fattening, pockmarked period
with a schismatic's pointing diaresis: "Here is my bride!"
and so turn her into a comma, glaucoma, coma.

translated from the Russian by Eugene Ostashevsky

Cinema

I suddenly remembered the eighties
standing with a crowd by the cinema
Dawn, a load of hairy boys
and an early March thaw.

Iron smelted across the land
and tank building is planned.
Life's shitty, but floats past nicely,
girls come along to the dance.

Jeans are imported from America
and sold for half a month's wage
by intelligent lads who have found
their calling out on the square.

A pretty *Komsomolka* girl
slightly creased, on a balcony,
she's been flying all night like Thumbelina
in the arms of a deputy.

But still, the film comes to an end
and everything else does too:
The crowds are leaving and the son
of man is rolling on the cafeteria floor.

translated from the Russian by Sasha Dugdale

Manuscript Found by Natasha Rostova During the Fire

I will try to live on earth without you.

I will try to live on earth without you.

I will become any object,
I don't care what—

I will be this speeding train.
This smoke
or a beautiful gay man laughing in the front seat.

A human body is defenseless
on earth.

It's a piece of firewood.
Ocean water hits it.
Lenin puts it on his official shoulder.

And therefore, in order not to suffer, a human spirit lives
inside the wind and inside the wood and inside the shoulder of a great dictator.

But I will not be water. I will not be a fire.

I will be an eyelash.
A sponge washing your neck hairs.
Or a verb, an adjective, I will become. Such word

slightly lights your cheek.
What happened? Nothing.
Something visited? Nothing.

What was there you cannot whisper.
No smoke without fire, they whisper.
I will be a handful of smoke
over this lost city of Moscow.

I will console any man,
I will sleep with any man,
under the army's traveling horse carriages.

translated from the Russian by Ilya Kaminsky

to A.K.

Are you still frightened, my clueless devochka?
Take a morsel of the Lord's bread (and a spoonful of wine, no?)
Imagine how we will reside in Paradise, in the skies,
and how we (finally) will see everything—
our currency, all we have lost or stolen on Earth
will glitter below: like the minute droppings of an iron bird.
And the proud angels, those tall sexless bitches,
will again blend into their ruthlessness the sweetest honey,
which they will pour down your throat, your exquisite throat.
And you are now mute and cautious, now small and tranquil,
now you will forget what you desired, now,
who you were, now, this lamentable city

where we have lived together.
Are you still frightened, girl? Already I am a bitter stranger.

translated from the Russian by Ilya Kaminsky, Kathryn Farris, and Rachel Galvin

— DARYA SUKHOVEI (b. 1977) —

Spring Scales

1
we'll smoke a couple cigarettes
each third a unit of time

toss out a computer
or trade in a hard disk

buy a new mouse and two books
what for what for

2
with a new mouse and two books
in a semitransparent polyethylene
bag

with dreams like a refrain

take the trolleybus take the trolleybus
what for what for

3
hello—insert someone's name here
I won't report anything new to you
absolutely nothing
except for that I have time for nothing

therefore I won't plan to meet you
in the very near future

4
our affairs however require supplemental
agreement and discussion
th-ere wh-ere we get together

I sincerely hope
a cup of tea (martini/mug of beer)

to choose the essentials
they'll be guaranteed

5

you know material complexities
I look through the window to the sky

the mini-bus is twelve rubles, metro six
I have to buy two books a month
a computer mouse polyethylene bag
shoe repairs analgesics contraception

6

       a continuation of the enumeration
quick noodles
cigarettes telephone bills rent
flowers

it's not yours to worry about

as usual our everyday things are fine
I'll tell you my news when we meeet

7

a signature *sincerely / regretfully*

what for what for

send by fax send by fax
pasting in new names and more new names
discovering new names for myself
which live like me

8

instead of the mini-bus I'll buy a beer

I even have enough for klinskoye
and if there's no klinskoye
then a light bavarian, baltica

eight sixty eight sixty
spring waits won't go winds whistle

9

first spring in the city center
like an unpretentious color scale
drink back a beer drink back a beer

too late to experiment with anything else
+
too early to go back
=
something else will work out

10
I go somewhere to argue with someone
I might even go far away
with this very goal

to the other end of the city for example
or to another city
under the same sky

11
strictly speaking there's nothing more I can say

I open the first door I come across
a bar or the scientific institute it doesn't matter

they let me in because of my honest eyes
hair washed in the morning
unfamiliar face

12
I can't even explain why
this text is called spring scales

probably some old inertia
trajectory

previously established laws
of ecumenical equilibrium

13
It's already a sort of egor letov*
twenty-third of march in club polygon
squeeze an order of tickets an order of tickets
press here

the author indicates the heart
and leaves the scene

translated from the Russian by Christopher Mattison

---

* Egor Letov is a key inventor of Soviet punk rock, having founded in 1984 the Siberian band Grazhdanskaya
  Oborona (or GO), which roughly translates as "Civil Defense."

⤚⟨ LITHUANIA ⟩⤛

— EUGENIJUS ALIŠANKA (b. 1960) —

from the case of bones

for six hundred years the bones ached in the Middle Ages they were stretched
according to the Gothic canons of beauty during the Renaissance soldiers
whipped them on pillars with lashes of ox-leather in the era of Classicism
the architects put into practice the rule of the golden section for some reason
called the bed of Procrustes in Soviet times during the First World War dogs
dragged them from one line of the front to another during the Second World
War soap was rendered from them in postwar times each small bone was stripped
there where it was even difficult to piss in the cold as well as here at Cathedral
Square buzzing with flies in the century's last decade one could see mechanisms
crushing bones but more often arthritis and radiculitis bent them but as pseudo-
eugenijus writes in the year two thousand bones will disappear and the earth
will ascend into the new eon of a new boneless god

translated from the Lithuanian by Kerry Shawn Keys

— GINTARAS GRAJAUSKAS (b. 1966) —

World in Your Pocket

the world is huge
that's why you need to range over it
in order not to be so small
nor persistently pout
and deliberately not move about
until the circle comes around

in fact one way or another
there's no difference
the end is the same

you sit down somewhere in a meadow
and you notice: the world is
just the size of an eyeball

it fits perfectly into the eyesocket
starkly here

translated from the Lithuanian by Eugenijus Ališanka and Kerry Shawn Keys

The Night Watchman

in a room warmed
by sleeping breath
the night watchman leans
his shoulders against the wall.

he watches the dark, his head
cocked, so he can see better,
winds a thread, torn
from his jacket about his finger.

he smokes: the flame at the tip
of his cigarette crackles.
someone turns over.
someone talks in his sleep.

don't answer, watchman, as long
as they dream, you needn't worry. time,
like an eighteen-wheeler, doesn't chase
after you in their dreams.

and when the wall clock strikes
four, don't jump, watchman.
hold on to the edge with your nails,
crumbling bones, cracked teeth.

it is yours: the dreamers
the name in the dark, it isn't only your
dream that i'll never enter,
watchman, poor night watchman.

translated from the Lithuanian by Laima Sruoginis

— DAIVA ÈEPAUSKAITË (b. 1967) —

Love, a Last Glance

Which branch will you string that rabbit,
the fruit of our love, from?
I neither got drunk, nor killed myself:
just let the snow smack my forehead.

And I stopped in the middle of the square
and paid them not to play.

Once Noah had faded downstream,
the animals converged behind bars.

Nothing else had any point.
Mice all fled their nests.
At any rate, there wasn't enough snow
to snub me off for good.

translated from the Lithuanian by Vyt Bakaitis

— NERINGA ABRUTYTE (b. 1972) —

The Beginning

the beginning can be like this: your shoes new
for two hundred litas, your coat without a lining,
your face peeling, your head full of dandruff, and
your love old, boring, you stop alongside such a beginning,
move a little: from home to the library, from there to the café:
I yearn for someone to shake me up, forcefully make me move,
the beginning can also be there—you'd want it there, where there are
unknown places, unfamiliar people and even language—
the beginning can be speech: you learn to speak, words—
for now only a melody, the beginning can even be different:
you go somewhere, not knowing where, who you'll meet, what you'll do—
a tower appears, flies—a crow on the roof, you hold on
with your last strength—you want to jump and struggle to save yourself—
the beginning is bad: it could be better—sometimes
the beginning: nonsense and daydreams,
the beginning which you cannot have.

translated from the Lithuanian by Jonas Zdanys

— LAURYNAS KATKUS (b. 1972) —

Later On

. . . later, Autumn. We walked into the avenue.
A sudden gust of freshness: chests relaxed,
briefcases lighter. The hearts of cars were beating
faster than ours. A small, bearable dose
of anarchy.

Later, we moved toward the pure grocery
of the universe. Robertas suggested his place.
We disappeared into large armchairs,
intoxicated without even drinking yet, outrageous
with our joking, suddenly not recognizing
each other. Later the alcohol swam
in our brains.
We were smoking cheap cigars and seeing who
could howl the longest, no cheating—
to waken the dark yard, stir up the natural forces,
overcome the phobia of squares, the Fabijoniskes syndrome
I saw drops of sweat on your forehead,
and the neighbor who died yesterday
knocked at the door.
It snowed in the TV. Some folks were gone.
Laughter hoarsened. Guzas fell asleep in his armchair.
At the cockcrow of the polar dawn,
I put my arms around you and whispered:
if we don't start everything anew,
Sophia, we are lost.

translated from the Lithuanian by Kerry Shawn Keys

Žvёrynas in Winter

Darkness strikes suddenly
like lightning strikes the chosen ones,
and whispers: don't fight; give up; calm down . . .
Shadows sneak into the house across the street,
melting into the bluish blaze of the TV screens.

A blind cyclone tosses between
the roof and the dream.
The sun's rays reach out stronger and stronger.
They draw open the curtains, and the newborn,
fleecy snow astonishes my eyes.

This sparkle, tearing the body apart,
speechless, and for a moment . . . myself.

translated from the Lithuanian by Kerry Shawn Keys

Simpleton

I would so much like to be
a Rosicrucian, Mother,
to live secretly in a cellar
in a castle, accessible
to no one

I would have
lots of good intentions
a pronounceable surname
and a fiefdom of peasants

I would perform rituals
after swearing fealty by candlelight
to the Master of the Order

and in the morning
I would ascend the ramparts
the tallest tower
the North Wind
fluttering my cloak
spurs striking sparks
good

good

what can be better
when no one knows
how secret and good you are

translated from the Lithuanian by Kerry Shawn Keys

⊁ LATVIA ⊁

— LIÂNA LANGA (b. 1960) —

Galanteria N. 1, 7, 9

1.

A woman between 38 and 45, maybe younger
overweight by 30 kilos more or less, face puffed, trampled from lack of sleep
dressed in mall-glitz, a shiny black leather coat
—her fat, humanly-acquired, the carcass of her soul
                on display in a smoke-filled dive

"A real bitch," thinks the alchonaut sitting at a table. "No wonder she's alone,
barely noon, but she . . ."

at the bar the woman orders "a brandy and something else"
the bartender stares through her muddied flesh through the bar window
at the slush-covered face of Brivibas Avenue
reflected back in the naked leather, its shiny lure
thrown out to catch small fish under ice, she sees
the surface of the brandy iced over with a crackling, roach-colored net
countless small hooks push from her underbelly, armpits, shoulders

                        outward—

but they're without bait, bare—

flies and worms have died in the cold

7.

The all-night store is stuffy, and the clerk in a padded jacket, deaf.
Santimes jingle in slot machines, bitterness settles in kefir packs.
After midnight, a newcomer who has no one to call drops by
to diffuse his madness. He buys a pack of Wallstreet, then begins
to tell the deaf man:
"I met her in a bar. The dark walked outside. O how the dark walked outside!
Alcohol roared in my brain. Probably my cradle was hung under a table.
But she had the eyes of a sea lion and swayed my mind." The store clerk nods,
loyal, ready to listen to anyone, shelving the recently delivered milk.

"Parentheses, parentheses!" the newcomer exclaims. "My parentheses. I lost them!
    I finally
fell in love with a good-for-nothing in a dump! My lioness. We talked some and
    then she

229

disappeared by stepping inside me. I drank till dawn. No longer in parenthesis!
    Flight,
despair, joy! I stepped outside myself! Of my own accord, suddenly, aware and
    free!
For the first time in my life, without limits,

now I can. . . ." The deaf man didn't see what happened next.
He was told that the newcomer left, slipped on trash by the doorstep, then lit up
    a smoke.
In the store window, the neon sign had waved like red algae in a strong current.
The man had vanished in the fog, his body leaving a rose-colored scar with fresh
stitches round it.

9.

Space has its scars, its splinters,
its scabs, fairy tales and towers
where unborn birds briefly rest
and felled trees compose songs.

Space has doors only the blind see,
garden lamps where blood congeals
shed for the nightmare and the dream,
lit by a bat once every hour.

There, as you climb an invisible stair,
you look in the face of hours and pain
now ended. And see the whirlwinds
that lovers leave when they have gone,

spirals turned by an incessant wind
and blown through sheets toward us

    translated from the Latvian by Margita Gailitis and J. C. Todd

           — INGA ĀBELE (b. 1972) —

Autumn Recipe

Porridge of hornets swallowed from syrup glittering cupped hands.
    In the livestock kitchen women pound meat for midday.
    The black pods of peas hard as a corpse's teeth.
    Day burns the sorrow from cemetery wreaths.
    In cool rooms at televisions children ripen.

The full moon melts the stars into ploughshares.
The dog with its last winter before it guards the infant in the garden on a yellow
blanket.
Snakes in the dike become slow, but in the shed, breathing heavily, pigs grow
ready for slaughter.

translated from the Latvian by Inara Cedrins

— INGA GAILE (b. 1976) —

The wind smooths out all the wrinkles and light beacons in our eyes,

The wind smooths out all the wrinkles and light beacons in our eyes,

we are on deck, we are on track; we find

the well and begin to live, we will survive, in order to say

"we love," we will survive, in order to say "we are coming," because

only at the very crest is it apparent that this is simply and solely

the beginning, sparrows chirp, the well's windlass turns, from green
grass the dew vanishes, a child comes through mist heading home

and only looks over where someone gathers berries, in the morning the kitchen

smells of autumn, and sheepdogs bark to bring in the day, over fields
a man wades, he has a woman in his head, a girl sits

alone on the shore, with wind-tossed hair, with
pebbles and desire to live, with great hope, with great

obstinacy, with wide eyes and love.

translated from the Latvian by Inara Cedrins

To leave, flee, lope, swim away with

To leave, flee, lope, swim away with
horses, break that instant, Mr. Pascal, crack it
like a nut, hide it under the pillow, so that night
remains, so that a son is delivered head first, to travel
away, leave this woman sitting with a polite smile,
sitting at a faux marble table in the center of
Europe, dashing through green lights and dividing the
clouds. To soar off as if somewhere beyond the forest

were a city, just such a city as was needed. In order
to return. Through mist, through darkness, through
sticky chatter—dash into the woman sitting calmly at
a faux marble table, bringing a blush to the cheeks,
look, she's at peace, she is here, and moisture on the table
from beer.

translated from the Latvian by Inara Cedrins

— RONALDS BRIEDIS (b. 1980) —

Silence

Silence
Like the one before the world was created

Fog slides over the river
Tangles in bushes on shore

Dew trembles on a branch
A bud bursts open
A fledgling moves in a nest

Silence
Like the one before the first word was spoken

Church bells lick their lips

translated from the Latvian by Margita Gailitis and J. C. Todd

Before addressing the people

Before addressing the people
The prophet on return from the desert
Bends over the well
To quench his thirst
But freezes
When he sees his reflection—

His open mouth a zero

translated from the Latvian by Margita Gailitis and J. C. Todd

⤜ ESTONIA ⤛

— ASKO KÜNNAP (b. 1971) —

O night, my car

O night, my car
My car's windshield
is covered in trains.
These train couplings
are free from carriage platforms.
But Ajax washes off blood and oil
and night is swifter than ever.
My car moves southward.
Little travelers, with nightcaps inside
rest above the roof,

fleafaces on the skylight glass.
The murders are rinsed away in the car wash
and night smooths the slats and bolts.
My car, a most beautiful car,
has driven through the swarm of trains
pushed off up by my foot it smooths
down into the hills in the south,
already having forgotten
those faces, play cases, sacrifices.
My night, my car!
Beetle cities, cockroach cities
In the night, falling asleep, you forget
the window open into the garden going gray
and the hard disk of the brain revolting.
Onto your pillow creep
beetle cities, cockroach cities
where you wasted your soul;
you sniff, a whiff of London—the cockroach,
you feel, Madrid—the black bumblebee,
Barcelona—the hornet with the broken snout,
St. Pete—a cloud of bluish blowflies,
Budapest—the checkerboard cicada.
And one by one the cities whisper,
whisper the images and words into your air,
what, the following silent morning,

banging your head against the pillow, on the verge of tears,
you can't remember—the thirst, the fear, the patterns.

> *translated from the Estonian by the author with Eric Dickens and*
> *Richard Adang*

— FS (b. 1971) —

[we are born in hospitals]

we are born in hosptials
long dreary corridors
footsteps echo in the silence
the suffocating smell
of chlorine and medicines
the walls steeped in disease
our names are recorded
all is in order
papers are filed
the files locked away
a guard desk stands at the door
no more visitors
for you today
outside it grows dark
round the corner the morgue
move your feet
says the cleaner

> *translated from the Estonian by Miriam McIlfatrick-Ksenofontov*

[the hangover in our shared body]

the hangover in our shared body
under the ceiling like mist
on the hall door handle
like thick dust
a dream at the window
your stockings on a chair
something of mine on the floor
the bed unmade till evening
into the warmth again

the hangover in our shared body
shelters us
husband and wife

the machine is way above and beyond

translated from the Estonian by Miriam McIlfatrick-Ksenofontov

— KARL MARTIN SINIJÄRV (b. 1971) —

I Am a Poemmaker

I am a poemmaker—soul but a strip but a share.
I am a poemmaker—ass toward trousers but bare.
I am a fruitful stranger of some weirdoish upbringing,
I have a hundredmoneyed purse but cursed to sad my heart,
I am a poemmaker.
A loser whose shares are high at high midnight.
A stupido working all day and enjoying dark hours.
Poemmaker: semicolon, literally sentenced.
A poet as a paragraph. But there's no law for that.
I am a poemmaker—white is red-colored black

translated from the Estonian by the author with Eric Dickens and Richard Adang

Arcadia

Arcadia, so red the rose.
And oh so trivial its simple name.
Together they may beautyfully pose.
Arcadia, so red the rose.

Wine withers, sloughs congest the hose,
high brows get low, shame is to blame,
Arcadia! So trivial the rose
and all so red its very drunken name.

translated from the Estonian by the author with Eric Dickens and Richard Adang

The Extraordinary Importance of a Private Life

Husband goes to work. Runs into breasts, a belly, mental health, legs, buttocks, a
retail prospector of war criminals, a family center's new perspectives, a belly.

Wife goes to work. Runs into a belly, legs, a belly, breasts, buttocks, the im-
partiality, legs.

Husband returns from work. Runs into breasts, breasts, a belly, legs, buttocks,
the masses.

Wife returns from work. Runs into breasts, a single-edged sword, legs, buttocks,
legs, a belly.

Husband goes to work. Runs into buttocks, breasts, pension, legs, buttocks, legs, an
ambassador, the extraordinary importance of a private life.

Wife goes to work. Runs into breasts, breasts, a belly, buttocks, legs, legs, buttocks,
the role of an intellectual in a society, a public opinion poll (according to you, is
it necessary to make superfluous movements?), buttocks, breasts, legs, a belly.

Husband returns from work. Runs into buttocks, buttocks, buttocks, legs, a belly,
legs, breasts, a belly, a belly, taxpayer's money, a belly.

Wife returns from work. Runs into legs—buttocks—a belly—breasts—social
security. Legs, legs, legs.

Husband enters the grave. Runs into buttocks (?), breasts (?), a primrose (?),
legs (?), a belly (?), 2 maggots, a policeman (?), a belly.

Wife enters the grave. Runs into her husband (?), legs (?), buttocks (?), a pine
needle (?), breasts (?), (??), a man, a belly (?), a woman (?).

From the grave, from their depths come buttocks, breasts, legs, a belly (the editorial
staff of the magazine Movement), they go to their final resting place for awhile.

*translated from the Estonian by Kalju Kruusa with Brandon Lussier and
Elin Sütiste*

⤹ FINLAND ⤸

— TUA FORSSTRÖM (b. 1947) —

It's beautiful in Sicily in the spring when the lemon trees are in bloom

I'm writing because I attended
your concert, it was the sixteenth
of September. You played Prokofiev, and
it's strange about music: you return
to places that don't exist. Two questions
keep me busy. One has to do with
conditions and destiny. The other has to do with
Procris. That it occurred to her to run into the forest.
That she couldn't trust her mate! I visited a
museum of Renaissance painting and then, everywhere,
in the streets, in subways, I saw: light, silky blue and that
special tenderness. In everyone! In the animals! I teach at a
high school here. It's beautiful in Sicily in the spring when
the lemon trees are in bloom. Perhaps you prefer to travel
according to your own plans but I wanted to ask because music
restores us, and a cloud drifts in through the window into
my apartment as the clouds sweep by every
morning over the park where I walk.

translated from the Finland-Swedish by Stina Katchadourian

from Minerals

I dreamed I was too dirty to go
to a doctor in Grand Popo, Benin, West Africa.
The doctor turned my ears inside out. It
hurt. There are things that can't be buried
or dug up, one doesn't know what they are and there
are many rooms in the underworld and glitter from
spaceships that have crashed.

translated from the Finland-Swedish by David McDuff

Septet to the Great Bear

Night's trailing its blue tongue,
the lakewater's cracking its ice roof
with a vocal pulse
and, fallen from their path, a couple of clouds
are drifting the shores with snow.
A thin shriek,

and a diamond writes
an icecrack like a sentence graved on a window

and the black signs on the earth's lines go silent

Maneuvering three machines in a stone cleft
a caretaker's shifting
the autumn leaves

The little one's sleeping.
The eldest of the eider ducks has gone
and come back again.

The littlest is eating her porridge herself.
Most of it

stays on the spoon.

translated from the Finnish by Herbert Lomas

A Sliced Guitar

On the restaurant's table the prayer meeting of the
Windsor chairs, overturned, legs toward heaven,

A house-sized pen which in the city of sleep
writes on my retina;

a crack between the thighs of the moon, the chafing shoe
of midnight, the hepatomas of words,

life-long verses. The cuticle of thinking.
The hairs of memory. The window's knife thrust,

a brief history of sleep, the tooth decay of Time and
the brass rail of inevitability,

death's customer discount, a sliced guitar and
the eyelashes of light and

death's customer discount, a sliced guitar and
the eyelashes of light,

translated from the Finnish by C. B. Hall in cooperation with the author

— MARTIN ENCKELL (b. 1954) —

Saint Petersburg

in the city of the sphinxes, and the mothers,
in the city where death's sphinx
rests in double majesty, and where the mothers
bear the bread home, out to the infinities of kneeling concrete,
where the children, the children increasingly often refuse to find their way
     home,
in this city of the mothers, and the sphinxes,
life writes its shadow script, as in fever,
as if an enormous tubercular angel had lain down to die
over the Neva's delta, over the mirage of stone and the marsh river's dark reflections,
over golden pinnacles and cupolas, over feverish gold, over façades doomed to
     beauty,
over palaces and portals where raw cold mist drifted in, over the trampled jewel
and the suburbs that mock, over the weighed-down marshes, and over weighed-
     down fates,
dizzying fates, and harrowed, that were scattered,
and are still scattered, into nothingness—in the city of the sphinxes, and the
     mothers.

— —

she is old and bent, she begs, begs her way in
behind your eyes, by one of the passages down to the underworld,
and you implore her, implore her not to look like your mother,

night after night her youth rolls in over you,
night after night you approach requiems she will never write,
night after night she freezes into pictures you have no access to

— —

in a white dress, by the window, in that light cool room,
she stands listening to the lingering echo
from a gate that has slammed shut, watching as through veils
the retinue of phantoms from the Marinsky, sylphides and future doomed
who silently stride across the Neva's frail dark ice

— —

dawn after dawn death stands
and polishes, caresses, caresses her doorknob,
dusk after dusk she locks you
in her gaze, a gaze that has swept over a whole century

— —

and in a black decolleté dress, in the icy palace,
she dances then, all night long, her bridal waltz
with ghost after ghost, until she dances with the dawn
in whose eyes red spiders gleam, and she hears the iron gates
slam shut about the rooms, the rooms where the taiga and the tundra begin

— —

night after night she freezes into the memories where death constantly divides,
night after night she approaches those she loved, over the Styx,
night after night she rolls a waxworks of torments over you,

she is one of the many, one of the dumb, she is all and each,
who stood and waited, for months and years, who stood and queued
and waited, outside Kresty, the martyrdom, the prison that sanctified the word.

— —

life writes its corroding shadow script over the most beautiful of cities,
as though an angel, an enormous tubercular angel, were trying to bless all
    that is doomed,
by letting itself be blessed down in the slowly sinking foundations of beauty,
while death, indifferent, apparently indifferent, watches death, in double
    majesty,
out of frozen stone, above the river, above the Styx—in the city of the
    mothers, in Saint Petersburg.

      translated from the Finnish by David McDuff

Herbal Wisdom

New churches, old
    harmonized organs and repetitions

like a prayer or a psalm for seven
voices.

Against scant blue

  a hundred people
believe in pilots and safety belts. The
wind

    just a little too strong.

But my heart it was, that loaded institution
through four expectations it came

    here. Exactly here

where you, with both hands,
  almost inaudibly
intend to break
    the fragrant life of a sprig of thyme.

That soundless break, the speech of dust, said all
    I understood.

      translated from the Finnish by Anselm Hollo

from The Poetry Track

4. In No Man's Land

In no man's land there's a lovely hill

surrounded by valleys suffused by magic
and perennially greening mountains.

No poet will ever find his way here.

And when he, poorer by a day,

having penetrated the traffic's infuriating routine,

beaten by aimless wandering and idleness,
returns home, meets an expression

that is like an iceberg's summit,
how demanding,
and with armies altogether too huge
considering the adversary,

does evening come with its autumns
being
lit in the parks

translated from the Finnish by Anselm Hollo

— HELENA SINERVO (b. 1961) —

Postcard

I saw your picture in the paper yesterday, and today
though the report concerns a tragic accident
and apparently you're avoiding us, your relatives
I felt the urge to tell you a couple of things:
A singer should always be smiling
and your smile won't sell if you don't soon get your teeth fixed.
Furthermore you should sit on a stone and listen to how
your inner teeth are grinding.
There's nothing to beat it! Especially in the morning
when you can stare out over the open water and see its hugeness,
an enormous colored lens from which the sun's iris detaches itself
in order to study the people of this town.
Don't ever let the same terror walk the same path three times,
it leaves the tracks of a forestry machine in the brain, instead
you should walk these paths, across water
everything appears in a different light, absolutely everything:
a robin is chirping wildly, there are violets, and lungwort!
I know what I'm talking about, I too
have been reading the paw of a tiny creature.

translated from the Finnish by Donald Adamson

Fete

The park's dark-green evening dress,
the soft sleeve, the tunnel—
the avenue we walk along.
We feel our way inside the sleeve
like a strange arm searching for light.
A pliant, longing arm of a strange body.

We listen to the sounds of the night, sawing, tapping,
hammering in the bushes.

Fete, we keep whispering
the password to each other.
This is a fete.
Cannot decline the invitation.
Cannot even leave the room,
the fete is about to begin.
No time to go back home
before the fete starts anew
in the middle of the road.

Seagulls shine on the lawn—
bird shit on the wet, black statue.
You have found people of your own kind, your look-alikes,
carved out of the same coffin.
Black boats float under their eyes, too.
They, too, believe that the spring will come again,
every instant will start a fete.

Skyrockets explode outward from their own core,
rockets bring something distant close to us
and then explode it, explode your face.
Exactly the right experience for a fete,
isn't it, you can imagine something changing.
The celebrants like the Furies,
the Erinyes, exude confetti, empty bottles.

Your image on the surface of the water:
it is you, but you are not it.
The stone wall crumbles, dissolves in the water
sculpted out of darkness.

Lamps of three colors light up
in the park: red, blue and purple.
The sea in some places so deep
that it swells like black chewing gum,
a black rubber raft slips into your ear.
Sand rustles into your ear,
the hourglass of your head.
The nose casts a long shadow
as if your face were a sundial,
a sundial in the dark night.

Someone slams a red clown nose
right in the middle of your face,
you swing around to look.
The Furies dance, waddling
ceremoniously, unintentionally comic,
holding up their hems in the whirl,
quiet in the accompanying currents.

Tell me what the celebrants'
abandoned kids said
when they passed you running
and shouting bang bang bang.
Did they wish to comment on something?
Sounds grow into a language for the children,
the language is a great death rider on its motorbike,
driving in a circle in a ball-shaped cage.

Do you already know everybody at this fete?
Names float around like flags in a stream.
Names drift among garbage scows.
Names are collected on a tray like disposable plastic cups
and eventually thrown away.

Where the trees end,
where the avenue ends,
a blind arm protrudes from the sleeve.
The fete is over
before it began,
we lose our way in the unonstructed darkness—
into the lime white painted darkness.

translated from the Finnish by Sarka Hantula

⚜ SÁPMI ⚜

— NILS ASLAK VALKEAPÄÄ (1943–2001) —

from Trekways of the Wind

My home is in my heart
it migrates with me

The yoik is alive in my home
the happiness of children sounds there
herd-bells ring
dogs bark
the lasso hums
In my home
the fluttering edges of parkas
the leggings of the Sami girls
warm smiles

My home is in my heart
it migrates with me

——

You know it brother
you understand sister
but what do I say to strangers
who spread out everywhere
how shall I answer their questions
that come from a different world

How can I explain
that we cannot live in just one place
and still live
when we live
on all this tundra
You are standing in my bed
my privy is behind the bushes
the sun is my lamp
the lake my washbowl

——

How can I explain
that my heart is my home

that it moves with me
How can I explain
that others live there too
my brothers and sisters

— —

What shall I say brother
what shall I say sister

They come
and ask where is your home
they come with papers
and say
this belongs to nobody
this is government land
everything belongs to the State
They bring out fat grimy books
and say
this is the law
it applies to you too

What shall I say sister
what shall I say brother

— —

You know brother
you understand sister

But when they ask where is your home
do you answer them: all this
On Skuolfedievvá we pitched our *lávvu*
during the spring migration
Čáppavuopmi is where we built our *goahti* during rut
Our summer camp is at Ittunjárga
and during the winter our reindeer are in Dálvadas

You know it sister
you understand brother

— —

Our ancestors kept fires on Allaorda
on Stuorajeaggis' tufts
on Viiddesčearru

Grandfather drowned in the fjord while fishing
Grandmother cut her shoe grass in Šelgesrohtu
Father was born in Finjubákti in burning cold

And still they ask
where is your home

——

They come to me
and show books
Law books
they have written themselves
This is the law and it applies to you too
See, here

But I do not see brother
I do not see sister
I say nothing
I cannot
I only show them the tundra

translated from the Sami by Lars Nordström, Ralph Salisbury, and Harald Gaski

✳ SWEDEN ✳

— ARNE JOHNSSON (b. 1950) —

from Changes

Sketch XXV

The water carrier's bucket is full,
he spills his love over
cattle, hunters and people. Now it is
August, the month of the predator:
                             Water, ashes, hot earth,
the month of fire. We are children who for a time
banish death. I can do no more, you tell me. Don't forget
the river, I say to you with the tongue of the lion. It is August,
the carrier spills
his rain over our
backs, raises us up. I want you to
tell me that there is no
death. He lowers his bucket, fills it
spills our earthly heaven over us. We
become again and again
                      (what you do not say I die of)

translated from the Swedish by Rika Lesser

from Part of this and separate as everyone

what you see: the lilac tree in bloom, the scents from their clusters of blossoms catching in clothing and skin. I woke up, my body stiff and aching, sentimental, mourning the dream I had just left. I move through the apartment, go out and the air is, yes a river spreading as it flows. Memory, now I search for everything, that which unites and divides. What I see is how we crossed the bridge over the river, it was night, land and water were one

translated from the Swedish by Rika Lesser

*

I return
to my mother's grave
lift her out of the earth
like a dim figure
and look into her eyes
for a long time
we stand silent and gaze
into each other

translated from the Swedish by Victoria Häggblom

*

the lake slept
under a blanket
a blanket of waves
the old
gravel roads slept
slept with their arms around the houses
the thunder slept
a comb
and a mirror slept
everything slept
everything that ever was slept
your face slept
a branch slept
slept in a vase

translated from the Swedish by Victoria Häggblom

— KATARINA FROSTENSON (b. 1953) —

Echo's Gorge

That red bone
the throat reef
where is she found

rasping and screeching
her saw

voice, what creature are you
beneath the stone

five fathoms
deep, the coral

translated from the Swedish by Frank Perry and Sarah Death

Sonnet from Shadow of a Gift

Cecilia Day, Celan Day
after and in each other
monotony's slender joy
slow colorless drizzle
Myopic music over the field
Weight should be what's felt
Only a kind of light's at work in
neon strips and graphic white
On a height a house
monolithic and mist-gray
is the condition,
what is urgent, what gentle
pervades, passes over
from you

translated from the Swedish by Frank Perry

— EVA RUNEFELT (b. 1953) —

Carnation

A bunch
of summer lightning,
deep pink flashes

Through the windowpane the great birds
of moisture and silver
divide the blue mountains with ease: inside
the blood-red shine of that elusive stone
as our hands get mixed up
in your black gloves

The orb of the sun behind a sheet of ash
and gray horses from out of the chimneys
The heads coming loose from their bodies
Between the right corner of my mouth
and my left cheek
you plant a sudden half-moon
with the taste of carnation

translated from the Swedish by Frank Perry

The Slowness

The flowers' glossy spoon-backs glazed in yellow
Just bought they stand and suck warm water, closed like
the eyes in the room next door
Eyes shutting outward into slowness, being drained of objects,
into another color
A clear-sightedness passes between the two of them,
like the chill from a half-open window, from foot to neck
There is space enough in the finger moving across a back.
How far in does the slowness go? To reach inside the touch and be obliterated.

translated from the Swedish by Frank Perry

— ELISABETH RYNELL (b. 1954) —

The Womb

The question of the womb of
woman   A boat anointed with honey
and then out onto the water
out with the boat   Who
does the rowing?   May
be it's a god who rows   He has
hands of gold   Takes hold of the oars

Strange   Now
she's being rowed   Now he finds
the rhythm   Now she is rowed
The water parts
for her

and she does not lose
her maidenhood.   Saving
for the one who never comes

   mothers labor
in virginity all   open themselves
untouched
for the child
while the men drink
full of their own strength   of teeth
drink the drink of women   burrow
into women's bodies   taste
taste those lips

The question of wombs   of cunt   what to
say   how to talk about them   All the uncleanness
cast upon them   Boat smeared
with honey   with milk   Boat
smeared with seed   Leaky boat

and as in the old days
there stands set
for an unexpected guest
there stands ready
in waiting   a platter   a glass   Drink
my friend

The womb. The question of
the womb

farthest in
in the midst of pleasure she remains
untouched   Row me
she says   Let me
part the waters

translated from the Swedish by Rika Lesser

three poems from **Soon into the Summer I Will Walk Out**

Into a field the fall sun fell down in clear dead colors. And the earth too fell down to the worms. They carried a swan out into the field and plowed her down into the black soil. A black-throated honey bird. A ray heart with paradise mouth. Famished she took deeper and deeper breaths. They plowed the feathers into the field. And sowed the swan with her own ugly white seeds. She smelled like the dead. But she came up like the beloved. A throat-rest with round beautiful eyes. Above the radiant earth collar. It formed a flower.

Out of the throat grows a white and beautiful swan with a dead head. And down below the trunk the silk limbs stick out. Or the blank mother-of-pearl leaves. She has a strong and brazen tile mouth. Which opens over the speckled neck. A coarse Lord pushes his coarse lord-stalk into her mouth. *It is a creek so lovely its current is like emerald gulps.* She is a simple swan rose. With tile-red ginger-sized mother leaves. O these mother leaves. That penetrate the silver vessels beneath *the soft tiling.*

The big valley is a vast mother-of-pearl mirror. There walks the large dead swan in her dead shroud. And there walk the mother-of-pearl children. Or the fragile found-ling clumps. That grow out of the virgin mother's throat. They led the swan into a forest and placed beautiful white stones of mother-of-pearl on her back. *Go now and eat that which you have taken from the swans.* Then one ran up and cut a branch from the tree and grabbed a *burning branch* and stuck it into her throat. And scrubbed her both up top and down below. Until the swan's flesh fell off in beautiful heavy clumps. For some time the swan lay in the bushes and slept. And black merchants came riding on black mother-of-pearl horses. Then they took the swan and carried her away.

translated from the Swedish by Johannes Göransson

(Analogia)

This poem could be a face
Not the right one, but the true one. Analogies deal with relationships that hold. It

Speaks. The poem's similarity to the face consists, among others things, in the
poet's capacity to see it from inside and struggle to regard it as an outsider.
Without

ever entirely succeeding. A mirror might be helpful.

In Pindar's seventh Nemean Ode he compares song to a mirror. Memory's.
  The face
A sounding mirror. The poem. A mirror of sound. Can we call this an analogy?

I try to imagine what you see. How I look when I think of this topos of from
    inside or outside. To reveal
is to conceal. To oscillate between things which cannot be made one

As a metaphor for theoretical knowledge transparency is comically opaque, at least
    with respect to poetry. High clear space. Gaze deeply into the well of the poem,
    where the moon glitters in the black

water. I saw a long line of antique mirrors in the museum. Archaeological goods, a
    dime a dozen. Burnished metal. Dark inside. But isn't song always transparent?
    Words never. Yes maybe

it is only when the poem longs for simplicity
that it can actually become like

like a face

translated from the Swedish by Rika Lesser

— HÅKAN SANDELL (b. 1962) —

Nature Morte: iv. **On an Eggshell**

The matter's dead, I imagine.
Once, back there in the twentieth century,
I found left behind in my cabin
on the Berlin train, in the cars bound for Poland,
a sucked-out eggshell pierced with
a piece of straw like a ray of sunlight.
Empty and hollow as a ping-pong ball,
rounded as soundly as a silkworm's cocoon,
a little cranium—a mouse's, maybe—
from which someone unknown, a god of fate
or a demon, had sucked out the life
yet left completely undivided
heaven and earth as one in that oval.
As if listening to a seashell that holds the ocean
I listened at that hard shell
to vanished summers, silent tears,
to the wing-beats over childhood fields

of birds, bees and dragonflies;
heard the echo of empty schoolyards
and touched that chalky armor
as if poking at sketches on the asphalt,
those naive pictures' depictions
of the mysteries of the darker sex.
A world preserved and enclosed
behind brittle walls and fully alive,
almost as on that liquidated sun.

translated from the Swedish by Bill Coyle

⤜ NORWAY ⤛

— BJØRN AAMODT (1944–2006) —

Five untitled poems

The big semis arrive at night from Rouen and Rovaniemi, roll up Bishop Street
fueled by black oil, black coffee and blue music, cross the Dyveke Bridge with
    10 inches of clearance
and half a pound of fried bacon. *Perkele!* This is not the road to eternal life.

— —

And then the Universe bends our straight line of sunlight,
grass and stone fences, as Grandfather's and Father's backs
bent over the twilit fields.

— —

The past wears a dark suit. Like tonight. The future wears a dark suit.
Like the next night. And Now stands there in a dark suit and pulls on the clock
    chain.
A dark suit bends over with three heads, deep in an infant's sleep.

— —

The song of the number 1, stiff and blind as a penis under silk and wool,
oak leaves and falling stars, sitting heavily on children's backs, 1/2, 1/4, 1/7,
the endless series of the condemned, crossing worlds of skin and milk, on its way
    toward zero.

— —

The only earth is a treadmill that crushes wheat in the half-darkness,
as 5 billion humans haul themselves up to the next step. The only heaven
is the movement of dust particles in a sunbeam. The only connection is distance.

translated from the Norwegian by Roger Greenwald

— TOR ULVEN (1953–1995) —

[They dance far]

They dance far
into the woods
accompanied by the silence
of fiddles
without strings.

Only the brook's clatter
that snakes through
the stone age.
And for the sharpest
ears—the sound
of erosion.

They dance and dance,
without thinking of you.

translated from the Norwegian by Siri Hustvedt

— ØYSTEIN WINGAARD WOLF (b. 1958) —

The Soapmaker

I remember the old soapmaker
at the Lilleborg Works
when we were twelve years old and
counted pubic hairs, betrayed Jesus, Mother and Father
and Fatherland, strong, vulnerable,
half unconscious in the crossfire
between history class and pop culture.
I remember the red, cracked face
that looked like a cake of soap in a hotel sink
and showed how you become what you do.
I remember the long arms that stirred and stirred
in circles and figure eights and kept the world moving
and the tattoo with the name "Esmeralda."
We asked him some simple questions
that didn't annoy or flatter him,
and the smell that followed us home from the huge factory
made it dizzying just to exist.

Now that I've grown up I know
it was soap that kept me alive,
round and oblong pieces that Mama painted
with Donald Duck, Porky Pig and Popeye
so they became small works of art that rich kids
could splash with in their bathtubs at Christmas;
yellow perfume bottles with foreign names
that Papa packed carefully in boxes and cartons
and sent to shining towns all over the country.

Grandpa became a small pile of soap and ashes
that the Nazis wanted to wash Europe with.
He was of the people of Israel.
Anyone who wants to know how everything hangs together
can just come to me and ask.
When I catch the smell of a lady on the street
I want to stir the world's cauldron like the old soapmaker
and follow her to where purity loses its meaning.

translated from the Norwegian by Roger Greenwald

[Your left hand]

Your left hand
fights a hopeless battle
wants to shake but doesn't reach
wants to caress but gets a stiff rap
it writes notes about the body's shyness
inspires no one with its preludes
about the dark side of the moon, its passing
other cars at high speed
goes jig-fishing, raises its guard
against imagined blows from language,
on the way to school, frantically leafs
in search of a postage stamp or a hymn verse
that can be sent out like Judas,
a grave-robber at the burial place of holy men
it arranges the flip side of your life
until it resembles the wardrobe of a clumsy comic
it will inherit you in the end
with all the wretched words you used
to keep love at a distance

translated from the Norwegian by Roger Greenwald

— HENNING KRAMER DAHL (b. 1962) —

Practicing Ballerina

The large gymnasium in morning light
Filled with notes from a tired piano,
Mirrored walls' staring images of mirrors.

She scratches her right armpit
Through a hole in her worn leotard,
Does stretches and lays her palms
On the floor's scuffed parquet,
Presses her ballet slippers together
Before the kaleidoscope is shaken
And movement explodes time's musty immobility.

A hazy conception of rhythms and patterns
In secret union with an ancient sun.
Inklings that sharpen into burning certainty
As the blood races ecstatically toward the heart.
The primeval gods' passionate breath
Where they whirled above the earth as newborn titans
Glimpsed here in an empty practice room
In a decrepit century
That's wearing a smooth pubescent mask
Over its torpid old-man's skin.

The ballerina in sweaty concentration
Hides in her taut body
The sacred source
Of life's rebellious daughter, Dance.

Not even death can obliterate her:
Her imprint, clear and sharp, remains
As the universe's glowing chaos hardens
Into the shape of the new world.

translated from the Norwegian by Roger Greenwald

— CATHRINE GRØNDAHL (b. 1969) —

Selected Exercises in Case Law II

What shall we learn from John Doe? Look at him
Do not act like him
He commits the same crimes year after year,
no matter how much we punish him
But no matter how often we learn
that we must *not* end up like him,
it isn't crimes and prisons we fear the most
here at the Faculty of Law,

or meeting John Doe in exams year after year
No, the most frightening thing is simply
to be named John Doe and to land in Smalltown,
with defective title to a mortgaged house full of construction flaws,
in debt up to your eyes, with creditors at the door
and a wife, Jane Doe,
who always wants to divorce you and get the lion's share
of your assets and your inheritance
and throw you out onto the street,
where you end up in a fistfight with your neighbor Richard Roe
because of that big new garage of his

translated from the Norwegian by Roger Greenwald

The Law Is the Mediterranean

The Law is the Mediterranean: Take long, slow strokes
You're rowing across the strait in one day
Jews, Christians, and Muslims
live on each their shore
You think the Law comes from the heavens
and that the shiny surface of the sea mirrors God,
an eye for an eye, a tooth for a tooth
There is a sea between you
The Law ties you together
and keeps you apart,
and every wave moves the Law: Take long, slow strokes
You're rowing across the strait in one day

translated from the Norwegian by Roger Greenwald

— PEDRO CARMONA-ALVAREZ (b. 1972) —

60 Minutes

There's a war, it starts and is already missing
from histories, tales
under the light of lamps that sparkle
and lean over bodies
There's a war and there are pebbles. The presence
of myths, blood running from the forehead puddles
in the eyes

resembles make-up and puddles in the eyes resembles war
in the eyes that tremble from being windows,
shaking from knowing the inside

There's a war and all the generals have drowned.
There's a war
and my sweetheart comes home
her hair pulled up in a knot that tightens her face
till it's unrecognizable.
There's a war and the ones who know are heading home
to watch themselves on screens.

Make me happy and it won't help much.

translated from the Norwegian by Roger Greenwald

— CORNELIUS JAKHELLN (b. 1977) —

Sèma (sign).

Each sign is a demon that has murdered its match.
The boldest ones survive in the book, realm of the dead.

translated from the Norwegian by Roger Greenwald

[Not to be is Nothing's only quality.]

Not to be is Nothing's only quality.
She decks herself out with feathers to blend in with what is.

Being: Heraclitus. Golgotha. Black Forest. Microsoft.
Being came like a kiss from a stun gun.

She'd thought Being was gone for good.

Nothing smokes gigacigarettes in her house by the sea.
Nothing weeps in her yellow Corvette.

No one cares about Nothing.

translated from the Norwegian by Roger Greenwald

⤙ ICELAND ⤚

— ELÍSABET JÖKULSDÓTTIR (b. 1958) —

The Divorce Children

The divorce children had parents who parted company and went their separate ways. The children were left behind, looked by turns to east and west and saw their parents receding into the distance until they disappeared in a blue haze beyond the further field of vision. Then the children hatched a plot and later many people were surprised that they did not seem to have any interest in widening their horizons. In the place where the family had stood together before, a tree now grew upside down, into the ground. The divorce children still crouch there, carving their roots.

translated from the Icelandic by David McDuff

— GYRDIR ELÍASSON (b. 1961) —

Nocturne

I dream a man
who is dead,
he is driving a new
car and invites me
for a long journey.
Thinking I
understand his
drift I decline
cautiously. We
are on Nylendugata;
the car doors open
and I look in,
at my dead
friend. "Thanks all the
same, I'll join you
later," I say,
but nonetheless get in
and we follow
the road,

in the dusk north
to where
the graves are
deeper than coal mines.

translated from the Icelandic by Bernard Scudder

— KRISTÍN ÓMARSDÓTTIR (b. 1962) —

Closed Bridal Night

A veil cushioned the bottom of that coffin.

In a grave lies a bride
with gifts in
her lap.

Ribbons in pale colors and white
tissue paper.

Visiting cards.

Dressed

in a crocheted dress,
lace stockings, shoes
and gloves.

Serpentine locks.

A veil cushioned the bottom of that coffin.

A face of salt
and sensitive
dusty eyes.

A veil cushioned the bottom of that coffin.

Many messages from bottles
were written there.

translated from the Icelandic by Bernard Scudder

And Your Tears

The bed stands
in the middle of the floor
the sheet sweeping cold tiles
I know you're thinking of here
day and night
that's why I'm lying still as the grave
beneath the white ceiling
which soon will blossom
for you are dying from me
night and day
I promised to lie
in the middle of the island
in the deepest valley
dearestdarling
and your tears glide down on parachutes of tulips
onto my quilt
that I may sleep

translated from the Icelandic by Bernard Scudder

— PIA TAFDRUP (b. 1952) —

A Thousand Times Recalled

Green here too, where since early summer the soil's crust
has resembled the furrowed skin that hangs from the cheekbones of aged women;
where the houses carry scars and memory's images fall, as dense as raining bullets
The eucalyptus trees on the hillside do not remember yesterday
just as the sparrows do not long for tomorrow

Horned cattle and flocks of sheep, spread across Jerusalem's plains;
flowers poised to spring out, and people who dance up the slopes
to pick them too early, reaching deep into silence so the yellow butterflies
are shaken loose and sail up into the air
in a radiance of signs, a gentle metallic swaying:

One of many or each single one—that makes all the difference
when refugees are hidden in the bottom of fishing boats
on their way to another country
with each their prayer for the same thing
To be lifted across the water.

translated from the Danish by Roger Greenwald

— PIA JUUL (b. 1962) —

Novel

I let them wake up one morning in a big house with
almost empty rooms. The bedclothes don't rustle
because they are soft from use.
One of them is thin
The other is not naked—it is a woman,
she is dressed in lots of layers of fabric, there is silk and cotton,
tulle that prickles, wool that itches, all of them black,
she won't take them off
she never takes them off, but he has touched her,
now he touches her again,
and she sighs, she is warm,
there are so many clothes
she says nothing, she touches back,

he is lying almost under her side,
he is nothing but skin,
that's how it should be, that's how it is, that's how it
has been all night long. I let them lie where they have woken,
they can go on lying there, let them lie, let his clothes
be lost, let the doors be locked, let them always
lie there, let her be warm, let it rub off on him, let
the rooms echo around their sounds, let them be.
Let them be

translated from the Danish by Barbara J. Haveland

— NIELS FRANK (b. 1963) —

Conspiracies

The parrot kicks. You could say
that. The parrot answers himself
in a profound voice. You
could say that. In his own way
the parrot is a genius. But no one *is*
in his own way and least of all
him. But how do you tell him that.

My coffee is hiding
in the cup. You could say that.
But from whom? Some steam rotates vaguely
when I look into the depths, a kind of dread
that makes itself invisible right
before my eyes, the purest nothing
which in reality is water. But
how do you tell it that.

And that many mediocre dreams
just rumble blindly through darkness.
And that the stars blossom in it,
high up. And that all the consequences of this
start quoting themselves brilliantly
as soon as you turn your back on them.

In the most taciturn language, for example
this, such enormities occur
all the time. The parrots start squawking.

The coffee keeps mum. To my credit I repeat
its silence, a way of life I go around
bragging about. In this way the incantations
won't recognize each other, but will
constantly combine. Yes. You could say that.
They combine into a powerful theory.
Forgive me for continually proving it.

translated from the Danish by Roger Greenwald

In the Californian Back Yard

(after Hockney)

The water splashes and the palms rise above
the most worldly banalities we romp around in.
The rest merely looks on, casually studying
the external, the extroverted side of itself.
It's a friendly day, a good day for living.

Everything is so simple, but simplicity
is a tremendous art. For if every detail suddenly vanishes,
dissolved in sunlight, only the conception itself remains, its might,
and it can't distinguish between the day side and the night side.
For it, reality is only an imprint.
For it, reality is flawless: it erases all its tracks
so each remaining thing can indicate a self-contained *here*.

But the water too is a track, especially if someone dives into it
from a yellow springboard. The splash fizzes up in spangled coolness
and gives him away, destroys the surface's perfection,
makes it craze: it indicates a *here*
that is absent. The most attractive thing is hidden,
you can only dream of it, unless the most attractive thing
is precisely whatever you can only dream of. Everything else
is indifferent in its distinctness.

Maybe you can get to know him better, sit in the unfolded chairs
and eat ice cream with him, while the sinking sun glistens
in every one of the thousand pearls on thighs and shoulders.
In this way the conception keeps groping
for more and more details, until a light rain falls
over the abandoned pool and all scenarios are consummated.

translated from the Danish by Roger Greenwald

The Nth Day of the Nth Month

Today I upended a huge oak tree and saw
that it had no roots. Furious, I razed the whole forest.

The flowers smell as lifeless as wax.
But wax here is no more lifeless than flowers.
Wax and flowers.

I put the moon and the sun at the same height. All creation fell still.
Before too long I remembered I had done this before.
And it hasn't amused me this time either.

I visited Libella's grave. I created her
and killed her to have something to give me joy
and sorrow. The truth is that she left me cold.
—Can I classify that as an action?

I created the Cult of the Horse—and of the Cat.
I equipped their members with certain traits of my own
as well as the conviction that the highest of all goods
is in one case the ability to see sideways like a horse
and in the other the ability to leap like a cat.
The beginning was amusing but the outcome
was determined in advance. I didn't stay to see the end.

Staring at the sky is the only thing I haven't grown weary of.
I can even feel some doubt about which of us came first.
This doubt is so pleasant that I evoke it only rarely
so I can enjoy it fully each time.
If I leave it untouched long enough perhaps
it can develop a certain independence?

I took ten drops of water and filled them with infinity.
Eight turned black. Two stayed clear.
Now, how can that be? I thought and was delighted
to have a little puzzle to start the next day with.

I think I'll move tomorrow up to today.

translated from the Danish by Roger Greenwald

⤜ GERMANY ⤛

— ULLA HAHN (b. 1946) —

Respectable Sonnet

So why not write a respectable sonnet
—ST. H.

Come bite me right and bite right in again
and leave off merely nibbling. Here's where
it's good, and here, and you know where, yes, there,
and take my measure mouth to mouth. Paint then

considering these eyes, rings around
them, let me hide behind beneath my hand,
then spring to yours. Pleasure me in sixes and
in sevens. I scream I know no sound.

Stay with me. Wait. I'll come again,
back to myself, to you, and once more tell
you too, I'll be your lovely old refrain.

Rub rings of sunshine into belly's shell
so that the warmth remain.
Then keep my eyelids open, my lips as well.

translated from the German by Oliver Grannis

— URSULA KRECHEL (b. 1947) —

My Mother

I.

When my mother had been mother
for a quarter century long, and wife, tho she could forget
about that in those days, when she had become
the way all upstanding wives had to be,
cleverer than the grandmother, more devoted than the aunts
more sparing in the kitchen and in love than one
in whose lap luck had fallen
when she flicked enough crumbs from the tablecloth
when she buried the hope to someday be a lady

in fur like before the war in the fashion magazines
still hidden behind the shelves in the pantry
when she began to search her daughters' faces
looking for a trace of what she did not find
in her own, when she ceased waking in fear
because she dreamed of the hot iron
left on, when she sometimes even
dared in the early afternoon
to cross her legs, a cancer
gnawed away at her uterus, grew, became overgrown
and little by little crowded my mother out of her life.

2.

Ten days after her death she was suddenly there again
in a dream. As if someone had come calling, I was drawn
To the window of our old apartment. On the street
four guys waved from a beat-up VW.
One of them honked the horn looking something like
the Berlin friends five years ago.
Then from the backseat a woman waved:
my mother. At first I see her
half hidden behind her new acquaintances.
Then I see only her
huge like on a movie screen, then her skinny white arm
on which not even a tiny little hair can be seen not even up close.
The flames from the stove used to singe them
as she bustled around the kitchen.
On her wrist she wore the silver bangle
my father had given her on their engagement.
She had handed it down to me. Me running down the polished stairs.
At the front door I hear giggling: Mama!
I call, the next words won't go over my lips.
My mother sits wedged between two boys
laughing. She hasn't been this happy for some time.
Why don't you come along? she asks. But there's no room
in the car I say and look awkwardly
through her silk blouse,
which during her life she never would have worn
over her still-perfect young girl's breasts,
and I think, I have to get father. Then the engine
roars, the rickety door slams shut

from inside. At the front door I could kick myself.
I didn't even take down her license plate.

translated from the German by Elizabeth Oehlkers Wright

— ANGELA KRAUSS (b. 1950) —

Leipzig, 1999

So perfectly natural, everything we inhabit. Like our body,
whose dilapidation escapes our notice, just like its constant renewal.
Everything perfectly natural as long as it lives.

The way that we open a door and close it again
makes partitions between body and dwelling place vanish,
for only a moment.
But naturally enough to remind us
that we're not just the ones who come and go in this place.

Or the shadow, headstrong and summer-like, placing
a collar of new row houses round its neck,
before the warm, humid breath of the street after a cloudburst,
as ever, flows surging through its own.
What we inhabit is what we are.

Even ten years are nothing,
were there not someone here
who ten years ago lost his faith
and has searched for it ever since.
And another encountered the person
he's been searching for half his life.

All this in just one city.

Both can remember exactly, to the very day,
how every connection was somehow lost,
or perhaps was revealed in a single exchange of glances.
And both remain locked in their dispute over which is more true.
Good or bad fortune.

And meantime our actions draw us, as they have for centuries,
at once alert and blind
expectantly into the future.

translated from the German by Michael Ritterson

You sleep

you sleep and lie beside your hair
your white leg propped up in the air
and me, on whom it rests, I am the world
oppressed by your sleep, am the danger
that gently keeps your dream alert

you sleep and lie beside your hair
a whisper I've sent to sleep inside your ear
speaks to you, says I was the evening,
the drunkenness, the shiver in your pessary,
it speaks to you the language saving me

translated from the German by Elizabeth Oehlkers Wright

Disoriented

I.

Even the word for it fails, even so.
Even so, everything else.
But my name plate, on the entrance,
unadulterated. This new,
this other house.
Where I will have been.
Where I will not have been.

II.

Who spoke when what to whom.
I count the buttons
on my coat,
whether yes or whether never.

III.

(. . .)

IV.

So I arrived there one day,
always on the way there,

and there I was. But I could not
find her language,
gave up and turned back,
where to.

The open and the shut room.
The wrong, the lost keys.
Cipher, stones, death.

translated from the German by Elizabeth Oehlkers Wright

— BERT PAPENFUSS (b. 1956) —

on edge

there is only one truth is there   & it is unspeakable
as well as unspeakable   & it is typical
i wear myself out in its pursuit   wearing out suit after suit
just enough to respectably pass   realizing waiting lies fundamentally
closer the closer you are to yourself   all the more probable
getting close to someone one   embodying truth
without regard for the truth you must wait   to get there
lies obtain truth   & truths unite & turn personal
applied truth stinks   keep it to yourself

translated from the German by David Perry

— THOMAS KLING (1957–2005) —

stratum I (petrarch)

the peak ahead, the slope behind me,
yet she is what I always see. wind

wounds that will not heal. protruding
roots, underbrush, cropped sparse grass

amid the hard gravel, thorny in
the northern wind . . . as he wrote

in a letter. then two helicopters,
black and suddenly out of nowhere,

circling over the square. rotors
whir; the jagged escape of the swifts

which dive, shrilly
in the scarce, decap-

itated air. air! each breath a crampon!
by noon, thin air. then distance.

translated from the German by Peter Filkins

stratum III (beatrice)

this hair is snow-white, this hair
is black, growing again at the root.

we became liquid. eventually we were
liquidated. so we drifted off, bees

saved in dawn's shimmering honey.
sacrifice, invocation, food for the dead.

how your voice unfolded!, its lowland
luminosity in the blacklight of the sunflower

we flow into, sleepless, honey, the liquefaction
of words: a hunger, deeply felt, for everything.

translated from the German by Peter Filkins

— UWE KOLBE (b. 1957) —

Never now anywhere

On the bridge they'll stay, detained,
each one in the other's arms,
kissing, and their eyes, wide-open,
up into the moon they'll stare.

Yes, they'll have a father, mother,
have forgotten both.
Are so young and yet so heavy,
all their turning circular.

To the heavens and the street lamps
love and their escape they'll swear.
But the lights, the streets stay silent,
nothing but the wind moves there.

From the bridge they will not stir,
not for parents but in vain,
only to themselves belonging
never now go anywhere.

translated from the German by Michael Hamburger

— DIETER M. GRÄF (b. 1960) —

While Dancing: A Paradigm

how much, after being perceived,
it is refined, how it pulverizes
and, a force drifting off, charges
the cells: coming from me, who
wants something, a girl who
stands before me, skipping rope.

                              Her

ever repeated motions—a belly
button being. Went back while
dancing, intentions suspended
and came again: this switching to
gether; *this balance without weight.*

translated from the German by Andrew Shields

— ZEHRA ÇIRAK (b. 1961) —

Friendly Fire

A random shot goes off
people begin to stir
unusually inconspicuous
they duck at the slightest breeze
always in fear
it might carry the bullet
many know
only hits in the back
most have had eyes
stitched into their shoulder blades
and many join in the shooting

no one looks ahead anymore
out of fear his own bullet
might find his own back

translated from the German by Elizabeth Oehlkers Wright

— KERSTIN HENSEL (b. 1961) —

At the Flea Market

Someone's selling love
for no money, no lie. No one
stops. My lover
at the next stand
buys a golden ring.

translated from the German by Elizabeth Oehlkers Wright

— ZAFER ŞENOCAK (b. 1961) —

M

maybe maybe not
who could it have been
who
gave the princess a shot of morphine
instead of kissing her awake
and leapt from the roof of an unfinished building
instead of staying there overnight undercover

the whole city keeps its lights on
to catch the murderer
until lights go out
in the last movie theaters
and couples make their way home
why don't people ever lose their way on these roads

the great dreams
lose their men
they fall on their beds
emasculated by their sleeplessness

maybe maybe not
a night like this never was
no princess ever slept on this construction site

translated from the German by Elizabeth Oehlkers Wright

hyacinth colic

you slept still i sat
your breath was going day
was pushing forest fieldward
the meadow now began
to flash in shadow fed a
pair of pigeons she with claws
so hot a small fleck on his
neck. still soft their calls
as dear as childhood mornings
(all asleep but sun and
dove and quiet roof) you
went your chest was oiled
nude you went the disc had
struck his forehead cooled
and warmed and hardened.
trying is a game the guilt and
every bed on floors is hard in
its pot the hyacinth is testing
whether quite without you
i will bear its scent

translated from the German by Iain Galbraith

In the Provinces 2 (In Gotland)

From a distance, this was all there was to see,
An undulating landscape assembled in a buzzard's eye,
The bare hills, a track and at the edge of it
A rabbit's foot in the undergrowth, ruffled by the wind,
A well-gnawed ankle joint that weighed no more

In the hand than a baby bird,
Still moving, still warm, that leapt
Out of the frying pan, bloodied as the prey
Of the gray butcher bird, on the rowan spike—
A little lump of bone beckoning with a flap of fur.

That was all that was left of a rabbit after
The shadow of a wing crossed his path,
After its zigzag dash had been cut off by a claw, its panting
Breath by a well-aimed beak. How comfortless
This death must have been, helplessly splayed
On the wintry earth, the last convulsions.
The sole survivor of the slaughter perched in the boughs,
Which, like bribed witnesses, had no recollection of anything.
The grass, which had long since picked itself up, sees to it
That this was all there was to see, this rabbit's foot.

translated from the German by Michael Hofmann

— LUTZ SEILER (b. 1963) —

concrete

two gray remarkable children leaned
overhead in the doorway one
held the establishment in his arms the

other read *once upon a time*
too early every morning and
a desire that

did not recognize itself
kneeling in the muscovite in the granite
of the great gravel surfaces *thou*

art myne thus we stood and looked
up above for ever ex-
changed with heavy ink on

the fingertips spastic
hooded kisses *i*
am thyne; from gravel, cement, reinforcing iron.

translated from the German by Tony Frazer

Jargons IV (2)

what still remains of "songless"—"an earnest bird"
brings up. no earnest bird discusses what
seemed essentially the fact. he as it were cancels
himself out. you mentally shake your head. you nod.
you say i see. this must the essence of negation be.
and what's confusing at a second glance: . . . NO X

HORSES (. . . carry you away) at a third holds
up and fast. no one horse holds so fast.
eleven horses or else nine: carry
you away. just as no ten. they hold you
fast. then let's have at it at no zero
horses—to sidle/bridle up! a matter

(to remove last lingering doubts): not not to be
neglected. not to forget: forgotten. to
hunger. simply done. resolved: to cut
the bread. forgets. is now (the bread harder
and harder) to cut to be called to "saw"?
may your speech be yea yea / nay nay!

what's likewise hard to clarify: if probably perhaps
exists. tendency: perhaps. probably not.
but here you quickly stand alone. and can't help make
a stand for "nonsense absolute" as having making
sense some. unprofitable enterprise: not only not
to say not / to do un. but then its beauty too.

translated from the German by Rosmarie Waldrop

— MARCEL BEYER (b. 1965) —

Snow

Now which do you mean, the seagulls, the boots
on the dock at night, the snow at night? Trieste
or Turku, Turku, Trieste—where are the flakes,
where are the forms, our soles, treading what down?

Do you mean the glimmer on the edge, the deep,
the look in the eye, the open sea? No

snow, snow, dirt, chewing gum, ice and
no snow—the falling snow is all I remember,
blue hands, blue everything.

translated from the German by Michael Hofmann

— NICOLAI KOBUS (b. 1968) —

anna

anna was a word game. she
could be taken from behind
as well as from the front. her body stands out
against the clinical white
of the tile walls. the bars
measure her cries lengthwise
back to front until far
down the branching halls.
every heart
is a slaughterhouse, there is no
end of blood.

translated from the German by Elizabeth Oehlkers Wright

— JAN WAGNER (b. 1971) —

fall villanelle

the light goes out of the days
and an hour lasts ten minutes.
the trees have played their final colors.

in the sky the stage scenery is being changed
too swiftly for the little drama in each of us.
the light goes out of the days.

your gray coat separates you from the air,
a passe-partout for a sentence like this one:
the trees have played their final colors.

ice-blue windows: on the weather maps
on the television the thumbprints of the deeps.
the light goes out of the days,

out of the empty park, the pond: the ducks will
be rolled away on invisible threads.
the trees have played their final colors.

and someone, who with three sunflowers
feels his way in the darkness, three black points on yellow:
the light goes out of the days.
the trees have played their final colors.

translated from the German by Donna Stonecipher

— JAN VOLKER RÖHNERT (b. 1976) —

Longing Is a Blind Sail . . .

—look up in the index of French poetry.
The morning with throbbing kidneys
is like the last page of a black and white
photo album your hands in the dream
keep flipping through until the secret
is aired—a topped-off fir forest.
For I love most deeply what only
happens once, he wrote, then
set up the imaginary scene where
Pierre Reverdy looks for the last time in Coco
Chanel's eyes, in those days the instruments
were extremely sensitive stuff. You know
it's true when I step in front of
the mirror now and behind me the day
begins as if love were an appointment
we've scheduled in sleep, very
far away from here and in
considerably better light.

translated from the German by Elizabeth Oehlkers Wright

a social still life in the line of vermeer

the piano teacher fingers an especially
sweet fifteen-year-old sundays strolling with the family
in the countryside and still
puberty, later out of this onanism will come love
and a tender adoration for juliette
binoche the seasons pass by unnoticed
which is really terrible
and sometimes the revolutionary étude of frederic chopin
new fingering but the same mistakes

translated from the German by Donna Stonecipher

5 aphorisms

1. You have to be a master of disguises to leave the same impression with everyone.

2. Ever since the invention of freedom, slaves have been in constant competition.

3. Democracy discriminates against the apolitical majority.

4. Tolerance is the largesse of the small-minded.

5. A slave uses every free minute.

translated from the German by Elizabeth Oehlkers Wright

Silvae (lit)

Sap runs out of the trees, as usual
the forests stand, wooden and green
before my window, and everywhere on the earth
where there is no field, no garden
no house like mine.

Sometimes an insect, on the under edge of a leaf,
a fawn-brown target with few
bull's-eyes from last year—

two ancient horses
pull wood out of the debris, with the darkness
come the hunters, you can see their yellow
                              tennis shoes shine.

translated from the German by Donna Stonecipher

— ULJANA WOLF (b. 1979) —

Recovery Room

recovery room I

oh had i only stayed in the recovery room
lost in dreams tied to drips beneath white sheets

next to others who also couldn't find themselves
a flock of sheep close to sleep close to god

and consolation and large nurses in white fur
—our shepherds bending softly over us—

if we surrendered one another to the human
riddle of numbers: on a scale of one to ten

how heavy is your pain?—and if there were
no borders that could again define us in

these fields in post narcotic sniffling—
we would stick very close to this our i

indiscernible from other sheep grazing here
beside themselves in the recovery room

recovery room II

oh had i never been in the recovery room
stranded deaf and rocking in a white boat

tied alongside other boats—yes this is
the last harbor yes this is the damp canal

of sleep where threatening nurses in black
robes stand like judges on the shore

each finger a strict syringe: drip and
devil my darling can you hear me

and in the locks you can hear nothing
only stillness this *purifired* water

that feeds you drop by drop from tubes—
with each swift wave beneath your bed

the sea steals you back into the dream of
star and muzzle far from the recovery room

translated from the German by Christian Hawkey and Uljana Wolf

⤜ AUSTRIA/LICHTENSTEIN ⤛

— EVELYN SCHLAG (b. 1952) —

Lesson

I wanted to list
What I have learned
How I hold a cool
Name in my hand when
I touch the doorknob how
I turn the road sign around
Kill the fish by striking
Their heads on the stone
I have practiced till I have
The knack and how I change
Dresses while the splashes of
Gill-blood are drying
from red to black

The cat which was sitting
On my lap laid his paw
On the back of my hand
And I did not know whether
It was to calm me or because
He so believed in the dead fish

translated from the German by Karen Leeder

— MICHAEL DONHAUSER (b. 1956) —

The Apple

For Brigitte Mahlknecht

I say today, apple.
As if to make the apple speak.
While the apple lingers this side of.
Beyond language within the language.
And longing practiced: on itself.
Beyond opposites, opposing.
Makes itself into the object of the apple.

Comes full circle.
On this bruised afternoon.
Where the apple is not the city.
Where the apple is the not-city.
Proxy in place of city.
Where the city is not smoking from its manholes.
Where it does not glitter, where it is dilapidated.
Revitalized.
Where it has nothing to do with round.
Yet not as a contrast to the apple.
But rather raised up: within the apple.
Centered around, forgotten by, unforgettable:
The abstract does not exist.
Not in spite of this moment.
Not in spite of this loss.
I eat the apple with every word.
And produced, weighed, labeled.
Every reflection, every blush, every reflex of light:
The apple unentangled: undescended into contradiction.
Unchallenged, unmolested, lit up by the sun.
In the winter light, the best of.
Beyond the unbridled apple growing.
Of the craze to grow, of the half kilo apples.
That is not crushing the moment.
To benefit the imagination.

Yet the apple says nothing, is what I say.
As if the apple would say nothing.
As morning apple now, taciturn.
As if I would celebrate the nonsphere.
The saying of nothing, the not yet, the never completely.
Imbalance in the name of the apple.
Name of the shadow, migratory bird, flying, stars.

The apple has no pure accent.
Meaning no trained tongue.
Instead a crooked stem.
It lodges a complaint on my behalf.
It insists on its meaninglessness.
It returns to its gestureless pathos.
No one, who reaches it now.

Or: plucked, brought to the mouth, tossed.
With the tossing gesture of the dancer.
Or: held up front, holding forth.
In a triumphal procession, a trick of words?
Nevertheless triumphantly of the moment.
In its speechlessness as moment.
Brought like this from the moment into the language:
As triumphant apple crossed by street noise.
It does not melt on the speaker's tongue.
Not like a Mozart kugel or a praline.
Does not lie in the snow, is not warmed by tears.
I do not cry.
I write the year of my rebirth.
As apple, through the apple, in the apple.
No apple dawning, no mass of molten speech.
I hold fast to the illusion: to the apple.
The apple held fast, yet at liberty.
Yet in the language in tranquility.

Apples galore, as they say.
In the apple depot, on the fruitfill.
like the landfill; under open sky.
Yet the sky doesn't speak.
Yet the language doesn't speak.
The apple speaks as language.
The languagelessness speaks as apple.
Even if in no one's interest.
Un- or overproduced:
In the interests of the economy.

I praise the applesilence in the apple
The inaudible boiling away of the juices.
Those slow silent of the silence.
The aroma of silence as sweetness.
Imperceptible, the loss of weight.
The imperceptibleness, so verily begun.
From the very beginning as apple as silence
Little by little the apple loses its juice.

translated from the German by Elizabeth Oehlkers Wright

About What Is a Hand
And What Is in the Hand

You take a piece of wood in your hand and say:
Me and the holidays. A great thing turns into
a particular held confidently at the far end of the arm
but rarely. Why?
Rarely.
Hands are not rare, but rarely open to the other
side of steady. Fingertips feel holidays
in their fingertips: wooden, a weight, positing
an unnameable particular world. Our cautious hands celebrate
this particular holiday.
Particular holiday.
Slow. What is slow? In trees the wood acts
slow. Out of one particular and another particular it grows
particularly tall. Long hesitation among
rows of trees. In this long hesitation we love to take
walks and the air.
It has grown rare around us. How sad. We
are sad. We have big questions that we won't pose. We
don't pose, we walk. We're posited as confident woods
by a great many steps below. May we say: a particular step?
Everything is still called wood. We take a particular holiday in hand.
Wood.

translated from the German by Rosmarie Waldrop

[Only, sometimes coast herons fly in a low V]

Only, sometimes coast herons fly in a low V
over the trickling lines unsurfaces, like a swaying
inverted beach, it and enclosed groups—the points
flocks noise-bright

threaten . . . happen, land-overlapped
quays and pier-posts in which plunge basins
of the carrier ships, on refill boats of the whole
swim-vest West,

everything, which in repetition fallows and
doubles, cuneiform of the fore-herons climbed
into the backlight, cuffed, the V in views
to the lynxes x-optional lurking.

Yes-yes, the basin-bird flowers nodded upwards on the underway-
dams of the forenight, grass flats and plaster-rhomboid field-glass
luminous-blue lashing rotors stamping distance spinning (within
themselves), moving along nearly hand over hand and stripe-lighters
sand-times by daybreak. And the breath (breathes): AND AND.

Look back into the valley ("tell a tale").
There are sources which I can clarify, and then the sand at the sea.

translated from the German by Michael Pisaro

— RAOUL SCHROTT (b. 1964) —

Twilight   Phenomena   II

the marble slabs of the clouds · and your
head hewn from the dark with gestures
lean and hard · the stands of hair gathered
on your neck eyes like the shadows of
eucalyptus leaves that fall on the chair by
the wall and your brow bright beneath both
hands · on the tiles of the terrace the night
stands as still as an insect its legs apart
raised antennae trembling · at four fingers
breadth above the horizon lies a segment
of the dawn · the curve of a wing closing
bluish-black on the wind and spreading
again · earthlight · and nothing now that
could be touched · your lips taut the smell
of cold wood and the lull in which you
draw your shirt to your left shoulder · the
morning is something that comes over the
crest of the hill vast and unending in
indian red · we ate oranges in the dark

vathi, 24.8.97

translated from the German by Iain Galbraith

[Reading into the face how the skin]

Reading into the face how the skin
is written on from the inside, the shimmering off-
sounds of looking spread out: your breath,
then. Adapting oneself, perhaps, to a present,
mutual, fabric, without unlicensed
access to the grid net over the landscape, some
quadrants without inhabitants, the coordinates pair
without a place, fictional lucky numbers. Fingerless
I grope the length of you, fingerless and quite tightly
under the skin of your face, when I hear and listen to
the stories: it's a dead certainty I would go
mad, if you suddenly told that one fairy story,
that wakes up the colors of your image in the blind spot,
of which it is suspected that I am in it,
at the spot where the evidence runs out.

translated from the German by Andrew Duncan

❧ THE NETHERLANDS ❧

— EVA GERLACH (b. 1948) —

Leda

You think a god is coming his wing
makes a kind of shadow *I*
you say and you are changed

You were just sleeping but now you can
never stop the shock even
if he hands you hat and whip bit and rein

like lightning he rises with you, memory
blows off you where were you first casually
you stroke the down that is burning on you

translated from the Dutch by Alissa Valles

Fed Up

A god comes to you in the night and beats you
almost to death. He doesn't know what dead is,
thinks it's like dark moon. Years you served him,
you're fed up you don't laugh at his jokes.

Stop it you say I'll start stinking remember to eat
when I'm dead. I won't come back,
what will you eat then? He beats and he beats.

Later he'll sit around weeping the god
there's something about before and after
he doesn't get isn't it all the same thing?
For a god it's all the same thing,

that's why he doesn't know
how much a man can take in his bed
of human flesh under the stars.

translated from the Dutch by Alissa Valles

There was a man

There was a man—nothing more than a thought,
a song of the times, strict upbringing,
chaste as the morning—who dreamt (cry me a river)
of performing naked.

In the Oasis Bar,
where he sometimes went with a shirt on,
where people knew him.

His parchment figure a family heirloom.
He waited in dark rooms. Every time he looked up
something cracked in his neck.
A woman with hands like picks
rented him vaginal fluid,
read other books.

He expected to be exposed
by impersonal music, by artificial light;
but not everyone is an imposter.

His nakedness retreated inside, humming little verses,
to tempt him. The man, a song of the times,

a dancing man.

translated from the Dutch by Deborah Ffoulkes

Button Box

They stood stiff-backed as gas flames
around the cold heater in the room under the eaves.
Below, graves were still breaking open.
Such a crush on the stairs, they were creaking.
Indistinct voices: "Button box!
Look in the button box!" That's what they shouted.
A child's body disfigured by growth
lay in its bed, bereft of movement.

translated from the Dutch by Deborah Ffoulkes

Secret Agent

I took care of everything: the alias,
the hotel where no one would look for us.
His muscle, his being short and taciturn,
his smooth brown soles were my idea.

The calm with which he did what he did
to force a confession out of me.
Shock, ice-cocktail, bamboo, false hope:
he was a master in the third degree.

When I left I'd sworn to what he wanted.
I had killed, betrayed and lied,
and ranted more than he had ever heard
and agreed: our meeting never happened.

translated from the Dutch by Alissa Valles

— MARJOLEINE DE VOS (b. 1957) —

Mrs. Despina sees a rhinoceros

Now she's crept up on it from far
her breath is cut off by its horn.
It turns out that she's a mother.
Grey and distant, the eye looks
out from the antiquity of life—
the body molded out of earth
so little known that she herself
feels lost, no thread to lead her,
erring across the earth's surface.
Would she be a calf, would she
exist and be as heavy as she—
clad in thick leather lope slowly
into brush known for centuries?

translated from the Dutch by Alissa Valles

Mrs. Despina goes swimming

She is rose on hills, clear gray water
she is the sun on its hands of gold—
no Aphrodite rising laughing on waves
No one is watching. What state is this
of languid rapture? Without any guide
skin scalp and breasts swim in the sea,
all silent in perfection. A breeze blows,
a wave arches, rock holds itself intact.

No word on duty here, she is nothing
but a single life, a morning in the sea.

At sunrise she turns and the world falls
back into itself. A sudden soprano sings
what she's forgotten: *Pray, but do pray*

> *translated from the Dutch by Alissa Valles*

Death he had your voice

Where you are, there am I, my dearling
I see you always, your blush and laugh
even at night I visit you in guise of sleep
and sing you a lullaby in my arms
you're mine and if you could see the god
who loves you is a devotee of darkness

My marrow is cold my kiss is soft
you stroke my rough morning chin
your hand gropes in the dark—
do I still sigh not yet fallen prey
you are so lovely when you move
your eyebrow slightly over your rainy
eye, in trepidation, oh my soul
don't let me go, whom you belie
with joy of life and dreams of man
so evanescent is my world power
I am doomed, I am taking you down
with me, and further down, deep down
never to come again.

> *translated from the Dutch by Alissa Valles*

from Picnic on the Spiral Staircase

Prologue

They are standing in a white field.

"Where are the things?" asks the Romantic.

The head looks all around.

"Not here," she says.

"This is as white as the end," says the Romantic.

"Come over here," says the head. She puts her arm around him; he feels thin and warm.

Old looks down at her feet. She cannot see very well where the ground ends and the air begins and hopes that her feet know that. "But we are still here," she says.

"Everyone has gone," says the Romantic. "Soon we too will be gone."

"There were too many secrets," says the head. "Now there is only one secret left. How it is to be gone. But if we are gone, we will no longer be able to comprehend that."

The Romantic buries his nose in the head's neck. As long as he feels warmth, he still exists.

"But we wanted to leave, didn't we?" asks the head.

"Not me," says Old. "I wanted to stay with you. Grow to be big someday."

"I want to touch and smell things," says the Romantic.

"May we stay?" the head asks of the white.

"You're asking the wrong question," says the Romantic.

"May we be read once again?" the head asks of the white.

Highs and Lows

When the Romantic sleeps, the slide turns into a staircase. He is sitting somewhere in a tower, a stone staircase that reaches the stars. Life is walking, thinks the head. You climb and climb and when you are tired, you are old. And if you can go no farther, you die.

Old tries to think of something nice and friendly besides. "Walking and talking at the same time is really great," she says. "All of us walked along there. Every now and then a break to eat something. A picnic on the spiral staircase."

"You don't get it!" says the head in dismay. "There is nothing, nothing, only that staircase. It's pitch black there, you have to do everything by groping around. It gives you a real fright when you run into someone!"

"So there are other people?!" asks Old.

"Now and then someone walking down," says the head. "Who has already been to the top, who knows what it's all about, he has seen the answer at the very top. But we're still climbing and we are dumb, so someone like that won't talk to us. And the rest are climbing to the top, below us and above us, but we never see them, for they are walking at the same speed as us. That is why we think we are all alone, except for those few wise people, that is. And we cannot see them in the dark. We can feel their clothing brushing past, once in a thousand years or thereabouts, and maybe we have been so confused by the silence and the climbing, that we think a witch is walking around there, or a hippopotamus, or God."

"Why don't we just go back down?" asks Old. "Away from there, two feet on the ground?"

"That's impossible," says the head. "We're alive, so we climb. That is, if it's true about that staircase."

"And if it isn't true?"

"Then we just lie here in bed. Then what we see makes sense, then this here is the truth. The wall, the chair with the clothes, the black curtains, the sleeping sisters."

"At least we know the way up there," says Old. "We can only go in one direction: up. We can't get lost there."

"That's the nice thing about that staircase," says the head.

Sisterly, they stare at the ceiling. They say nothing and climb, say nothing and climb.

Light and Shadow

The highest clouds are red and gold hills surrounding a lake. The edge of the lake is made of flatter clouds. The lake is made of clouds that are so thin you can see through them. They see through them.

"Let's go and live there," says the Romantic.

"It's in our heads forever. We can always think about it," says the head.

"Thinking is not enough," says Old. "If we think about it, we miss it. Missing is a kind of stomachache."

"Missing is loving something," says the head. "If you miss something, it has truly been there. You have had it for all time, it has to be that way, because you feel it."

"Missing is wanting to go back," says the Romantic. "We want to go back so badly it hurts."

"There was once a little cottage on the edge of a dark forest," says Old. "In the cottage lived a father and a mother and their children. That was the way it used to be. I can still remember it."

The head says: "Me too. I still remember the edge between light and shadow where we used to walk. The shadow was full of trees. Light shone from the cottage. We saw the cottage from the distance and ran toward it."

"Then we were no longer lost," says the Romantic.

They look at the landscape above their heads.

"Getting lost there wouldn't be so bad," says the Romantic.

translated from the Dutch by Scott Rollins and Katheryn Ronnau-Bradbeer

I Am a Doctor

I let the rain destroy my clothes
and stay awake at night and then fall asleep
on the back seat of my car, on my horse.
When I find a dead body in the street
I look for letters and keys in the clothes
and I try to find someone who recognizes the body
(sometimes it's the dog or the horse).

Look at me, I'm a doctor.
Give me your hand, I'm a doctor.
Let me through, I'm a doctor, no a policeman.
No, a doctor and a policement were walking down the street.

Here are two envelopes.
In one there's a joke that's twice as good as in the other.
You can keep one of the jokes.
Pick an envelope, open it, and read the joke.
The joke in the other is twice or half as good.
If I let you switch, would you?

What's it about, I asked whom I found,
and they all told the same joke about themselves
and gave me lists of their character traits
as if they wanted a place in a better one.
It's me, talk to me.

I'm a doctor, they called me to be sure.

I'm going to make a joke that will last ten years.
I have all the ingredients.

translated from the Dutch by Alissa Valles

Psalm 22

Listen.
The words that I cry out

like

a herd,
stampeding the field,
and there is no other field.

There is a drowning horse at the bottom of a waterfall,
there is blood on half my face.

Doesn't it distract you to listen to me
from your sure and constant loss?

But I keep an eye open for you
so that you can look through it
and look again and can think of an answer
and want to take it back like an unintended but relinquished sacrifice.

Like saying: I don't want
to lose you.

translated from the Dutch by Alissa Valles

In the dream of an angel

Brought into being by the pronouncing of a word,
the first letter, a beginning of opening
of mouth around word.

Word that, if it could be part of a proof,
would make the proof be understood
as soon as the word was spoken, even if it weren't halfway the proof.

As in the dream of an angel

whose sleep has not yet come into being around it
despite the words he cried out to bring that about;

an angel has to prove his sleep.

translated from the Dutch by Alissa Valles

⤨ BELGIUM ⤪

— WILLIAM CLIFF (b. 1940) —

Ballade of the Mouse

After Charles d'Orléans

there are some who say that I'm dead
well what with all these illnesses
we hear so much of now lives blink
out in a heartbeat   and the instant
I stopped appearing in the spots
where once I used to perch my puny
build, they made a grave pronouncement
I hereby trounce as tactless jive
this little mouse is still alive

at my age, granted, quite a few
have traveled to the other side
and I who trawled so many ports
should long ago have snapped my neck
though I climb trees and haul myself
up rotten or worm-eaten ladders
and though I hike down slippery slopes
slathered with sodden clay and goo
however recklessly I strive
this little mouse is still alive

I have no child   I have no wife
my home's a creaky tenement
with ceiling plaster so crazed and cracked
a falling chunk could split my skull
the other tenants here belong
to the "Lumpenproletariat"
but those who hang out in the hood
have mugs you'd take a stroll to look at
even in this disgusting hive
the little mouse is still alive

ten I see fall down on my right
roughly as many on my left
so come fair weather or come rain
I go out in the streets to scratch

myself just where it tends to itch
or stretch out in bed like a sleeve
in order to watch vicious shadows
parade across the wall beside me
how is it I possess the drive?
can the little mouse still be alive?

and if the telephone should ring
despite the rumor of my death
it must be people would prefer
to think I haven't yet stopped breathing
though the sun won't give the sky the time
of day though cars blare and our city
heaves a death rattle worthy of
rat nation   still there are kind souls
one of whose honorable feats
is believing that my heart still beats

oh my friends you who'll laugh to hear
I'm not yet six feet under   may
surprises please us when they arrive
my god the mouse is still alive

translated from the French by Alfred Corn

— WERNER LAMBERSY (b. 1941) —

from Linnaeus' clock

The finite and the infinite
were on the road together

One of them said
now I've arrived

Do you think so said the other
and he lifted his still-
too-young brother
onto his shoulders

He
from the height of his perch
told about the road
interpreted the landscape

For the other was blind
from birth
and could only look
within himself

But that was why
the song had chosen him

— —

There's a cry
we don't hear it

But there's a cry
uttered by the dead
within their death

A cry so long
that those who utter it
no longer need
to move their lips or
close their mouths

So we confuse it
like a star
behind another
closer one

With the great silence
which came before

— —

May an unanswered mystery
fill and impregnate
your song

May it be a warm garment
in the sweat of those
who, for a long time, wore it

and may it speak of time but
no more than the broom bush does

Whose seedpods scatter
in the sunlight like
holiday firecrackers

translated from the French by Nora Makhoul

Death on a pale horse

after William Turner

Within the contours of details
He was vague, but he was very precise
In what lay outside accuracy.

A hand, in a still Phrygian scene
Points to a distant core, a place,
The weapon that was lost.

But as the rider tips to his fall—
His red-lit torso more like
A bull's head that has gored

The pale horse through the guts—
He rives the future open
In my eyes, spewing out

Of the picture like a bloodshot
Vision of what was still to come.

It's not conceivable that
It was plain to see that anyone
Painting could be so lonely.

translated from the Flemish by Gregory Ball

First steps

He ran into the street without a glance
and I, beginning to be like him more and more,
thought he could make it to the door.

But he turns around, cars racing
along the prom. Now he's almost there
I'll never get to him in time.

Just so my father, all his life,
could dream of my hand, as small
and quick, able to slip between bars
into the depths of rock and water.

Life rushes in a blink.

Then I grab him—he unafraid,
His eyes wide open and so calm—

I with that fatal smash
That will never leave
My life and body.

translated from the Flemish by Gregory Ball

While sketching

It's an old wall.
The stones run their faces
Staring at you, huddled
Shoulders racked on a row,
year on year painfully hunched,
drawn tight.

Some of them monstrous, sunken-eyed,
Others with mouths that have sung into silence,
Witnesses piled in a mass grave.

I count some hours off beside them,
Sun-shift lends them some expression,
A moment's wavering as yet another century's
Gone with never a blink.

Everything you've still got to do—
Warming milk for the child,
Turning fruit in a basket to ripen,
Sharpening a lover's fingernails,
Filling the car up as you cheerfully stand there smoking—

Comes poking out of their sneer,
Unmoved by the dusty wake
Of the wind's eraser.

translated from the Flemish by Gregory Ball

from **Susette**

> *Frankfurt (June 1802)*

1. Red lungs

I wear no jewels. Yet alabaster is
my skin, stone catches winter light.
Brown cotton or white atlas silk become
me now. Consumptive flesh is rouge-like.

The canopy exists? Madder-dye shrinks
the heart, the endless coughing tires the lungs.
The voice is drowning. The rose of the
cabinet closing for good, wilting round

my decay. It runs in foliage, iron on
the sole. No one sees how the source lures
and time heals. The god's too strong for any
power. His sphere spins ever inwards.

2. Susette's sickbed

What burns my lip with bitter taste?
And whose kiss kindled my disease?
Fine bed (satin, cotton, white lace)
so dank. The lance-tip's lodged deep in

my side. No hand sweeps dreams away
from sleep. Will my breath sing once more?
No bird calls. The pears sleepy and the
tree raven. A foreign will disturbs

the curtain. His hand lies coolly
on me? Is it the fever, an
  open window?
    Is it

3. Susette's grave

A thaw warms frosted ground. No willow
still mourns her. High in a tower
lives the ink, in which the temple ruin
sinks. Each lime-tree, now past flowering,

scatters pale flakes. In stone gravel gazes
at him—a frieze, triumphal arch built in
decay, three pillars, pollarded, with fragments
spread across a floor, until them too

the white whirlpool engulfs. A snow-field concludes
each story. The sun rises, descends.
The circle turns, obeying its own law.
(*Thus I wrote. More presently.*)

translated from the Flemish by John Irons

⇥ ENGLAND ⇤

— MIMI KHALVATI (b. 1944) —

Ghazal

after Hafez

However large earth's garden, mine's enough.
One rose and the shade of a vine's enough.

I don't want more wealth, I don't need more dross.
The grape has its bloom and it shines enough.

What can Paradise offer us beggars
and fools? What ecstasy, when wine's enough?

Come and sit by the stream. Rivers run dry
but to carry their song, a chine's enough.

Like the sun in bazaars, streaming in shafts,
any slant on the grand design's enough.

When you're here, my love, what more could I want?
Just mentioning love in a line's enough.

Heaven can wait. To have found, heaven knows,
a bed and a roof so divine's enough.

I've no grounds for complaint. As Hafez says,
isn't a ghazal that he signs enough?

— SELIMA HILL (b. 1945) —

North Carolina

Everything about you's a bit like me—
in the same way that North Carolina's a bit like Ribena
but rhymes with Vagina, which is nearly the same,
but much darker—
brutal and sweet like disease,
sweet as an asphalt dealer.

Imagine a cloud.
Imagine eating a cloud.
Imagine your mouth being full of the cloud like the world.
And imagine a person like me with a person like you.

I have turned you into a cloud.
Prepare to be eaten.

— DENISE RILEY (b. 1948) —

Milk Ink

Don't read this as white ink flow, pressed out
Of retractable nipples. No,
Black as his is mine.

Rain-streaked glass, burnt orange cherry leaves, eye drape of sugar pink.
Don't pin me to frou-frou incident
But let me skate—that

This ganglion cluster should have been born with better eyes
More glowingly deer-like—then instead of being horrified might not
One lift its banging head up off the ground and stroke its streaming hair
And, and, and never go away.

Don't read his as white ink flow, shot out
Of retractable. No,
Black as this is mine.

— SEAN O'BRIEN (b. 1952) —

Cities

and still some down to go
—KEN SMITH

What are cities made of? Steam vents. Blue light. Murder.
Steps going down from the dark to the dark
Past yellow helmets aiming anxious lamps, past padded coats
Making sorrowing bearlike gestures of general
But hopelessly inarticulate love, past men
And their haircuts, their eyebeams, unspoken advice.
Everyone knows. Whoever it is must already be dead.
Eviscerated, eyeless, boiled—in a thousand conditions
They wait to be found and lamented, chained
Amid the perpetrator's stinking hoard of symbols:
Nail-clippings, fingerbones, rat hair, milk,
Scorched pages of an ancient book
That holds the key. But down you go

And the hours stretch, and the clocks in the offices
Stare at each other in rigid hysteria.
Your colleagues in the daylight world
Yawn with despair, an hour from sailboats and beer.
But you go on descending until you have left
The last outpost of order some far landing back
Before cast-iron stairs gave way to wood.
Isn't it tempting to dump the aluminium suitcase
And stop here, making a place of this nowhere?
The staircase folds back on itself
And the silent tunnel plunges further in
Under the last of the railbeds, the last bottled river,
Graveyard of oystermen, library of masons, latrine of the founders,
Stained glass temple of carnivorous Morlocks,
Deadlight, corridor, cupboard, box.
Sit with your torch playing over the brickwork
Still hoarse with graffiti—*"looks like Aramaic"*—and listen
To the silence breathing *This is and this is and this is,*
Endlessly folding and reading itself,
A great book made of burlap and dust,
That is simply digesting the world—
Its drips and rustles, the screams from old cases,
Trains that were heading elsewhere
In a previous century. Soon
You will come to believe you have eaten this book,
That your gullet is lined like a tenement room with its print,
That your tongue has illustrations
And your breath must smell of pulp.
Isn't it tempting to answer, *Just give me the reason*
And then we'll go up to the air—it is dawn above ground
And the manholes stand open, steaming
For the resurrection, straight up in the blue
Where we seek reassurance—*go up there*
And start to forget it all over again.

— JO SHAPCOTT (b. 1953) —

Phrase Book

I'm standing here inside my skin,
which will do for a Human Remains Pouch

for the moment. Look down there (up here).
Quickly. Slowly. This is my own front room

where I'm lost in the action, live from a war,
on screen. I am an Englishwoman, I don't understand you.
What's the matter? You are right. You are wrong.
Things are going well (badly). Am I disturbing you?

TV is showing bliss as taught to pilots:
Blend, Low silhouette, Irregular shape, Small,
Secluded. (Please write it down. Please speak slowly.)
Bliss is how it was in this very room

when I raised my body to his mouth,
when he even balanced me in the air,
or at least I thought so and yes the pilots say
yes they have caught it through the Side-Looking

Airborne Radar, and through the J-Stars.
I am expecting a gentleman (a young gentleman,
two gentlemen, some gentlemen). Please send him
(them) up at once. This is really beautiful.

Yes they have seen us, the pilots, in the Kill Box
on their screens, and played the routine for
getting us Stealthed, that is, Cleansed, to you and me,
Taken Out. They know how to move into a single room

like that, to send in with Pinpoint Accuracy, a hundred Harms.
I have two cases and a cardboard box. There is another
bag there. I cannot open my case—look out,
the lock is broken. Have I done enough?

Bliss, the pilots say, is for evasion
and escape. What's love in all this debris?
Just one person pounding another into dust,
into dust. I do not know the word for it yet.

Where is the British Consulate? Please explain.
What does it mean? What must I do? Where
can I find? What have I done? I have done
nothing. Let me pass please. I am an Englishwoman.

Fish

I envied my wife her nightly visions.
She'd lay each one proudly on the bed

like a plump, iridescent fish,
and ask me to identify it.

Some nights I'd even manage to trap
my own by concentrating hard,

submerging the net into blue-black waters.
I'd place my catch on the rippling sheet.

So we'd have our own two fish, almost
indecent, nuzzling each other's mouths,

soul-fish, awkward in our hands,
hungry, as if our lives were a host

of crumbs to gulp in greedily.
They'd beat their tails very fast

until we could only see the one dream
moving between us, or feel stirring

one enormous fish, with our own lives
grieving, joyful, growing in its belly.

White Comedy

I waz whitemailed
By a white witch,
Wid white magic
An white lies,
Branded by a white sheep
I slaved as a whitesmith
Near a white spot
Where I suffered whitewater fever.
Whitelisted as a whiteleg
I waz in de white book
As a master of white art,
It waz like white death.

We Crave

attention, then come over all coy, and start fiddling
with watchstrap and buttons, or talking about a friend
of a friend who claims to own the world's largest collection
of aquarium ornaments, yet has no aquarium. In the mean-
time the tough-minded argue each of us is loved not
so much for his or her oddities, as in spite of them, or even
faute de mieux! Familes form, squabble on long
car journeys, invent nicknames for strangers; the tyres hum
their own tune, and in shimmering forecourts
the baked atmosphere presses from all sides, searing
the lungs. We commend, internally, the wisdom of the soft-
voiced tycoon who acquired the land, only
to flatten it, then skilfully divide it into distinct
yet related lots; a spongy layer of wood-chips lines
the criss-crossing paths, and whispers faintly underfoot.

As it was drummed into me, I would drum it
into others: the art or science of management never
pauses, though it occasionally lies low, or enacts
retreat like a Parthian archer. Invariably, speed and stealth
take advantage of the famous, non-existent "margin" poor
Herbert Pocket kept urging upon Pip; a sound decisive
as the whirr and double click of a computer mouse
signals the arrival of the inner bailiffs, and an era
of thrift. Listen harder, and through the virtual prison-bars
comes swarming the buzz of creditors and debtors over
lunch, each pledging allegiance to the other, to knowledge,
to the mysteries of living on thin air . . .

State of the Nation

Now any word from you is a new word,
As gnarled and unawaited as the new
Could ever be, the tongue of the grim few
Who burnt my flag, and I did have a flag.
I had, like we all have, the shape of shroud
Or swaddling with me gone from it. That flag.

And any news of you is propaganda.
In that I can believe it well enough,
Or that it was concocted by your staff
To be believed. All but the oldest pictures
We mock as forgeries, and my children wonder
What I am always burning and I go *Witches*.

No, I have let them clean across my country,
The people of your land, in happier times.
I've neither known nor cared about their crimes,
But neither have I let them stay. I trust
They know the points of exit and of entry
Can still be told apart in the red dust.

And yes, I have corresponded with your greats,
Translated work, remembered stanzas, lines,
Partaken of your wisdom as your wines,
And told my countrymen: They are the Past,
But they had jokes and hopes and secret dates,
They thought their paste-and-paper homes would last,

And that their prayers were heard.—But it's the Law,
Or is it here. Your earth is blown and lost.
You work forever in a birdless west
In binary. You will not be received.
Your immigrants will be turned out at door,
Their fantasies and nothing else believed.

Your treasures we will lick into clean plates,
And wring the loaded clouds so very tight
They bulge apart and wash your picnics out,
We sorely hope. Our likeliest to die
Will dream you up when he hallucinates.

The best of us will cross and pass you by.

But don't assume we do this to our other
Neighbour, where they whistle the To-Come.
Her citizens are made to feel at home
As long as they require it. They belong.
All borders are the same, except the border
Between our kind and you. That's barbed and strung,

Uncrossable, too long for the pinched age
We have as nations. Say there's still some meadow
Where we could meet or send in place a shadow
To make the signs we would. That would be news.
Perhaps in your gone country there's a stage
For puppetry. It would at least amuse.

My motorcade went miles along the border
One April night. I listened and saw nothing.
Then there was distant rocketfire, then nothing,
A pitiless cold dark. It's said we're winning
(Admittedly by me, and it's an order)
But when the morning breaks I think we're winning,

The salmon light falls freshly on the schools
I built, and loyal students in the squares
Are gulping down espressos as I pass,
And every evening all the theatres shine
With characters we know and love, and tales
That never were, but happen, and are mine.

— SIMON ARMITAGE (b. 1963) —

Kid

Batman, big shot, when you gave the order
to grow up, then let me loose to wander
leeward, freely through the wild blue yonder
as you liked to say, or ditched me, rather,
in the gutter . . . well, I turned the corner.
Now I've scotched that 'he was like a father
to me' rumour, sacked it, blown the cover
on that 'he was like an elder brother'
story, let the cat out on that caper

with the married woman, how you took her
downtown on expenses in the motor.
Holy robin-redbreast-nest-egg-shocker!
Holy roll-me-over-in-the-clover,
I'm not playing ball boy any longer
Batman, now I've doffed that off-the-shoulder
Sherwood-Forest-green and scarlet number
for a pair of jeans and crew-neck jumper;
now I'm taller, harder, stronger, older.
Batman, it makes a marvellous picture:
you without a shadow, stewing over
chicken giblets in the pressure cooker,
next to nothing in the walk-in larder,
punching the palm of your hand all winter,
you baby, now I'm the real boy wonder.

— FIONA SAMPSON (b. 1963) —

Hayfever portrait

Air-motes are stellar, ideations rambling
convection by convection through satisfied
evening. At dusk they gather under the tree by the septic tank,
fag-ends aglow,

their group movement a conversation of forms
made out of elbow-space.
Imagine their planetary zoom.
Imagine (close up now) their toppling roll on air

as you and the dog head out past,
swishing currents.
And it's good not to be too apologetic about this—
you could fill up your brain with your self

that goes bruising and galumphing through the thigh-high meadow-sweet
(also brain-shaped) and nettles.

⤜ WALES ⤛

— SHEENAGH PUGH (b. 1950) —

Golden Rabbits

He came up for the peace, the scenery,
the stepping back in time, but mostly
because someone told him the rabbits here
were golden. At the time, he'd never
seen rabbits, and if he had, in truth,
they'd have been psychedelic, the stuff
he was on. But somehow the vision
stuck long enough to get him on a train,

a ferry, a bus, out to the far end
of a peninsula. The crofters were kind,
but they all laid bets he wouldn't last.
Around that time, a lot of folk lost
in the twentieth century took this road,
looking for peace, the truth, themselves, God.
Whatever they'd mislaid, the first storm
saw them give up on it and head for home.

But he's still here, after so long, growing
enough to get by, writing a bit, doing
small driving jobs. "You can't eat scenery,"
someone said, but he can, very nearly.
The red rocks nightly catching fire,
a pod of whales, the odd meteor shower,
are what sustains him, like the peat stack
in his shed, or the big winter sack

of tatties. Most of the rabbits are brown,
same as anywhere, but just the odd one
isn't. His only road blocked by snow
each new year, he scrapes ice from his window
and watches them edge close to his scatterings
of crusts, carrot tops, potato peelings,
his heart stopping when, against the white,
one shape glows like clear honey in sunlight.

Mother Tongue

"I started to translate in seventy-three
in the schoolyard. For a bit of fun
to begin with—the occasional 'fuck'
for the bite of another language's smoke
at the back of my throat, its bitter chemicals.
Soon I was hooked on whole sentences
behind the shed, and lessons in Welsh
seemed very boring. I started on print,
Jeeves & Wooster, Dick Francis, James Bond,
in Welsh covers. That worked for a while
until Mam discovered Jean Plaidy inside
a Welsh concordance one Sunday night.
There were ructions: a language, she screamed,
should be for a lifetime. Too late for me.
Soon I was snorting Simenon
and Flaubert. Had to read much more
for any effect. One night I OD'd
after reading far too much Proust.
I came to, but it scared me. For a while
I went Welsh-only but it was bland
and my taste was changing. Before too long
I was back on translating, found that three
languages weren't enough. The 'ch'
in German was easy, Rilke a buzz . . .
For a language fetishist like me
sex is part of the problem. Umlauts make me sweat,
so I need a multilingual man
but they're rare in West Wales and tend to be
married already. If only I'd kept
myself much purer, with simpler tastes,
the Welsh might be living . . .
                              Detective, you speak
Russian, I hear, and Japanese.
Could you whisper some softly?
I'm begging you. Please . . ."

⤚ SCOTLAND ⤛

— JOHN BURNSIDE (b. 1955) —

De Humani Corporis Fabrica

after Vesalius

I know the names of almost
nothing

      not the bone
between my elbows and my wrist
that sometimes aches
from breaking

         years ago

            and not
the plumb line
from the pelvis
to the knee

less ache than hum

         where
in my nineteenth year
a knife blade slits through nerves
and a nicked vein

leaving the wall intact

         the valves
still working
so the blood kept flooding out
till Eleanor

      a nurse on evening shift

opened the wound
and made me whole again.

I have no words
for chambers in the heart
the smaller bones

         the seat of gravity

or else I know the names
but not the function:
ganglia

                    the mental foramen
the hypothalamus
                         the duodenum.

Once
         in our old school library
                              I took
a book down from the shelf
and opened it to stripped flesh
                              and the cords
of muscle
         ribbed and charred
like something barbecued

the colours wrong
                    the single eye exposed:
a window into primal emptiness.

I sat for hours
                 amazed
                    and horrified
as if I had been asked to paraphrase
this body with the body I possessed:
hydraulics for a soul
                    cheese-wire for nerves
a ruff of butcher's meat
                    in place of thought.

I've read how Michelangelo would buy
a stolen corpse
                 to study
                    in the dark
the movement of a joint
                    or how a face
articulates the workings of the heart

how Stubbs would peel
the cold hide from a horse
and peer into the dark machinery
of savage grace

but I have never learned
                    nor wished to learn
how bodies work

other than when they move
and breathe
            corporis fabrica

is less to me than how a shudder starts
and runs along the arm
                            towards the wings
that flex and curl
between the shoulder blades

—so I will lie beside you here
                            unnamed
until my hands recover from your skin

a history of tides
                a flock of birds
the love that answers love
                            when bodies meet
and map themselves anew
                            cell after cell
touching after glancing touch
                            the living flesh

revealing and erasing what it knows
on secret charts
                of watermark
                            and vellum.

— ROBERT CRAWFORD (b. 1959) —

A Scottish Assembly

Circuitry's electronic tartan, the sea,
Libraries, fields—I want the lot

To fly off and scatter, but most of all
Always to come home to roost

In this unkempt country where a handicapped printer,
Engraver of dog collars, began with his friends

The ultimate encyclopedia.
Don't expect any rhyme or reason

For Scotland remaining an explosion reversed
Or ordinariness a fruited vine

Or why I came back here to choose my union
On the side of the ayes, remaining a part

Of this diverse assembly—Benbecula, Glasgow, Bow of Fife—
Voting with my feet, and this hand.

— W. N. HERBERT (b. 1961) —

Scaldfoot

The stumps of the old bridge
                              curve across the river
in a sperm whale smile:
                              krill-swilling, squid-crunching.
I press my ear to that giant acetate,
the bandstand of the Magdalen Green,
that oompahpah omphalos of the known world,
that July when I was ten, back when
McGonagall meant to be funny and
Ossian hadn't made it up yet about the Gaelic.
I'm listening for the tunes they would have hummed
when the bridge went down, if
the bridge hadn't actually gone down,
those creatures in corsets,
those types in toppers—
and maybe it did, the engine I mean,
whistle as it slid through the liquid coal,
to boil the sludge it bothered on the bottom.

With fish in their ribs and weeds through their hats
the passengers still sit, their singing piped
to the well-studded concrete of the stand,
that giant showerhead brimming with hymns.
How hot the concrete gets against your cheek and ear
in the memory's July, how choleric, as though
you were embracing some fever-face,
some slum-girl crushed into the pustular grey,
the tenement porridge that rebuilt Dundee.
How strange the current-coldness of the dead
should seem to blast the ear with so much heat.

My grandmother's father must have known them,
the men who swapped shifts and lived,

or did a fatal favor: he must have known
the space before in which such gestures seem
to lack significance—and did it make
his ear suspicious of such innocence?
We only know he was meticulous in listening
to every psalm his engine knew, each air
it could recite, and that its exhalations were
harmonious beneath his care, so that
he would have understood, in the seconds before
that blaring release that boiled his foot
(which then went septic and drowned out his blood
with hotter poisons), that someone had
broken through our harmonies to where
the corpses sit and hit their keener note
that wipes out melody and tone and breath.

— JACKIE KAY (b. 1961) —

Virus

The mice come first. In our bedroom
at the top of the house we hear the cunning
scraping, scuttling inside the skirting.
It is the first sign.

The plague of flies are next. In our kitchen
at the bottom of the house, they swarm in sick
thick circles. It is late October.
The Pied Piper calls. "Something big," he says.
"Must be something big and rotten.

Look for the eggs, tiny, white."
This the time of the Wests.
"Do you mean a body," you say, anxious.
The Dalston train thunders by like fury

at the bottom of our town garden.
And yesterday the wasps came.
Two thousand strong. An army in my study
and the wee toilet. The Pied Piper returns.
"Vicious bastards," his eyes gleam with job satisfaction.

This is our love nest. I see you, looking at me.

Wee wifey

I have a demon and her name is WEE WIFEY
I caught her in a demon trap—the household of my skull
I pinched her by the heel throughout her wily transformations
until
she confessed
her name indeed to be WEE WIFEY
and she was out to do me ill.

So I made great gestures like Jehovah: dividing
land from sea, sea from sky,
my own self from WEE WIFEY
"There," she says, *"that's tidy!"*

Now I watch her like a dolly
keep an eye,
and mourn her:
For she and I are angry/cry
because we love each other dearly.
It's sad to note
that without
WEE WIFEY
I shall live long and lonely as a tossing cork.

— DON PATERSON (b. 1963) —

An Elliptical Stylus

My uncle was beaming: "Aye, yer elliptical stylus—
fairly brings out a' the wee details."
Balanced at a fraction of an ounce
the fat cartridge sank down like a feather;
music billowed into three dimensions
as if we could have walked between the players.

My Dad, who could appreciate the difference,
went to Largs to buy an elliptical stylus
for our ancient, beat-up Philips turntable.
We had the guy in stitches: "You can't . . .
er . . . you'll have to *upgrade your equipment.*"

Still smirking, he sent us from the shop
with a box of needles, thick as carpet-tacks,
the only sort they made to fit our model.

(Supposing I'd been *his* son: let's eavesdrop
on "Fidelities," the poem I'm writing now:
The day my father died, he showed me how
he'd prime the deck for optimum performance:
it's that less I recall—how he'd refine
the arm's weight, to leave the stylus balanced
somewhere between ellipsis and precision,
as I gently lower the sharp nib to the line
and wait for it to pick up the vibration
till it moves across the page, like a cardiograph . . .)

We drove back slowly, as if we had a puncture;
my Dad trying not to blink, and that man's laugh
stuck in my head, which is where the story sticks,
and any attempt to cauterise this fable
with something axiomatic on the nature
of articulacy and inheritance,
since he can well afford to make his own
excuses, you your own interpretation.
But if you still insist on resonance—
I'd swing for him, and every other cunt
happy to let my father know his station,
which probably includes yourself. To be blunt.

— DREW MILNE (b. 1964) —

A modest preposition

for the people of East Timor

Gnosis means simply knowledge, of whither
we are hastening, though in other times
it is as if one met song murderers,
death hands whose sacrifice is body fact.
            It is not so difficult
                to see the advance stand still
                    on circle line excursions,
swan-dancing over the pre-scribed pages
still cultivated as our last chapter,

whose neck turn thought is to be all the same
        though its pain never is,
        while the tread 'essential'
        is nought but read ends,
where that something to be said is here blown
before an altar of bad-mouthing calm
that has every thus crust appearance
of being consecrated now to prose;
        perhaps a sophist delight
        first composed dissoi logoi,
        if fraught, mark the old turn,
with the vengeance of communication
whose firsts are a thousand island dressing
cooked in fine archaic illustration.
The result is a disaster, flesh lows
        as the spits turn critical,
        the state of delirium
        signs its fault, and its purpose,
like so much else politic dullness, is
not to cure one single flesh rash richness,
much less deliver us from the old stall
        of some moment dress
        whose tardy expatiation
        is a fashion of *other*.
In a very framework of city, law,
or our covering stillness, is only
a drift, striving to obscure that poor will
the polis spent its meaning creating,
        like whether to wage slaughter
        or just send observers:
        our own plenty questions
        face us like blocked capital,
apologies on part half of people
do not ring true, and besides, nothing here
indicates what is still called election,
as to pass, from divided opinion
to bloody confrontation, is rather
        the current of this *stasis*.
        In the other form of trance,
        on sponsored Dionysus
or the bold insomnia of sold news,

the wine has a happy dish, with brilliant
shivers drunk deep, singing home sweet heimat.
      A clumsy proposal, then,
      for the swift abolition
      of *all* our advertising
      from cable to leader and hope,
      whose possible first pleasure
      may be a beginning
      on vultureless beauty
drained of litanies and winged messengers
whose further angels assist the carved drapes
of actually existing capitalism.

⋊ NORTHERN IRELAND ⋉

— CIARAN CARSON (b. 1948) —

The Words

Yes—someone lived here once. You know it by the pungent dragon-whiff,
The way a zephyr blows a ghostly music from those conches, like the hieroglyph

Of where we are. The dog-rough breath that slabbered here is now a mere miasma,
Baffled that the structure of the universe should be corpuscled in its plasma.

Hear? The deep vast stratum of a limestone sea still broadcasts sound-waves, and
The guardian angels of its threshold are connected to us by an ampersand

When we talk in our sleep. There have been other revenants, of course: whole
    asylums
Of escaped lunatics, diatribes of Vandals reared on horse-shit, Crusaders and
    credendums.

Here, consonants have been eclipsed, and vowels carry umlauts, like the moan
Of lovers who repaired here to strip off their shadows before swoon-
Ing into one another's arms. Now, it is a reservoir of silence, or a Twilight Zone . . .

— MEDBH MCGUCKIAN (b. 1950) —

On Ballycastle Beach

for my father

If I found you wandering round the edge
of a French-born sea, when children
should be taken in by their parents,
I would read these words to you,
like a ship coming in to harbour,
as meaningless and full of meaning
as the homeless flow of life
from room to homesick room.

The words and you would fall asleep,
sheltering just beyond my reach
in a city that has vanished to regain
its language. My words are traps
through which you pick your way
from a damp March to an April date,

or a mid-August misstep; until enough winter
makes you throw your watch, the heartbeat
of everyone present, out into the snow.

My forbidden squares and your small circles
were a book that formed within you
in some pocket, so permanently distended,
that what does not face north faces east.
Your hand, dark as a cedar lane by nature,
grows more and more tired of the skidding light,
the hunched-up waves, and all the wet clothing,
toys and treasures of a late summer house.

Even the Atlantic has begun its breakdown
like a heavy mask thinned out scene after scene
in a more protected time—like one who has
gradually, unnoticed, lengthened her pre-wedding
dress. But, staring at the old escape and release
of the water's speech, faithless to the end,
your voice was the longest I heard in my mind,
although I had forgotten there could be such light.

⊁ REPUBLIC OF IRELAND ⊁

— NUALA NÍ DHOMHNAILL (b. 1952) —

The Language Issue

I place my hope on the water
in this little boat
of the language, the way a body might put
an infant

in a basket of intertwined
iris leaves,
its underside proofed
with bitumen and pitch,

then set the whole thing down amidst
the sedge
and bulrushes by the edge
of a river

only to have it borne hither and thither,
not knowing where it might end up;
in the lap, perhaps,
of some Pharaoh's daughter.

translated from the Irish by Paul Muldoon

— VONA GROARKE (b. 1964) —

The Riverbed

There is sun in the mirror, my head in the trees.
There is sun in the mirror without me.
I am lying face up on the riverbed.
My lover is swimming above me.

The ribbons he tied in my hair are gone,
gone back to their net in the water.
Instead I have silverweed, speedwell and rue,
where once I had his hands to lie on.

Instead I have silverweed, speedwell and rue,
where once I had his arms beneath me.
His body may come as his body has gone—

and the marl will close over again.

Where are your silverweed, your speedwell now?
They have all gone under the water.
Where is your face in the river now?
Drifting upstream to the moon.

I have walked on the floor of the river with you.
I have walked on the floor of the river.
I would lie on the bed of the river with you.
I will lie on the bed of the river.

— CONOR O'CALLAGHAN (b. 1968) —

The Pilot Light

Every night the spare cylinder's yellow
has shone in the bathroom window
like one of those lop-sided moons
dangling out over Clare,
that stray's bray carried thirty Augusts
and the island's intermittent pinhead
run aground on day.
There have been afternoons
when the white manes flattened
and even the cement out front
was warm underfoot.
I'm leaving the gate stoned back,
the pilot light budding in your name.
Is it safe? Sure, and I like what it says.

ABOUT THE POETS

BJØRN AAMODT (1944–2006), from Norway, published his first book of poems in 1973; five more followed, and a volume of collected poems in 1995. Aamodt worked as a merchant sailor, a metalworker, and a social worker; much of his work reflects his experience in those jobs. He was the recipient of the Halldis Moren Vesaas Prize (1997), the Gyldendal Prize (1997), and the Dobloug Prize of the Swedish Academy (2003).

INGA ĀBELE (b. 1972) has written three plays and several screenplays as well as two collections of poetry, one collection of stories, and a novel. Her most recent poetry collection is *Atgâzenes stacijas zirgi* (*The Horses of Atgazenes Station*).

NERINGA ABRUTYTE (b. 1972) studied Lithuanian language and literature at the University of Vilnius and has currently published two poetry books, *Autumn of Paradise* and *A Confession.*

KURT AEBLI (b. 1955) was born in Rüti (canton of Zurich, Switzerland) and today lives near Zurich. Best known for his prose miniatures, he has also published several books of poetry, including *The Clock* and *Ant Hunt,* for which he was awarded a 2004 Literature Prize from the Swiss Schiller Foundation. Most recently, he has received awards from the Canton of Zurich in 2004 and 2005.

ANNA AGUILAR-AMAT (b. 1962), born in Barcelona, teaches translation at Barcelona Autonomous University. Her works include *Music and Scurvy,* winner of the Màrius Torres award in 2001. She has also published, together with Francesc Parcerisas, *Small Things,* illustrated by Miquel Plana, and the book *The Pleasure of Reading. Music and Scurvy* was published in English an an e-book by Sandstone Press.

MIMOZA AHMETI (b. 1963) grew up in Kruja, Albania, and emerged poetically in the late 1980s and early 1990s, when Albania was just beginning to transition from isolationist communism to a more open society. Her third collection, *Delirium,* published in 1994, received wide attention and secured her position as a major poet. Ahmeti's work is seen as bridging the gap between Albanian culture and the traditions of the West.

MARIGO ALEXOPOULOU (b. 1976) studied philosophy and classic Greek philology in Athens, where she was born. She holds an MA in classic studies from Glasgow University, where she also did her PhD. She teaches Greek at Athens College and ancient Greek drama at the University of Peloponnese and has published three books of poems: *Faster Than Light, Which Day Is Missing,* and *The Envymeter.*

EUGENIJUS ALIŠANKA (b. 1960) has published three collections of poems: *Equinox, City of Ash,* and, most recently, *Godbone.* He is also the author of two books of essays, *An Imagining Man* and *Return of Dionysus.* Currently Ališanka is a director of international programs at the Lithuanian Writers' Union in Vilnius and secretary general of the Lithuanian PEN Center.

URS ALLEMANN (b. 1948), born in Schlieren, Switzerland, now lives in Basel. Since 1986 he has been arts editor at the *Basler Zeitung.* His books of poetry are *Fuzzhare, Holder the Polder: Odes, Elegies and Others* and *beautiful! beautiful!* In 1991 he was awarded the Prize of the Land Kärnten for the winning entry in the Ingeborg Bachmann competition.

GABRIELLE ALTHEN (b. 1939) was born in Algeria. She is a professor emerita of comparative literature at the Université Paris X-Nanterre. She is the author of a novel, a book-length study of Dostoevsky, and seven collections of poems. She is on the editorial boards of the literary journals *Aujourd'hui poème* and *Siècle 21*.

MONIZA ALVI (b. 1954) was born in Lahore, Pakistan, and grew up in Hertfordshire. Her books include *How the Stone Found Its Voice, Souls,* and *Carrying My Wife.*

ZORAN ANČEVSKI (b. 1954) is a professor in the Department of English Language and Literature at Sts. Cyril and Methodius University in Skopje. He is the former secretary of the Macedonian PEN Center, president of the Struga Poetry Evenings, and author of five books of poetry, including a *Selected Poems,* published by the Macedonian press Blesok.

RADU ANDRIESCU (b. 1962), born in Iaşi, Romania, has authored five books of poetry: *Mirror Against the Wall* (which won the Poesis Prize), *The Back Door, The End of the Road, the Beginning of the Journey* (which was awarded the poetry prize of the Iaşi Writers Association), *Some Friends and Me,* and *The Stalinskaya Bridges.* Longleaf Press published *The Catalan Within,* translated by Andriescu and Adam J. Sorkin, in 2007. Andriescu teaches in the English Department at the University of Iaşi.

YURI ANDRUKHOVYCH (b. 1960), from Stanislav, is credited with having radically renewed Ukrainian poetry in the mid-1980s by establishing with poets Viktor Neborak and Olexandr Irvanets the Bu-Ba-Bu (which stands for Burlesque-Farce-Buffoonery), a poetic performance group that attacked the accepted standards of socialist realism. He is also the author of several novels. His work has been translated into many European languages.

ANTONELLA ANEDDA (b. 1955), born in Rome, received her degree in the history of modern art. A noted translator of Phillipe Jaccottet and Ovid, among others, her own poetry collections include *Winter Dwellings, Nights of Western Peace,* for which she won the Montale Prize in 2000, and *The Catalog of Joy.*

LINDITA ARAPI (b. 1972), from Lushnja, Albania, studied at the University of Tirana and worked for several years as a journalist for Albanian television. She went on to receive a doctorate from the University of Vienna, has published four volumes of poetry, and currently lives in Cologne, Germany.

SIMON ARMITAGE (b. 1963) is a novelist, poet, and essayist. His books include the novels *The White Stuff* and *Little Green Man,* and the poetry collections *Selected Poems* and *The Universal Home Doctor.*

BERNARDO ATXAGA (b. 1951) is the pseudonym of Joseba Irazu Garmendia, born in Asteasu, in the Basque Autonomous Community. He studied economics and philosophy at the Universities of Bilbao and Barcelona and worked a variety of jobs before dedicating himself to writing in 1980. Since, he has published several books of poetry in Basque, which have also been printed in a bilingual Basque-Spanish edition, *Poems & Hybrids,* and his work has been translated into more than seventy languages. The recipient of Spain's National Literature Prize, he has also written children's books, short stories, and novels, a number of which have been translated into English (from his own Spanish versions), among them *The Lone Woman,* published by Harvill Press.

KREŠIMIR BAGIĆ (b. 1962) is a prominent Croatian poet, literary critic, editor, and scholar. He has published several volumes of poetry, and his work has been translated into many languages. A separate collection of his poems, *Le Palmier se balance,* was recently published in France.

MIKHAS BAJARYN (b. 1970) lives in Belarus. His work has appeared in Radio Liberty broadcasts and other publications, and he is the editor of the anthology *Nihil.*

RAFFAELLO BALDINI (1924–2005) was born in Santarcangelo di Romagna (Forlì), and worked as a copywriter, journalist, and poet. He was the author of six collections of poetry and three theatrical monologues, all written in the Romagnolo dialect. His collection, *Furistír,* was awarded the 1988 Viareggio Prize, the first time the prize was awarded to a work written in an Italian dialect.

DANIEL BĂNULESCU (b. 1960) was born in Bucharest, Romania. He is the author of four books of poetry: *I'll Love You till the End of the Bed,* which won the debut prize for poetry from the Romanian Writers' Union; *The Ballad of Daniel Bănulescu; Daniel Bănulescu Federal Republic*; and *Daniel, of Prayer.* His two novels are *I'll Kiss Your Ass, Beloved Leader!* and *The Seven Kings of the City of Bucharest.*

POLINA BARSKOVA (b. 1977), born in Leningrad, studied at the University of California–Berkeley and currently lives and teaches in the United States. She is the author of several volumes of poetry and is generally considered one of the most interesting Russian poets of her generation.

EQREM BASHA (b. 1948) was born in Macedonia but has spent most of his life in Kosovo, living in Prishtina for the past three decades. The author of eight poetry collections, he works in the publishing industry.

ENİS BATUR (b. 1952) was educated at the Middle East Technical University in Ankara. Considered one of the pioneers of twentieth-century Turkish poetry, he has published numerous books of poems, including *The East-West Dîvan* (1997). *Ash Dîvan: Selected Poems of Enis Batur,* an English translation of his work, was published by Talisman House.

SAMİ BAYDAR (b. 1962), who is also a painter, graduated from the Mimar Sinan University Faculty of Fine Arts. Baydar has published numerous books of poetry in Turkey, most recently *Nicholas's Portrait* and *Between Being and Non-Being.*

ALEKSANDAR BEČANOVIĆ (b. 1971), born in in Podgorica, Montenegro, is a poet and film critic currently living in Bar. The author of four books of poetry, he received the Risto Ratković poetry award in 2002.

DARIO BELLEZZA (1944–1996), poet, novelist, and playwright, was born in Rome and died there in 1996 of complications resulting from AIDS. His early work was championed by Alberto Moravia and Pier Paolo Pasolini, among others. Among his eleven books, the best-known volumes of poetry include *Invectives and Licenses, Secret Death* (winner of the Viareggio Prize), *Book of Love,* and *Book of Poetry.*

MARCEL BEYER (b. 1965) was born in Tailfingen, Württemberg, grew up in Cologne, and currently lives in Dresden. One of the best-known story writers and poets of his generation, he is the author of numerous prose volumes and three volumes of poetry, including *False Fodder* and *Geography.* Among many honors, he is the recipient of the Berliner Literature Prize (1996), the Johannes Bobrowski Medal (1996), the Uwe Johnson Prize (1997), the Friedrich Hölderlin Prize of the City of Tübingen, the Spycher Literature Prize (2004), and the Erich Fried Prize (2006).

NATALKA BILOTSERKIVETS (b. 1954), born in Sumy, Ukraine, holds a degree in Ukrainian literature from Kyiv University. Her four books of poems are *Ballad about the Invincibles, The Underground Fire, November,* and *Allergy.*

BÉLA BODOR (b. 1954) was born in Budapest. He studied music and art before becoming a writer, essayist, and critic. His books include several volumes of poems, a novel, short stories, essays, and a book on the eighteenth-century Hungarian novel. He has won many awards.

ANDRIY BONDAR (b. 1974), a renowned columnist and critic originally from Kamianets-Podilsky, Ukraine, moved to Kyiv in 1994. He has published three books of poetry.

PETR BORKOVEC (b. 1970) is a prominent poet, a recognized master of traditional prosody, and a translator of literature from Russian, Hungarian, Korean, and classical Greek. He edits the Christian cultural journal *Souvislosti (Connections)* and the cultural weekly *Literární Noviny.* Poems from his six books have been translated into many languages and have received such honors as the 2002 Hubert Burda Award for younger Eastern European poets. His poems appear in English in the Arc Publications anthology *A Fine Line: New Poetry from Eastern and Central Europe.*

IVANA BOZDECHOVÁ (b. 1960) is a linguist, poet, and translator who teaches at Charles University in Prague. She has been a Fulbright Scholar at Stanford University and the University of Nebraska-Lincoln.

ROSA ALICE BRANCO (b. 1950), born in Aveiro, teaches the psychology of perception and contemporary culture at an Institute of Art and Design near Porto, Portugal. She is the organizer of an annual poetry festival in her hometown of Aveiro, serves as secretary to the Portuguese PEN Club, and attends international poetry festivals throughout the world. Her work has been translated into numerous languages, including French, Spanish, Italian, and Arabic. In 2004, her collected poetry was published, and more than fifty of her poems in translation have appeared in journals in the United States.

RONALDS BRIEDIS (b. 1980) is a Latvian poet and critic who has recently published his first volume of poetry. He manages literary projects for the Writers' Union of Latvia.

BALŠA BRKOVIĆ (b. 1966), a prominent Montenegrin poet and fiction writer, was born in Podgorica, where he still lives. He has published five collections of poetry and a novel, *A Private Gallery.* He is an editor of the Montenegrin daily newspaper *Vijesti.*

FLORA BROVINA (b. 1949) is a Kosovar poet who worked for many years in the pediatrics ward of Prishtina General Hospital. In 1999, she was kidnapped by masked Serb gunmen and spent the next year and a half in a Serbian prison before international pressure prompted her release. She has published three volumes of poetry.

HELWIG BRUNNER (b. 1967), musician, biologist, and poet, was born in Istanbul and resides in Graz, Austria. Besides poetry, he writes short fiction, reviews, and popular and technical science articles. He also edits the Graz literary journal *Lichtungen.* His book *Walking, Looking, Talking* won the Ernst Meister Förderpreis. Other poetry volumes are *Graz Partitures, Elevator or Stairs, On the Tip of the Tongue the Foreign,* and *Used Granite: Haiku, Senryu & Tankas.*

FRANCO BUFFONI (b. 1948), born in Gallarate (Varese), is professor of comparative literature at the University of Cassino. A prolific translator, he has directed the journal of theory and practice of poetic translation, *Parallel Text,* since 1989. His collection

Of the Master in His Workshop won the Pascoli Prize. Poems from his many collections appeared in the book-length English translation *The Shadow of Mount Rosa.*

EVGENII BUNIMOVICH (b. 1954) lives in Moscow, where he is known as an award-winning columnist and a politician. In addition to writing poetry, he is currently a deputy in the Moscow City Duma.

JOHN BURNSIDE (b. 1955) teaches at the University of St Andrews. In 2006, both his memoir, *A Lie About My Father,* and his *Selected Poems* were published. For earlier work, he has received the Whitbread Poetry Prize and the Scottish Arts Council Book Prize and been shortlisted for both the T. S. Eliot Prize and the Forward Poetry Prize.

MARIUS BUROKAS (b. 1977), from Lithuania, is the author of *Ideograms* and *Planning a Murder.* In 2001, he was a fellow at the Iowa International Writing Program.

RUI PIRES CABRAL (b. 1967), born in Macedo de Cavaleiros in northern Portugal, studied history and archaeology at the University of Porto, graduating in 1990. His first collection of poems appeared in 1994; since then, he has published five other poetry books, the most recent one—*Capitals of Solitude*—in 2006. He has contributed to many literary publications in Portugal and Spain. He currently lives in Lisbon and works as an English translator.

PEDRO CARMONA-ALVAREZ (b. 1972), born in Chile, moved with his parents first to Argentina and then to Norway after they were forced to flee their native country. He attended the Writers' Academy in Bergen, published his first book of poems in 1997, and has since published two more. He is also an essayist, a writer of song lyrics, and a vocalist with the band Sister Sonny.

CIARAN CARSON (b. 1948) lives in Belfast. Among his many books are *Breaking News* and *The Twelfth of Never.* He has also recently translated *The Inferno of Dante Alighieri.*

PATRIZIA CAVALLI (b. 1947) was born in Todi and lives in Rome. Her books of poetry include *My Poems Won't Change the World, The Sky, Poems,* and *Always Open Theater.* She is also well known for her translations from the French and English of various novels and plays, including works of Shakespeare and Molière.

BRANKO ČEGEC (b. 1957), a writer, editor, critic, essayist, translator, and poet, was editor of *Quorum,* one of the most significant literary magazines in the former Yugoslavia, and is the founder of the publishing firm Meandar. He is the author of five books of poetry.

RUXANDRA CESEREANU (b. 1963), was born in Cluj-Napoca, Romania, the cultural center of Transylvania, where she now teaches at the university. Her first book, a "micro-novel" entitled *Voyage through the Looking-Glasses,* came out the year Romanian communism fell. Two collections of poetry, *Garden of Delights* and *Live Zone,* soon followed—the latter translated as *Lunacies* with Adam J. Sorkin. *Crusader-Woman* is being published by Commonwealth Books in 2008.

YIORGOS CHOULIARAS (b. 1951) was born in Thessaloniki. He was educated in Greece and the United States, at Reed College and the New School, and has worked in both countries as a university lecturer, press officer, and journalist. He was a founding editor of the influential Greek reviews *Tram* and *Hartis,* and he is the author of six books of poems.

ZEHRA ÇIRAK (b. 1961) was born in Istanbul, grew up in Karlsruhe, Germany, and currently lives in Berlin. She has published several collections of poetry, including *Flight-Catcher, Bird on the Back of an Elephant, Strange Wings from My Own Shoulder,* and *Exercises*. She has won many prizes for her work, including the Hölderlin-Förderpreis for Lyric Poetry in 1994 and the Adalbert-von-Chemisso-Preis in 2001.

WILLIAM CLIFF (b. 1940) is the pen name of André Imberecht, born in Gembloux, Belgium. He is the author of *L'Etat Belge, La Sainte Famille,* and *Le Pain Quotidien*. In 2007 he received le Grand Prix de Poésie de l'Académie Française for his entire work.

ROBERT CRAWFORD (b. 1959) has published numerous books of literary criticism on Scottish literature and poetry. His own poetry books include *The Tip of My Tongue, Spirit Machines,* and *Masculinity*.

MAURIZIO CUCCHI (b. 1945) was born in Milan, where he continues to reside. He is an editorial consultant and publicist who contributes regularly to the newspaper *La Stampa*. His books of poetry include *The Missing, The Wonders of Water, Glenn, Woman of the Game, Poetry of the Source,* and *Glenn's Last Journey*. He has also edited several well-known anthologies of Italian poetry and has translated widely from the French, including Stendhal, Flaubert, and Lamartine.

HENNING KRAMER DAHL (b. 1962), from Norway, published his first book of poems in 1983 and has since published ten more, as well as a novel, essays, children's books, and some dozen volumes of translations (H.D., Plath, Walcott, Pessoa, et al.). He has one book in English, *Blue Note Boulevards,* translated by Jennifer Lloyd, with woodcuts by Magne Furuholmen.

DRAGAN JOVANOVIĆ DANILOV (b. 1960), born in Požega, Serbia, is studying art history at Belgrade University. The author of twelve books of poetry, two novels, and one book of critical essays, he has been translated into English, French, Italian, Bulgarian, and Macedonian. For his works he has received many literary awards.

ALEŠ DEBELJAK (b. 1961) is a poet, essayist, and professor of cultural studies at the University of Ljubljana. Internationally recognized as one of the best poets in Central Europe, he has published seven books of poetry, three of which are available in English translation (*Anxious Moments, Dictionary of Silence,* and *The City and the Child*). His nonfiction books in English include *Twilight of the Idols, Reluctant Modernity,* and *The Hidden Handshake*. He has won the Preseren Foundation Prize, the Miriam Lindberg Israel Poetry for Peace Prize (Tel Aviv), and the Chiqyu Poetry Prize (Tokyo). His books have been translated into more than ten languages.

REGINA DERIEVA (b. 1949) has published twenty books of poetry, essays, and prose. Her most recent book of poems in English translation, *Alien Matter: New and Selected Poems,* was published in 2006 (Spuyten Duyvil). Her work has been (or is being) translated into many languages, including Swedish, Arabic, French, and Italian, and has appeared in *Poetry, Modern Poetry in Translation, Salt, Poetry East,* and *Notre Dame Review,* as well as in many Russian magazines. She currently lives in Sweden.

KRISTIN DIMITROVA (b. 1963), the author of eight books of poetry and two books of prose, is a professor of foreign languages at the University of Sofia. She has received numerous awards for her writing, including the 2003 Association of Bulgarian Writers Poetry of the Year Award and, in 2004, the Translator's Union First Award for Poetry Translation for her translations of John Donne into Bulgarian. A collection of her poetry in English, *A Visit to the Clockmaker,* was published in 2005 by the Irish press Southword Editions.

LIDIJA DIMKOVSKA (b. 1971) grew up in Skopje, Macedonia, received a PhD in Romanian literature in Bucharest, and now lives and works in Ljubljana, Slovenia. In addition to editing an anthology of young Macedonian poets, she has published four books of poems and a novel in Macedonian, and won the "Studentski Zbor" prize for best debut Macedonian book. *Do Not Awaken Them with Hammers*, a collection of her poetry in English translation, was published by Ugly Duckling Presse.

ADDA DJØRUP (b. 1972) was born in Fredensborg, Denmark, grew up in Århus, spent 1999–2002 in Madrid, now lives in Florence. She has a BA in comparative literature and has held many jobs, including teaching Danish to adult immigrants and refugees in Copenhagen. Her first book, a poetic sequence whose speaker is the mysterious Monsieur, is titled *Monsieur's Monologues. In which Monsieur engages in nonsense / imagines things about reality / laments his lack of the same / and finally arrives*. Her second book is a collection of stories.

MICHAEL DONHAUSER (b. 1956) was born in Vaduz (Lichtenstein) and lives in Vienna. A poet of Lichtenstein and Austria, he has written *Of the Things, Land of Sargans, The Garden*, and, most recently, *I Have Long Not but Thought of You Alone*, among many other volumes of poetry and prose. He is translator of Arthur Rimbaud and Francis Ponge, and recipient of a number of important prizes, including the 2004 Meraner Poetry Prize and the 2005 Ernst-Jandl Poetry Prize.

MILAN ĐORĐEVIĆ (b. 1954), born in Belgrade, Serbia, is a poet, writer, essayist, and translator currently living in Belgrade. The author of seven books of poetry, he won the Vasko Popa poetry award and the Vladislav Petković Dis poetry award.

ULRIKA DRAESNER (b. 1962), born in Munich, lives today in Berlin. She has studied in Munich and Oxford, has published widely in newspapers and magazines, and has also worked for radio. Her books of poetry include *Bolt of Lightning, Cells Hired for the Night*, and *Memory Loops*. The recipient of several prizes since 1995, she has most recently been awarded the Hölderlin-Förderpreis in 2001 and the Preis der Literaturhäuser in 2002.

KURT DRAWERT (b. 1956) was born in the industrial town of Hennigsdorf, Brandenburg, in the former East Germany, and now lives in Darmstadt. He makes his living as a writer of poetry and prose. Among his numerous awards are the prestigious Ingeborg-Bachmann Award (1993), the Meran Poetry Prize (1993), the Uwe-Johnson Prize (1994), and an Arno Schmidt fellowship (2000), as well as the Otto Braun Medal of Honor from the German Schiller Foundation in 2001.

ARIANE DREYFUS (b. 1958) was born in Paris and lives and teaches in the greater Paris area. She is the author of ten collections of poems, including *L'Inhabitable* and *Les compagnies silencieuses*.

SYLVIANE DUPUIS (b. 1956) grew up in Geneva and received her university degrees in French literature, archaeology, and ancient Greek; she was also active in theater and archaeological excavations. The recipient of, among other awards, the Prix de Poésie C.F. Ramuz, she is currently a lecturer in Francophone Swiss literature at the University of Geneva and the author of several poetry collections.

FERIDA DURAKOVIĆ (b. 1957) has published five collections of poetry and two children's books. The recipient of the Hellman-Hammet Grant for Free Expression, she lives in Sarajevo with her husband and young daughter. In 1998, White Pine Press published a collection of her poems, *Heart of Darkness,* translated into English by Amela Simić and Zoran Mutić.

DAIVA ĖEPAUSKAITĖ (b. 1967), from Marijampolė, has published three books of poetry, including *Nameless* and *I Ate One Cranberry.*

OSWALD EGGER (b. 1963) was born in Italy and now lives in Vienna. He has published several poetry collections, including *The Earth of Speech, Summers,* and *Masses of Speech.* Egger has received many honors, most recently as Villa Aurora writer in residence (Los Angeles), the Meran Poetry Prize, and the Christian Wagner Prize.

GYRDIR ELÍASSON (b. 1961) grew up in the town of Sauðárkrókur in northern Iceland. He is the author of numerous books of poetry and prose and had translated the work of, among others, Richard Brautigan. He currently lives in Reykjavík.

MARTIN ENCKELL (b. 1954) is a poet, translator, and visual artist. He has written several volumes of poetry and prose, and in 1995 he was awarded the Young Art in Finland Prize.

CHRISTOPHE LAMIOT ENOS (b. 1962) was born in the Eure Valley and lived for fifteen years in the United States before returning to France in 2005. He is the author of three poetry collections, as well as books of literary essays. He is also a translator of contemporary American poetry.

ALEXANDER EREMENKO (b. 1950) was born in Moscow, where he studied at the World Literature Institute. His poetry began to gain recognition in the late 1970s in the Moscow literary underground.

HAYDAR ERGÜLEN (b. 1956), born in Eskişehir, graduated from the Sociology Department at Orta Doğu Technical University in Ankara. His most recent books include *Death and Scandal, The Cardboard Valise, Hafiz, Collected Poems,* and *40 Poems and One,* which won the prestigious Behçet Necatigil Poetry Award. Believing that the poet is more than merely an individualized voice, he sometimes publishes poetry under the heteronyms Salamander and Hafiz.

SEYHAN ERÖZÇELİK (b. 1962) studied psychology at Boğaziçi University and oriental languages at Istanbul University. Since then, he has worked as an advertising editor. The author of a number of books of poetry (most recently *The Rain Stone* and *Once We Were, Once We Weren't*), he edits the journal *Poetry Horse.* He was awarded the Unus Nadi Prize in 1991, the Behcet Necatigil Poetry Prize in 2004, and the Dionysos Prize in 2005. His book *Rosestrikes and Coffee Grinds* will be published in English by Talisman House in 2008.

MARIE ÉTIENNE (b. 1937) was born in Vietnam, spent part of her youth in Africa, and now lives in Paris. She was the assistant of the experimental theater director Antoine Vitez for a decade and has written widely of his work. She is the author of several novels and short story collections and nine books of poems, including *Anatolie,* which received the Prix Mallarmé in 1997, and *Dormans.*

DANIEL FALB (b. 1977) was born in Kassel, Germany. He studied physics and philosophy in Berlin, where he still lives today. His poems have appeared in a number of journals and anthologies, and his first collection of poetry, *The Clearance of These Parks,* was awarded the 2005 Poetry Debut Prize of the Literary Colloquium Berlin. He is also the recipient of the 2001 Prenzlauer Berg Literature Prize and most recently a 2006 Scholarship Prize from the Foundation of Lower Saxony.

GERHARD FALKNER (b. 1951) was born in Nuremberg, Germany, where he still lives. Poet, playwright, essayist, and translator, he has written many volumes of poetry, among them *Endogenous Poems, Nth Person Singular, Selected Poems,* and *Melancholy.* He has received many awards and fellowships for his work, among them the Bavarian Staatsförderpreis, the Schiller Prize and the Spycher Literature Prize Leuk.

SYLVA FISCHEROVÁ (b. 1963) teaches classics at Charles University in Prague and has published four collections of poetry. Her work has been widely translated into English, appearing in various American literary journals. *Tremor of Racehorses: Selected Poems,* a collection of her poetry translated into English, was published by Bloodaxe Books.

MARK FORD (b. 1962) was born in Kenya and lives in England. He has published two collections of poetry, *Landlocked* and *Soft Sift.* He teaches at University College London.

TUA FORSSTRÖM (b. 1947) was born in Borgå and resides in Ekenäs. She began to achieve wide recognition not only in Finland and Sweden but also in Britain with her sixth collection, *Snow Leopard.* For *After Spending a Night Among Horses*—conceived as a dialogue with the director Andrei Tarkovsky—she received the 1998 Nordic Council Literature Prize. Her latest collection is *Songs.* Books of her poems have also been translated into Danish, Dutch, Finnish, French, and Spanish.

NIELS FRANK (b. 1963), from Denmark, published his first book in 1985. He has published five books of poems, one of essays, two that mix genres, a collection of narratives about well-known artists (and one anonymous forger), and a volume of photos. He has also translated poetry into Danish (notably that of John Ashbery).

KATARINA FROSTENSON (b. 1953), born in Brännkyrka, is a poet, playwright, dramatist, librettist, and at the age of thirty-nine was the fifth woman elected to the Swedish Academy. In addition to writing many celebrated collections of poetry and works for the stage, she has both introduced and translated into Swedish some of the key works of contemporary French literature, in recognition of which she was made a Chevalier of the Légion d'Honneur. Her most recently published works are *Carcass* and *The Word—A Passion,* the former a book of poems, the latter an oratorio composed by Sven-David Sandström.

FS (b. 1971) is short for "François Serpent," the pseudonym of Indrek Mesikepp. Serpent's collections include *God is Human Too, book with white covers,* and *2004,* which won the award of the Cultural Endowment of Estonia. He works as editor of literary criticism at the literary magazine *Looning.*

INGA GAILE (b. 1976) is a Latvian poet. Her poetry collection *Time Had Grown Enamored,* won the Klavs Elsbergs Award; in 2004, a second collection of poetry, *While Crying One Dare Not Laugh,* was awarded the Anna Dagda Foundation Accolade for excellence in poetry.

RÓBERT GÁL (b. 1968) grew up in Bratislava and, after residing in Brno, New York, and Jerusalem, now makes his home in Prague. His collection of poetic aphorisms and fragmentary philosophical essays, *Signs & Symptoms,* was published in English translation by Twisted Spoon Press, and has been widely compared to the work of the Romanian aphorist E. M. Cioran.

EMILIAN GALAICU-PĂUN (b. 1964) was born in Unchiteşti in what is now the Republic of Moldova. He has published six books of poetry, among them *ABC-Desire, The Beaten Leading the Unbeaten, Yin Time,* and *Gestuary.* Galaicu-Păun has also published a novel, *Gestures (The Trilogy of Nothing),* and a collection of essays, *The Poetry After Poetry.* He serves as editor in chief of the Cartier publishing house in Chişinău.

MIHAIL GĂLĂŢANU (b. 1963) was born in Galaţi, Romania. He published his first book of poems, *News About Me,* in 1987, and his second collection, *Keeping My Fists Tight,* six years later. Since then, a book of his poetry or prose has appeared each year. Recent poetry titles include *My Grave Digs Itself* and *The Starry Womb.* Gălăţanu was editor in chief of *Playboy Romania* and now edits *Flacăra,* a glossy monthly magazine.

SERGEY GANDELEVSKY (b. 1952) was born in Moscow, where he became an active participant in the underground literary culture of the 1970s and 1980s. He is one of the few authors to have won both the "Little Booker Prize" and the "Anti-Booker Prize"—for his book *Trepanation of the Skull. A Kindred Orphanhood* was published in the United Statese by Zephyr Press, in Philip Metres's translation.

PABLO GARCÍA CASADO (b. 1972) was born in Córdoba in 1972 and studied law. His first collection of poems, *The Outskirts,* published in 1997, won the Critical Eye Prize and was a finalist for the National Poetry Prize that year. His second collection, *The Map of America,* was published in 2001.

LUIS GARCÍA MONTERO, (b. 1958) one of the most popular poets writing in Spain today, has received numerous awards for his work, including Spain's National Poetry Prize and the National Poetry Critics Prize. He was born in Granada and currently is a professor of Spanish literature at the University of Granada. In addition to his poems, he has also written the lyrics for songs by Spanish rocker Miguel Ríos.

GÜR GENÇ (Gürgenç Kkorkmazel) (b. 1969) was born in Cyprus and attended university in Ankara, Turkey, but left his studies to pursue poetry. His books include *Dividedness, Eat!,* and *Swallow the Road.* After living abroad for years, he returned to Cyprus, where he established B/6 publishing and the anarchist literary journal *Nettle.*

CLAIRE GENOUX (b. 1971) was born in Lausanne, where she also studied at the University of Lausanne. In 1997, her first collection of poems, *Oval Sun,* was published, and in 1999 she received the Prix Ramuz for *Seasons of the Body.* A collection of her short stories was published in 2000.

EVA GERLACH (b. 1948) was born in the Dutch Antilles and published her first poetry collection, *No Further Distress,* in 1979; it was awarded the Van der Hoogt Prize for young writers. In 2000, Gerlach received Holland's chief literary award, the P. C. Hooft Prize, for her entire poetic oeuvre. Since then she has published several further collections, including a second book of poems for children, *Eye to Eye to Eye to Eye,* and her most recent collection, *Situations.*

GUY GOFFETTE (b. 1947) was born in the Belgian Ardennes. He is the author of six collections of poems, among them *Manteau de Fortune,* which received the Grand Prix de Poésie of the Académie Française. He's also the author of books on Bonnard, Verlaine, and Auden. He lives in Paris and is an editor at Gallimard. *Charlestown Blues,* a collection of his poems translated by Marilyn Hacker, was published in 2007 by the University of Chicago Press.

DMITRY GOLYNKO (b. 1969), born in Leningrad, is a cultural theorist, poet, essayist. and historian who has published several books of poems. He lives in St. Petersburg.

PAVLE GORANOVIĆ (b. 1973), born in Nikšić, Montenegro, writes poetry, prose, and essays. He has published three books, and his poetry has been translated into several languages. Secretary of the Independent Association of Montenegrin writers, he is also coeditor of the renowned journal *ARS*.

GEORGI GOSPODINOV (b. 1968) is the editor in chief of a weekly Bulgarian literary magazine and a professor at New Bulgarian University in Sofia. He is the author of two collections of poetry, one book of short stories, and a novel, *Natural Novel*, published in translation by Dalkey Archive Press. His poems have won critical acclaim in both Bulgaria and abroad, and appear in English translation in the Arc Publications anthology *A Fine Line: New Poetry from Eastern and Central Europe*.

DIETER M. GRÄF (b. 1960) was born in Ludwigshafen and lives in Cologne. He has published three volumes of poetry: *Study of Intoxication: Father + Son, Driving Head,* and *Western Edge*. Recipient of the Leonce and Lena Prize from the City of Darmstadt (1997), he has held several fellowships, including one for the Literarisches Colloquium in Berlin (1996) and at the Villa Massimo in Rome (2004). In 1999, he was writer in residence at the Villa Aurora in Los Angeles and in 2005 at the Deutsches Haus at New York University.

GINTARAS GRAJAUSKAS (b. 1966), from Marijampolė, Lithuania, is the author of several collections of poems: *Tattoo, Hermit's Holidays, Catalogue,* and, most recently, *Bone Pipe*. He has also published a collection of essays, *By Ear*.

BRUNO GRÉGOIRE (b. 1960) was born in eastern France, and (as he puts it) he was born a second time five years later near the Red Sea. His travels, to Central America and Mexico in particular, inform his work. He is the author of three collections of poems and, with François Hatchondo, has translated the Mexican poet José Carlos Becerra.

VONA GROARKE (b. 1964) is from the Irish Midlands. She is the author of four books of poetry: *Shale, Other People's Houses, Flight,* and *Juniper Street*. *Flight and Earlier Poems* and *Juniper Street* are published in the U.S. by Wake Forest University Press.

TATJANA GROMAČA (b. 1971), a poet and fiction writer, works as a journalist for the *Feral Tribune,* a weekly magazine known for its political satire. Her first book of poems, *Something Wrong, Maybe?,* received significant critical praise, and was subsequently translated into German and Polish.

CATHRINE GRØNDAHL (b. 1969), from Norway, published her first book of poems in 1994; it won the Tarjei Vesaas First Book Prize. She has since published three more volumes of poems. She has studied philosophy and law and works as a defense attorney in Oslo.

DURS GRÜNBEIN (b. 1962), born in Dresden and now living in Berlin, has been Germany's most celebrated poet since receiving the Georg Büchner Prize in 1995. Among his eight volumes of poetry are *Mornings in the Gray Zone* and *Lesson at the Base of the Skull*; his most recent volumes are *Declared Night* and *Of Snow*. He is also an essayist and classical translator. His most recent awards include the 2004 Saxony-Anhalt Literature Prize and the 2000 Salzburg Easter Festival Literature Prize.

TOBIAS GRÜTERICH (b. 1978) was born in Karl-Marx-Stadt (Chemnitz), East Germany. He has been writing aphorisms since 1997, and studying geodesy at the University of Technology, Dresden, since 2000. His aphorisms have been published in anthologies, journals, and newspapers and he has received several awards for his book, *Earned Injustices: Aphorisms,* including the 2000 Literature Prize of the city university of Marburg. He was also the winner of both the eighteenth (2001) and the twenty-first (2004) Hessen-Thüringen Youth Literature Forum.

ULLA HAHN (b. 1946) was born in Brachthausen and now resides in Hamburg. Her first collection of poems was widely acclaimed when it appeared in 1981, and with the publication of six additional volumes since then, she is now considered to be among the finest lyric poets in the country. She worked for a number of years as a radio editor, has taught at several German universities, and is the recipient of many prestigious literary prizes, including the Friedrich Hölderlin Prize of the city of Bad Homburg, the 2002 German Books Prize, and the 2006 Elisabeth Langgässer Literature Prize.

MILA HAUGOVÁ (b. 1942) was born in Budapest, the daughter of a Hungarian mother and Slovakian father, and spent her early childhood moving from place to place in postwar Czechoslovakia. She emigrated to Canada in 1967, but returned a year later, and since 1972 has lived in Bratislava, where she worked as an agronomist and professor of agriculture. A highly regarded translator (of Plath, Celan, and Trakl, among others) and the former editor of the literary journal *Rhomboid* (1986–1996), Haugova has published twelve collections of poetry. *Scent of the Unseen* is a collection of her work in English translation.

KERSTIN HENSEL (b. 1961) was born in Karl-Marx-Stadt (Chemnitz), East Germany, and now resides in Berlin. Besides poetry, she has published three novels, several books of short stories, radio plays, libretti, and pieces for theater and film. Among her volumes of poetry are *To Understand the Train Station: Poems 1995–2000,* and *Free Throw.* She is the recipient of the 1987 Anna-Seghers Prize of the Academy of Fine Arts in Berlin, the Leonce and Lena Prize (1991), and the Gerrit Engelke Prize of the city of Hannover (1999).

W. N. HERBERT (b. 1961) writes in both English and Scots. His poetry collections include *Bad Shaman Blues, The Laurelude,* and *Cabaret McGonagall.* He is professor of poetry and creative writing at Newcastle University.

STEFAN HERTMANS (b. 1951) is professor at the Academy of Fine Arts in Ghent. He has published novels, collections of short stories, essays on literature and philosophy, theater texts, and poetry, and his work is widely translated throughout Europe. He has won several major literary prizes, including the Belgian State Prize for *Music for the Crossing,* a collection of five long poems on Paul Hindemith, Paul Valéry, Paul Cézanne, Vaslav Nijinsky, and Wallace Stevens, respectively. Most recently, Hertmans published *Cinnamon Fingers,* his twelfth collection of poetry.

SELIMA HILL (b. 1945) is the author, most recently, of *Portrait of My Lover as a Horse, Lou-Lou,* and *Red Roses.* The London-born author has received numerous awards for her poetry and been shortlisted for the Forward Poetry Prize, the T. S. Eliot Prize, and the Whitbread Poetry Award.

EMMANUEL HOCQUARD (b. 1940) is the author of more than twenty books of poetry and has collaborated on films and other visual projects. Editor and publisher of Orange Export Books, he was instrumental in the small press movement in France in the 1970s and 1980s and the founder of the still-active Un Bureau sur l'Atlantique, an organization that fosters French-American poetic exchange.

PETR HRUŠKA (b. 1964) lives in Ostrava, Czech Republic, and works for the Institute of Czech Literature in Brno. He has published three books of poetry and has been translated into French, German, Polish, and Dutch.

FLÓRA IMRE (b. 1961), born in Budapest, studied Hungarian, Latin, and ancient Greek at the University of Budapest and published her first volume of poems in 1986. She has also translated Horace and Lucanus, and she has written a handbook on prosody. She has won several literary awards and currently works as a secondary school teacher.

KÜÇÜK İSKENDER (b. 1964), an assumed name meaning "little Alexander," studied five years of medicine before devoting himself to literature. His poetry fuses a militant gay sensibility with a nihilistic mysticism. He has published prolifically since his first book, *My Eyes Do Not Fit My Face.*

MIRELA IVANOVA (b. 1962) lives in Sofia and is the author of six books of poetry. She is also an essayist, screenwriter, and translator of German literature into Bulgarian.

ANN JÄDERLUND (b. 1955) lives in Stockholm and is the author of nine books of poetry, from *The Streamer City* to her most recent collection, *In a cylinder in the water of watertears.* She has won numerous awards for her poetry, including the Erik Lindegren Prize and the Gerard Bonniers Poetry Prize of the Swedish Academy. She has also written two picture books, one in the name of each of her children; she writes dramatic works as well.

CORNELIUS JAKHELLN (b. 1977) is a Norwegian poet and musician with master's degrees in literature and philosophy from the Sorbonne. He published his first book, *Gebura Muse,* in 2001 and has since published two more volumes in his *Quadra Natura* tetralogy: *Yggdraliv* and *Fagernorn.*

KATHLEEN JAMIE (b. 1962) is lecturer in creative writing at St Andrews University. Among her poetry collections are *Waterlight, The Tree House,* and *Jizzen.*

FRANCK ANDRÉ JAMME (b. 1947) was born in Clermont-Ferrand, France. He has published twelve books since 1981, as well as numerous illustrated editions. In 2005, he was awarded the Grand Prix de Poésie de la Société des gens de lettres for his life's work. Black Square Editions in New York City has published two of Jamme's books: *The Recitation of Forgetting,* translated by John Ashbery, and *Another Silent Attack,* translated by Michael Tweed.

ESTHER JANSMA (b. 1958) was born in Amsterdam. She is a poet whose work is internationally recognized and published frequently—most recently in *Roof Turrets,* for which she won the Hughes C. Pernath Award in 2001. She has also been published in many poetry and prose magazines, anthologies, and collections. She is an archaeologist by profession, and currently serves as Head of the Research Department of the Dutch National Service for Archaeology, Cultural Landscape, and Built Heritage.

SAŠA JELENKOVIĆ (b. 1964), born in Zaječar, Serbia, graduated in literature at the Philology Faculty in Belgrade. The author of eight books of poetry, he is a member of Serbian PEN and Serbian Literary Society. He received the Matičev šal Award, the Milan Rakič Award, and the Vasko Popa Award.

MILJENKO JERGOVIĆ (b. 1966), born in Sarajevo, Bosnia and Herzegovina, is a writer, poet, and journalist currently living in Zagreb, Croatia. He is one of the most prolific Bosnian and Croatian writers, with more than twenty books of poetry, fiction, and nonfiction published. He won the Premio Grinzane Cavour Award, the

Friedenspreis Erich-Maria Remarque Award, as well as several major literary awards in Croatia and Bosnia and Herzegovina. His short story collection *Sarajevo Marlboro* was translated into English and published in the United States by Archipelago Books.

ARNE JOHNSSON (b. 1950) made his debut in 1985 with *Changes* and has published ten additional books of poems, among them *The ground shone even in the dream* and *Part of this and separate as everyone*. He has also published a book of essays and a CD. The recipient of many literary prizes, he has been translated into Belarusian, English, German, Greek, Hindi, Latvian, and Lithuanian, and for many years has worked as a librarian.

ELÍSABET JÖKULSDÓTTIR (b. 1958) was born in Reykjavík and grew up in both Seltjarnarnes and Reykjavík. She is the author of numerous short stories, plays, novels, and volumes of poetry—among them, *Dance in a Closed Room* and *Ella Stina's Book of Spells*. Her plays have been shown in New York, Macedonia, Austria, Denmark, Sweden, and Russia. An outspoken ecological activist, she currently studies theater in Iceland.

PIA JUUL (b. 1962), from Denmark, published her first book in 1985 and has since published four more books of poems. She has also published a stage play, three radio plays, a novel, and a collection of stories, as well as translations into Danish from English (Ted Hughes) and Swedish. She lives in Kragevig, Denmark, in the southern part of Sjælland (Zealand).

HÉDI KADDOUR (b. 1945) was born in Tunisia but has lived in France since childhood. He is the author of four collections of poems. His novel, *Waltenberg,* received the 2005 Prix du Premier Roman. He is also a theater critic for the *Nouvelle Revue Française* and a professor emeritus at the École Normale Superiéure/Lyon.

KATIA KAPOVICH (b. 1960) was born in Kishinev, Moldova, and studied foreign languages. In 1990 she immigrated to Israel, and in 1992 to the United States. The author of three books of poetry in Russian, she writes in both Russian and English, and her work has appeared widely in American literary publications. She currently edits the American magazine *Fulcrum*.

ZVONKO KARANOVIĆ (b. 1959) was born in Niš, Serbia, and lives in Belgrade. He is the author of seven books of poetry and two novels.

LAURYNAS KATKUS (b. 1972), a Lithuanian poet, is the author of *Voices, Notes,* and *Diving Lessons.* A volume of his poems was published in English under the title *October Holidays* in 2001, translated by Kerry Shawn Keys, with Sam Witt and John Burns.

JACKIE KAY (b. 1961) was born in Edinburgh to a Scottish mother and a Nigerian father. Adopted by a white couple, she was brought up in Glasgow and studied at the Royal Scottish Academy of Music and Drama and Stirling University. Her books include the novel *Trumpet* and the poetry collection *Life Mask*.

BOŻENA KEFF (b. 1948) studied psychology, Polish philology, and philosophy at the University of Warsaw, where she received a doctorate in 2001. She is the cofounder of the Polish Feminist Association and a translator of Maggie Humm's *The Dictionary of Feminist Theory*. In 2002, her book *A Figure with Shadow: Jewish Women in Polish Literature from the End of the 19th Century to 1939* was among the top twenty nominated for the NIKE, the most prestigious literary award in Poland. She currently lives in Warsaw with her son.

ANDREJ KHADANOVICH (b. 1973), from Minsk, studied French literature in graduate school. He has translated widely from French, English, Polish, Russian, and Ukrainian, and is the author of five books, most recently *From Belarus with Love*.

MIMI KHALVATI (b. 1944) has published six collections with Carcanet Press. The most recent, *The Meanest Flower*, is a Poetry Book Society Recommendation and is shortlisted for the T. S. Eliot Prize.

MARZANNA BOGUMIŁA KIELAR (b. 1963) was born in Gołdap and studied philosophy at the University of Warsaw. She is currently a lecturer in Warsaw and a collaborator of the journal *Krasnogruda*, published by the Borderland Foundation. She gained critical acclaim with her first book of poems, *Sacra conversazione*, which received the Kazimiera Iłłakowiczówna Prize and the Kościelski Foundation Prize. Her second volume, *Materia prima*, was shortlisted for the NIKE Literary Prize in 2000.

THOMAS KLING (1957–2005) was born in Bingen, Germany, and died at the age of forty-seven. A leading figure in experimental poetry and a controversial essayist, he was one of the most important German-language poets of his generation. Recent volumes of poetry include *Analysis of Flight Data, Excavations, Long Distance Trade*, and *Rot*. His most recent awards were the 2005 d.lit-Literature Prize from the Stadtsparkasse Düsseldorf, the Ernst Jandl Prize in 2001, and the Peter Huchel Prize in 1996.

MARIJA KNEŽEVIĆ (b. 1963) was born in Belgrade, Serbia, graduated in literature at the Philology Faculty in Belgrade, and earned her MA in comparative literature at Michigan State University. The author of seven books of poetry, she won the Đura Jakšić poetry award in 2006. She is a columnist for the daily publication *Politika*.

NICOLAI KOBUS (b. 1968) was born in Stadlohn, Germany, and currently resides in Hamburg. From 1993 to 1998, he edited the journal *Chiffre* in Münster. He has published poetry in newspapers, journals, and anthologies such as *sterz, du, das Gedicht, edit*, and *die taz*, and been widely anthologized, including in the 2004 and 2006 annual best of poetry collection, *Jahrbuch der Lyrik*. He has been the recipient of many honors and awards, including the 1999 Wolfgang Weyrauch Prize, the 2004 GWK Förderpreis for Literature, and the 2005 Ernst Meister Förderpreis. His first collection of poetry appeared in September 2006.

KRZYSZTOF KOEHLER (b. 1963) was born in Częstochowa and received an MA and PhD in Polish literature from Jagiellonian University in Krakow. His volumes of poetry include *Poems, Unsuccessful Pilgrimage, Guerilla of Truth*, and *Third Part*. He is generally associated with the "Barbarian" poets who publish in the Krakow quarterly *BruLion*.

UWE KOLBE (b. 1957) was born in Prenzlauer Berg, East Berlin, and currently lives in Berlin. Since his first book, *Born Into*, he has published poetry as well as crime fiction. His most recent book of poetry is *The Colors of Water*. Banned from publication between 1982 and 1985, Kolbe moved to the West, returning only after reunification. An acclaimed poet and translator, his latest awards include the 2006 award from the literaturhaeuser.net consortium of literature houses, the 1993 Tübinger Friedrich Hölderlin Award, and the 1992 Berlin Literature Prize.

IVAN KOLENIČ (b. 1965) is a poet and novelist considered a part of the "Barbarian Generation" of Slovak poets. He currently lives in Bratislava.

ANISE KOLTZ (b. 1928) was born in Luxembourg-Eich. She founded the "Journées de Mondorf" (biannual international writers' and poets' festivals) held 1963–1974 and

1995–1999. She lives in Luxembourg and writes in three languages: her writing in French dates only from the 1970s.

ABDULLAH KONUSHEVCI (b. 1958), from Prishtina, Kosovo, studied at the University of Zagreb and worked for many years as a journalist. He has published six volumes of poetry and has translated Ernest Hemingway and a number of other writers into Albanian.

BARBARA KORUN (b. 1963) lives and teaches in Ljubljana, Slovenia. She has published three books of poetry (*The Edge of Grace, Notes from Under the Table,* and *Fissures*). Southword Editions (Ireland) recently released her selected poems, titled *Songs of Earth and Light* and translated into English by Theo Dorgan.

GAZMEND KRASNIQI (b. 1963) was born in Shkodra, Albania, where he currently works for the Shkodra Art Gallery. He has published two volumes of poetry and an anthology of experimental poetry. He has also translated several English-language poets into Albanian, including Yeats, Eliot, Pound, and Auden.

ANGELA KRAUSS (b. 1950) was born in Karl-Marx-Stadt (Chemnitz) and resides in Leipzig. Best known for her novels and stories, she writes poetry only occasionally. She has been the recipient of many important prizes, including the 1988 Ingeborg Bachmann Prize, the 1996 Berlin Literature Prize, the 1996 Bobrowski Medal, and the 2002 Honor Award from the German Schiller Foundation. Her latest book is *What Next.*

URSULA KRECHEL (b. 1947) was born in Trier, Germany, and now lives in Berlin. Since the publication of her first book of poetry *To Mainz!* in 1977, she has published widely in several genres. Her most recent poetry volumes are *Middlewards, Voices from the Bitter Core,* and *Unangered: Poems, Lights, Bookmarks.* She has been awarded many honors for her work, including the International Eifel Literatur Prize (1994), the Martha Saalfeld Förderpreis (1994), and the Elisabeth Langgässer Literature Prize (1997).

KATA KULAVKOVA (b. 1951) is professor of theory and methodology in literature studies in the Department of General and Comparative Literature at Sts. Cyril and Methodius University in Skopje. A former president of the Macedonian PEN Center and a member of the Macedonian Writers' Association since 1978, Kulavkova is the author of numerous books of poetry and the editor of an anthology of Macedonian short stories and essays.

ASKO KÜNNAP (b. 1971) was born in Tartu, Estonia, and has published three books of poems: *In Defense of Coincidences, And the Lizards Replied,* and *The Fairest War.* In addition to writing poetry, Künnap works as an illustrator; he designs books, board games, and CD covers and runs an alternative micro publishing house, Näo Kirik (The Face Church).

VIVIAN LAMARQUE (b. 1946) was born in Tesero (Trento), but since nine months of age has lived in Milan, where she worked as a teacher for many years. Her books include *Teresino,* which won the Viareggio Prize, *The Gold Gentleman, Poems in the Formal, The Gentleman of the Frightened Ones,* which won the 1992 Montale Prize, and *A Quiet Dust.* She is also the other of many prizewinning books of fables and a translator of Valéry, Baudelaire, Prévert, Grimm, and Wilde.

WERNER LAMBERSY (b. 1941) was born in Anvers, Belgium, and now lives in Paris, where he is in charge of promoting Belgium's Francophone literature. The author of numerous books of poetry, including the widely acclaimed *Masters and Tea Houses,* he has published a bilingual (English and French) book of poems in Canada, titled *Despite My Growling Heart.*

BOIKO LAMBOVSKI (b. 1960) has published seven books of poetry in Bulgarian since 1986. He has received numerous awards for his poems, which have been translated into German, Russian, Serbian, Slovenian, Italian, and Arabic.

LIÂNA LANGA (b. 1960), former director of the Latvian National Council of Culture, was born in Riga and began publishing in 1988, winning the Latvian National Literary Award for two books, *Now Heaven, Now an Hourglass* and *Blow Your Horn, Scorpion!*

RADMILA LAZIĆ (b. 1949), born in Kruševac, is a prominent Serbian poet, editor, and activist. She is the managing editor of *ProFemina: International Journal for Women* and *Writing and Culture,* published in Belgrade. A book of her poems, *A Wake for the Living,* was published by Graywolf, in Charles Simic's translation.

LEEVI LEHTO (b. 1951) has published six volumes of poetry, a novel, and an experimental prose work. His most recent book is *Other Poems.* His translations, some forty books in total, range from mystery writing to philosophy, sociology, and poetry, including work by Louis Althusser, Gilles Deleuze, George Orwell, Stephen King, Ian McEwan, Arthur C. Danto, Mickey Spillane, Alexander Dubček, Josef Škvorecky, Walter Benjamin, John Keats, John Ashbery, and Charles Bernstein.

GWYNETH LEWIS (b. 1959) writes both in Welsh (her native language) and English. She was the inaugural National Poet of Wales. Her first three books of poems are published as *Chaotic Angels* by Bloodaxe. Both her books of nonfiction, *Sunbathing in the Rain: A Cheerful Book on Depression* and *Two in a Boat: A True Marital Rite of Passage* are published in the U.S.

LULJETA LLESHANAKU (b. 1968), from Elbasan, Albania, studied literature at the University of Tirana and has edited for the periodicals *The Voice of Youth* and *The Light.* She has published four volumes of poetry, and one of her books, *Fresco,* has been translated into English and published by New Directions in 2002.

ADÍLIA LOPES (b. 1960), born in Lisbon, self-published her first book in 1985 under the title *A Rather Dangerous Game.* Since then, she has published more than fifteen further collections, nearly all issued by alternative or underground presses on the margin of Portuguese publishing. She has emerged as one of her country's most controversial poetic voices, ardently defended by some critics for her originality, dismissed by others. Book-length translations of her poetry, especially the collection *The Poet from Pondicherry,* have appeared in Spain, France, Italy, the Netherlands, and Germany.

OLEH LYSHEHA (b. 1949), born in Tysmennytsia, Ukraine, published his first book in 1977, in samizdat. His first officially published collection appeared in 1989. James Brasfield collaborated with Lysheha on a selection of his poems translated into English, which was published by Harvard University Press and won the 2000 PEN Award for Poetry in Translation.

DİDEM MADAK (b. 1970), who likes resigning, resigned her jobs as a secretary, a salesclerk, a poll taker, and a marketing agent. After being expelled from the law faculty of September Nine University, she returned after an amnesty. She is currently practicing law. The manuscript of her first book of poetry, *The Cut Papers,* won the İnklap Şiiri Prize (the Poetry of Revolution Prize) in 2000.

VALERIO MAGRELLI (b. 1957) was born in Rome and currently teaches French literature at the University of Cassino. Poems from his five collections have appeared in the book-length English translations *Nearsights* (Graywolf, 1991) and *The Contagion* *of Matter* (Holmes and Meier, 2000). He has won the Mondello Prize, the Viareggio Prize for Poetry, and the Montale Prize. In November 2003, the Accademia dei Lincei awarded him the Antonio Feltrinelli Prize.

BRANKO MALEŠ (b. 1949), born in Zagreb, Croatia, is a poet, critic, editor, and essayist. He has published five volumes of poetry, and in 2002 he received the prestigious Goran's Wreath award for his work. His poetry had exerted a strong influence on younger generations of Croatian poets.

GLYN MAXWELL (b. 1962) is the poetry editor of *The New Republic* and the author of numerous poetry collections, including *The Sugar Mile, The Nerve,* and *Time's Fool.*

MEDBH MCGUCKIAN (b. 1950) was born in Belfast and educated at a Dominican convent and Queen's University. Her books include *The Book of the Angel, The Face of the Earth,* and *Drawing Ballerinas.*

ABDELWAHAB MEDDEB (b. 1946), born in Tunisia, moved to Paris as a student. He is now professor of comparative literature at the Université Paris X, Nanterre. Poet, novelist, essayist, and translator, he is the author of fifteen books of poems. His 2002 study was published in English as *The Malady of Islam* (Basic Books, 2003).

SEMEZDIN MEHMEDINOVIĆ (b. 1960) is one of the most prominent poets of Bosnia-Herzegovina. Since 1996 he lives in the U.S. In Sarajevo under the siege, he founded the literary magazine *Phantom of Liberty* (published today by Durieux, Zagreb). In 1993 he was cowriter and codirector of *Mizaldo,* one of the first Bosnian wartime films. His highly acclaimed collection of poems, poems in prose, and short fiction, *Sarajevo Blues,* as well as his recent book of poetry, *Nine Alexandrias,* both in Ammiel Alcalay's translation, were published by City Lights.

JOSÉ TOLENTINO MENDONÇA (b. 1965) was born in Madeira, He has published seven volumes of poetry, which were recently issued in a collected edition, as well as a play, a number of translations, and two books on theological subjects. A Roman Catholic priest, Mendonça is a professor of biblical studies at the Catholic University in Lisbon.

IMMANUEL MIFSUD (b. 1967) has published fiction as well as two collections of poems: *In the House of Clara* and *The Book of the Wind and the Flowers.* Most of his published work has been in the theater, which he also directs, and he has founded many theatrical companies, including the research theater group Theater of the Blind. He teaches at the University of Malta.

DREW MILNE (b. 1964) is the author of numerous books of poetry, among them *The Damage* and *Go Figure.* He is also the editor of Parataxis Editions and is the coauthor, with Terry Eagleton, of *Marxist Literary Theory.*

VALZHYNA MORT (b. 1981), born Valzhyna Martynava in Minsk, currently lives in the United States. She received the Crystal of Valenica Award and has read her poetry all over the world. Her first collection, *I Am as Thin as Your Eyelashes,* was published in 2005. Copper Canyon Press will publish her first U.S. book, *Factory of Tears,* in 2008.

EMMANUEL MOSES (b. 1959) was born in Casablanca, lived in Israel from 1968 to 1986, and then returned to Paris, where he has lived ever since. He is the author of six books of poetry and five works of fiction. His literary awards include the Prix Max Jacob. He is also a translator from Hebrew, German, and English. Other Press has published a collection of his poems in English translation, *Last News of Mr. Nobody.*

LALE MÜLDÜR (b. 1956) studied economics at Robert College, an American school in Istanbul, and then received a master's degree in the sociology of literature from Manchester University in England. She has published eight books of poetry, essays, and a novel, including *Voyager 2, The Book of Series, Virgin Mary's Smoke, mother am I a barbarian, Anemone: Collected Poems, 1988–1998, ultrasound in ultra-zone,* and *Byzansiyya.* Müldür is one of the central poets of the movement "Poetry of Motion."

SENADIN MUSABEGOVIĆ (b. 1970), born in Sarajevo, is a poet and political theorist. He has published three collections of poetry, and his books appear in Italian and French editions.

VIKTOR NEBORAK (b. 1961) is best known as a poet of the Bu-Ba-Bu (which stands for Burlesque-Farce-Buffoonery) poetic performance group that he founded with poets Yuri Andrukhovych and Olexandr Irvanets. The author of six books of poems, as well as a prose writer, translator, and cultural activist, Neborak is also a performer with the Ukrainian rock band Neborok.

ANDREAS NEESER (b. 1964) was born in Schlossrued, Switzerland, and today lives nearby in Aarau. Both poet and prose writer, he has published several collections of poetry, including *Driftwood, Grass Grows on the Inside,* and *The Sun Is a Wet Dog.* He has received many grants from Aargauer board of trustees for his work since 1991. Most recently he has been awarded the 2006 Meraner Poetry Prize: Media Prize RAI-Sender Bozen.

GIAMPIERO NERI (b. 1927) (pseudonym of Giampiero Pontiggia) was born in Erba (Como) and has lived in Milan since 1950. The volume *Natural Theater* includes his previous poetry collections, *The Western Look of the Suit, Lyceum,* and *From the Same Place.*

IOANA NICOLAIE (b. 1974) was born in Sângeorz-Băi, in Năsăud, in the north of Romania. A poet, novelist, and literary critic, she has published three collections of poems and a novel. Her first book of poetry, *Retouched Photograph,* appeared in 2000, and her next two, *The North* and *The Faith,* soon followed. Nicolaie also published her novel *The Sky in the Womb* in 2005.

NUALA NÍ DHOMHNAILL (b. 1952) was born in Lancashire, England. In 1957, her family returned to the Dingle Gaeltacht in Kerry, Ireland, where she grew up. Among her books are *Astrakhan Cloak, Pharaoh's Daughter, Selected Poems,* and *Spionain is Roiseanna.* She is also one of the few female Irish poets who writes exclusively in Irish.

LYUBOMIR NIKOLOV (b. 1954) grew up in the Bulgarian village of Kiryaevo and worked as an editor and translator in Sofia, before emigrating to the United States in 1990. He now lectures on poetry in American universities and broadcasts for the Voice of America and the BBC Bulgarian service. He has published three books of poetry in Bulgarian. A volume in translation, *Pagan,* was published by Carnegie Mellon University Press in 1992. His next volume, *Unreal Estate,* will appear from Carnegie Mellon in 2008.

O. (OVIDIU) NIMIGEAN (b. 1969) was born in Năsăud in Romania. He is the author of five books of poetry: *Selected Writings; Weekend Among Mutants; Good-Bye, Good-Bye, Dear Poems; Planet o;* and *Niculina Blues.* In 2003, he published a novel, *Mortido.* Nimgean is editor of the anthology *Ozone Friendly,* which collects works of writers from the region.

BORIS A. NOVAK (b. 1954) was born in Belgrade, Yugoslavia, and has lived in Ljubljana, Slovenia, for most of his life. He is the author of many books of poetry, including *Still-Life-in-Verse, Daughter of Memory, 1001 Verses* (based on *Arabian Nights' Entertainment*), and *Coronation*. He has also served as editor of *Nova revija (The New Magazine)*, one of the most important political-cultural magazines in Slovenia.

SEAN O'BRIEN (b. 1952) lives in Newcastle upon Tyne. Among his many books are *Inferno: A Verse Version of Dante's Inferno, The Birds: A New Verse Version of Aristophanes' Birds, Cousin Coat: Selected Poems,* and *The Drowned Book*.

CONOR O'CALLAGHAN (b. 1968) grew up in Dundalk on the Irish border. He has published three books with Gallery Press and Wake Forest University Press. The most recent, *Fiction,* was a recommendation of the Poetry Book Society in London.

BRUNO K. ÖIJER (b. 1951) made his debut in 1973 with *Song for anarchy,* followed the next year by *Photographs of doom's smile* and *Vesuvius,* a group anthology. Since then he has published a novel, *Chivas Regal,* an LP, a CD, four film monologues, and several volumes of poetry. Known for his unique stage performances, he has won many awards for his work, including the Winter Prize and the Grand Prize of the Foundation of the Nine, Swedish Radio's Poetry Prize, and the Bellman Prize of the Swedish Academy.

KRISTÍN ÓMARSDÓTTIR (b. 1962) has published six books of poetry, including *a maid in an old restaurant,* where the poem "Closed Bridal Night" appeared. She has also published novels and short stories and written for the theater in Reykjavík. Some of her work has been translated and published in France, Sweden, and Finland.

TONNUS OOSTERHOF (b. 1953), born in Leiden, studied Dutch literature and psychology at the University of Groningen, and psychology at the Free University in Amsterdam; he subsequently worked as a school psychologist. In 1990 he made his debut with the poetry book *Farm Tiger,* for which he received the C. Buddingh' Award for the best debut collection of that year. Since then he has published nine poetry collections; among them, *{Robust Tongue Work} a radiant assembly* received the Jan Campert Prize, and *We saw ourselves changing into a small group of people* received the VSB Prize.

IMRE ORAVECZ (b. 1943) was born in Szajla, a village in northern Hungary. Among his books are *The Book of Hopi, When You Became She, Szajla,* and *The Ideal Day. When You Became She* is available in an English translation by Bruce Berlind.

LAURI OTONKOSKI (b. 1959) is a poet, musician, essayist, and music critic who has published seven collections of poems, essays, and a children's book. He was awarded the Nuori Suomi (Young Finland) Prize for literature in 1995, Yleisradio's (the equivalent of the BBC) Tanssiva Karhu (Dancing Bear) Prize in 1996, the Pekkanen Prize in 1999, and the Engel Prize of Church Art in 2001.

BERT PAPENFUSS (b. 1956) was born in Stavenhagen, East Germany, and currently lives in Berlin. A Prenzlauer Berg poet long known in the West, he has authored more than twenty books of poetry, prose, and translations. His more recent poetry volumes include *Rumbalotte Gedichte 1998–2002, Rumbalotte Continua, Agitation, Poems 1994–1998, Mors ex nihilo,* and *Grief.* He is the recipient of many awards for his work, including the 1988 N. C. Caser Prize, the F. C. Weiskopf Prize in 1991, and the Erich Fried Prize in 1998.

JEAN-BAPTISTE PARA (b. 1956) has published four collections of poetry and has translated Indian, Italian, and Russian poetry into French. He is the editor of the literary review *Europe* and copresents a poetry program for France Culture with André Velter. He has received the Prix Nelly Sachs and the Prix Laure Bataillon for translation, and the Prix Apollinaire in 2006 for *Hunger of the Shades.*

ALEXEI PARSHCHIKOV (b. 1955) was born in Kiev, studied at Stanford University, and currently divides his time between Cologne and Moscow. He rose to prominence as a poet in the 1980s.

DON PATERSON (b. 1963) was born in Dundee and lives in Kirriemuir, Scotland. He is poetry editor for the London publisher Picador and author of *The Book of Shadows, Landing Light,* and *The White Lie: New & Selected Poems,* among others.

CHUS PATO (María Xesús Pato Díaz) (b. 1955) was born in Ourense, Galicia, in the northwest corner of Spain. She teaches history and geography at a high school in Galicia and has published seven books of poetry, including *m-Talá* and *Charenton,* as well as a selection translated into Spanish by Irís Cochón: *A Ganges of Words.* A selection from *m-Talá* was published in Canada by Nomados in 2003. Chus Pato is a member of the Galician Popular Front, which favors independence for Galicia.

VERA PAVLOVA (b. 1963) was born in Moscow, where she currently lives. After studying for many years to be a composer, she began publishing poetry at the age of twenty and has currently published ten books of poems. She is the recipient of the prestigious Apollon Grigoriev Award.

ANDRAS PETÖCZ (b. 1959) was born in Budapest, where he studied Hungarian and history at the University of Budapest. A poet, editor, and one-time video producer, he is the author of two dozen books of poems, autobiographical prose, and poems for children. His poems have been translated into French, Polish, and English, and he has won several literary prizes.

JOSÉ MANUEL DEL PINO (b. 1958) has studied at the University of Malaga and Princeton University. The author of numerous works of poetry and literary criticism—including several scholarly books on Spanish cinema, Spanish modernism, and the avant-garde—he is professor of Spanish at Dartmouth College.

KATERINA PINOSOVÁ (b. 1973) is a poet, graphic artist, translator, and an active member of the Czecho-Slovak Surrealist Group. Her work in various media has been previously anthologized in the University of Texas Press anthology *Surrealist Women,* and has been published widely in both the Czech Republic and abroad. She writes in both English and Czech.

LYSANDROS PITHARAS (1960–1992) studied international relations at Sussex University and worked as a journalist in London. He also worked as an actor and director at Hampstead Theatre. He was one of the founders of the Cypriot Arts Forum in Britain. After his death from AIDS in 1992, his book *I Am the Twentieth Century* was published in Nicosia. He wrote in English.

DANA PODRACKÁ (b. 1954) is a former editor who now serves as an MP for the People's Party Movement in the Slovak Parliament. She has published five collections of her poetry, as well as seven books of essays and four children's books. *Forty Four,* a collection of her poems in English translation, was published in Ireland by Southword Editions in 2005.

SIMONA POPESCU (b. 1965), born in Codlea, Romania, graduated from the University of Bucharest, where she now teaches. Besides a novel and two books of essays, she has published four books of poetry: *Xylophone and Other Poems*; *Juventus*; *Night and Day*; and *Works in Green; or My Apology for Poetry*.

STEFFEN POPP (b. 1978) was born in East Germany. He studied German literature and philosophy in Dresden, Leipzig, and Berlin, where he has lived since 2001. He has published two collections of poetry: *Like Alps* and the epic project, *Ohrenberg or the Way There*. For both his poetry and his prose Popp has been awarded several prizes and fellowships in Germany and Austria, including the Heimrad Bäcker Förderpreis.

JEAN PORTANTE (b. 1950) was born in Differdange, Luxembourg, and now lives in Paris. He is the author of some thirty books, among them the poetry collections *Opened Closed*, *Effaçonner*, and *Point*, and *The Work of Shadows*. In 2003, he received both the Prix Mallarmé for his most recent collection of poems and the Grand Prix d'Automne of the Société des gens de lettres for the entirety of his work.

YURKO POZAYAK (b. 1957) is the pen name of Yuri Lysenko, who works as a Ukrainian diplomat. He won the Bu-Ba-Bu Prize in 1997.

SHEENAGH PUGH (b. 1950) lives in Cardiff and teaches at the University of Glamorgan. She is the author of several poetry collections, including *The Beautiful Lie*, *Stonelight*, and *The Movement of Bodies*.

FABIO PUSTERLA (b. 1957) was born in Mendrisio (Ticino) and lives in Lugano, where he teaches at the Liceo Cantonale. A prolific essayist, translator, and poet, he is on the editorial staff of the literary magazine *Idra*. Among his poetry collections are *A Concession to Winter*, winner of the Montale Prize and the Schiller Prize, *Things Without History*, *Danse Macabre*, and *Blood Stone*, which won the Schiller Prize in 2000.

VIOLETA RANGEL's official bio claims "she was born in Sevilla in 1968 but has spent most of her life in Barcelona." In actuality, "Violeta Rangel" is a heteronym of Manuel Moya, who was born in Fuenteheridos, Andalucía, in 1960, and who has created a distinct poetic style and identity separate from his own in the works of the "poet" Violeta Rangel. In addition to three collections "by Rangel"—*The Possession of the Earth*, *It's Nothing*, and most recently, in 2002, *Four Roses*—Moya has also published eight books of poetry under his own name.

IRINA RATUSHINSKAYA (b. 1954), born in Odessa, was imprisoned in Russia for her dissident activities and exiled from the country in 1986. She is the author of numerous collections of poetry and two memoirs.

DELIMIR REŠICKI (b. 1960) was born in Osijek. One of the leading Croatian poets today, he is the author of six books of poetry, as well as an editor of the daily newspaper *Glas Slavonije*. For his collection of poetry *Arrhythmia*, he received the Vladimir Nazor national award for the best literary work of 2006.

DENISE RILEY (b. 1948) teaches at the School of English and American Studies at the University of East Anglia. She is the author of several books of nonfiction as well as the poetry collections *Dry Air*, *Mop Mop Georgette: New and Selected Poems 1986–1993*, and *Selected Poems*.

ANA RISTOVIĆ (b. 1972), born in Belgrade, has published several books of poetry, and her work has been translated into numerous languages. She has published four collections of poetry for which she has received a number of awards, including the Branko's Award, Branko Miljković's Award, Igalo Book Fair Award for Poetry, and a German poetry award—Hubert Burda Preis. She is an editor of the multilingual review *Balcanis*.

JAN VOLKER RÖHNERT (b. 1976) was born in Gera, East Germany, and lives in Jena and Dresden. His poetry has been included in such anthologies as the annual *Jahrbuch der Lyrik* in 2003 and *Lyrik von Jetzt*. His own poetry collections include *Castle Ruins Blues* and *Devotion, Endless Cocoon*. He also publishes essays and translations of poetry (Robert Creeley, Christopher Edgar, Michel Deguy). He is the recipient of a 2003 Poetry Debut Prize of the Literary Colloquium Berlin and a 2003 Walter Dexel Stipendium from the city of Jena. His most recent book, *Metropolis. Poems,* appeared in 2007.

DAVIDE RONDONI (b. 1964), born in Forlì, is the founder and director of the Center for Contemporary Poetry at the University of Bologna. A translator of Rimbaud, Baudelaire, and Péguy, his own poetry collections include *The Time Café,* which won several literary prizes, *He Would Have Loved Anyone, and To See Your Face.*

PAUL DE ROUX (b. 1937) was born in Nîmes and now lives in Paris. Admired for the simplicity and purity of his poetry, he has published many collections. His translation of Keats's "Hyperion" was published in 1989. Other writings include a novel and several essays on painting.

VALÉRIE ROUZEAU (b. 1967) was born in the Nièvre. She is the author of a dozen collections of poems, including *Pas revoir,* which received the Prix des Découvreurs in 2000, and is in its sixth edition, and *Va où,* which received the Prix Tristan Tzara in 2002. She is also a translator, notably of the work of Sylvia Plath, about whom she has written a critical study.

KATEŘINA RUDČENKOVÁ (b. 1976) is a poet, fiction writer, and playwright who has published three collections of poetry and one collection of short fiction. She studied songwriting and screenwriting at Jaroslav Jerek's Conservatoire and European agrarian diplomacy at Czech Agriculture University, and presently lives in Prague, where she edits the online journal *Dobra Adresa*. Her poetry was awarded the 2003 Hubert Burda Preis for younger Eastern European poets, and appears in English in the Arc Publications anthology *A Fine Line: New Poetry from Eastern and Central Europe.*

EVA RUNEFELT (b. 1953) made her literary debut in 1975 as both a poet and a novelist. Since then she has published six more books of poetry, most recently *In a scattered now,* and *In the beast,* as well as the prize-winning collection of short stories *Time Arrested.* Her nonfiction includes essays on film and articles in the national press on contemporary Swedish art. She has received many prestigious awards for her poetry, among them the Bellman and Ferlin prizes. She lives in Stockholm.

ELISABETH RYNELL (b. 1954) grew up in Stockholm but spent a year in London and traveled to India before making her poetic debut with *Lyrical Suite etc. grumbling.* Since then she has published fiction, nonfiction, and six more books of poetry, most recently *In My Houses.* Her novel *To Mervas* is forthcoming from Archipelago Books in Victoria Häggblom's translation. The recipient of many additional literary awards, she teaches creative writing and is active in several Swedish authors' organizations.

BORIS RYZHII (1974–2001) committed suicide in 2001. His work has been translated into many European languages.

AMINA SAÏD (b. 1952) was born in Tunisia and now lives in Paris. She is the author of seven collections of poems and has written stories based on Tunisian folktales. She is also translator of several novels by the Filipino writer F. Sionil José.

LIANA SAKELLIOU (b. 1956) was born in Athens, studied English at the University of Athens, and received her PhD from Pennsylvania State University. Her books of poetry include *Touches in the Flow* and *Take Me Like a Photograph*; she has also edited and translated Greek volumes of Gary Snyder, Denise Levertov, and H.D. She has received two Fulbright Awards and has been a visiting fellow at University of the California–Berkeley, Northwestern University, and Princeton University.

FIONA SAMPSON (b. 1963) has published fourteen books of poetry, philosophy of language, and writing process, including *Common Prayer* (shortlisted for the T.S. Eliot Prize). She has won the Newdigate Prize and the Zlaten Prtsen (Macedonia) and is the editor of *Poetry Review*.

HÅKAN SANDELL (b. 1962), from Malmö, Sweden, made his poetic debut in 1981 with *Cathy* and has published numerous collections of poetry since, including *The Midnight Fresco, The Oslo Passion,* and, most recently, *Sketches for a Century*. He has also published volumes of translations, essays on "retrogardism" and tradition, and art criticism. His work has been translated into English, German, Hungarian, and Spanish. Since 1992 he has lived outside Sweden, in Copenhagen, County Cork, and Oslo, where he still lives.

EVELYN SCHLAG (b. 1952) was born in Waidhofen an der Ybbs, Austria, where she lives today. She has written several poetry volumes, including *Do You Need Sleep Tonight, The Talent of My Wife,* and *Relocation of the Heart*. Among her many public recognitions, the novelist and poet has received the Bremer Förderpreis (1988), the Anton Wildgans Prize (1997), and the Otto Stoessl Prize (1998). She has also been short-listed for the Aristeion Prize (1998).

RAOUL SCHROTT (b. 1964), born on a ship between South America and Europe, grew up in Tunisia and Landeck, Austria, and today lives in Ireland. A prolific novelist, translator, and poet, his recent volumes include *White Book, Tropics,* and *Hotels,* as well as the novella *The Desert of Lop* (published in English translation by Picador), which skirts the line between poetry and prose. Among numerous honors, he has received the 1995 Leonce and Lena Prize, the 1996 Berlin Literature Prize, and the 1999 Peter Huchel Poetry Prize.

OLGA SEDAKOVA (b. 1949) was born in Moscow and currently teaches in the Philosophy Department of Moscow State University. She is the recipient of the Paris Prize and the Shiller Fund Award and her work has been widely translated. A collection, *Poems and Elegies,* was published by Bucknell University Press in 2003, translated into English by Slava I. Yastrenski.

LUTZ SEILER (b. 1963) was born in Gera, Thuringia (East Germany), and lives today in Berlin. He is founder and coeditor of the literary journal *moosbrand*. Among his books of poetry are *Forty Kilometers Night, Pitch and Blende,* and *Touched/Guided*. An award-winning poet since 1999, most recently he has received the Berlin Academy of Arts 2006 Literature Förderungspreis, the 2004 Bremer Literature Prize from the Rudolf Alexander Schröder Foundation, and the 2003 Ernst Meister Prize for Poetry.

MARCIN SENDECKI (b. 1967), was born in Gdańsk; he was an early associate of the magazine *BruLion,* which published his first collection, *From On High*. He studied medicine and sociology at Warsaw University, and he is currently managing editor of the weekly magazine *Przekrój*. With Marcin Swietlicki and Marcin Baran, he edited the poetry anthology *The Long Goodbye. Tribute to Raymond Chandler.* His collections include *Plots, Museum of Banners of the People's Movement,* and *Jump Ditch.*

ZAFER ŞENOCAK (b. 1961) grew up in Istanbul and Munich and currently lives in Berlin. He is the author of four essay collections, including *Atlas of a Tropical Germany,* translated into English by Leslie Adelson; a prose trilogy; several translations from Turkish; and seven volumes of poetry, most recently *Passage: Selected Poems 1980–2005.* In 2008, a translation of his poetry will appear with Zephyr Press under the title *Door Languages.*

VICTAR SHALKEVICH (b. 1959) was born in Grodno. In 1980, he graduated from Belarus State Institute of Theater and worked in the Grodno Drama Theater for many years. In addition to being a poet and theater actor, he also plays lead roles in films and is known as a singer whose albums have gained him awards and popular recognition in Belarus and Poland.

JO SHAPCOTT (b. 1953) teaches at Royal Holloway College, University of London. Her poetry books include *Transformers, Her Book: Poems 1988–1998, My Life Asleep, Phrase Book,* and *Electroplating the Baby.*

TATYANA SHCHERBINA (b. 1954), born in Moscow, published five collections of poems in samizdat before 1989. She has worked for Radio Liberty, and her work has been translated into many European languages. After living in France for a number of years, she currently lives in Moscow.

ELENA SHVARTS (b. 1948) was one of the best-known poets in the Leningrad underground culture of the 1970s and 1980s. The author of numerous collections of verse, she also writes prose. Her work has been widely translated.

HELENA SINERVO (b. 1961) published her first collection of poems, *Untold,* in 1994. Since then she has published six more, including *The Blue Anglia, Pairs of Darkness,* and *Human Worth.* Sinervo has translated into Finnish poems by Elizabeth Bishop and Yves Bonnefoy and has written lyrics for Liisa Lux's debut album.

KARL MARTIN SINIJÄRV (b. 1971) published his first collection of poetry at the age of seventeen, and to date has authored six poetry collections. The most recent is *Artutart & 39,* which in 2002 received the Poetry Award of the Cultural Endowment of Estonia.

DAN SOCIU (b. 1978) was born in Botoşani, Romania. His first book, *jars with tight lids, money for another week* received the National Prize for Poetry Mihai Eminescu debut award. In 2004, *brother flea* appeared, and in 2005, *eXcessive songs,* which won the Romanian Writers' Union Prize for the best poetry book of the year. Sociu works in Bucharest for the venerable Romanian Book Publishing House, now a subsidiary of Polirom Publishers.

DAMIR ŠODAN (b. 1964), from Split, Croatia, majored in English language and literature, and history, at the Faculty of Philosophy at Zagreb University. An important translator of English-language poets into Croatian and editor of the Feral Tribune Publishing House, he has published two critically acclaimed volumes of poetry, *Sound Changes* and *The Middle World.*

MARTIN SOLOTRUK (b. 1970) was born in Bratislava and holds a PhD in American poetry from Comenius University in Bratislava, where he now teaches. His first book of poetry, *Silent Wars,* won the Slovak Literary Fund Best Debut Award in 1997, and his second collection, *Mletie,* was published in 2001. He has translated many English-language poets into Slovak, including Ted Hughes, John Ashbery, Seamus Heaney, and Charles Simic.

PIOTR SOMMER (b. 1948) was born in Otwock, near Warsaw. He studied English at the University of Warsaw and now edits the Polish journal *World Literature.* He has taught at several American universities, and has been a fellow of the International Writing Program at the University of Iowa and the National Humanities Center in North Carolina. His poetry collections include *What we're remembered by, A Subsequent World, Lyrical Factor and Other Poems,* and *New Relations of Words,* and he has also published essay collections and an anthology of translations from English. In 2005, Wesleyan University Press published *Continued,* a collection of his poems in English.

EWA SONNENBERG (b. 1967) has published seven books of poetry, including *Hazard,* which received a Georg Trakl Award in 1995, and, recently, *Pisane na piasku/Written on Sand,* a bilingual collection of zen-inspired poems. She has also published a quasi tale, *The Queen's Page,* and a collection of short prose, *The Madman's Encyclopedia.* In 1998 she was the *Kultura* magazine Fellow for Independent Art in Paris. She's on the faculty of Jagiellonian University's Literature and Fine Arts Studies. She holds an MA degree in music and is currently completing her second master's in philosophy at Jagiellonian University.

ANDRZEJ SOSNOWSKI (b. 1959) was born in Warsaw. A poet, translator, and essayist, he studied and later taught in the University of Warsaw's English department. His collections include *Life on the Korea, Nouvelles impressions d'Amérique, A Season on Hel, Lodgings, Convoy: An Opera,* and *Zoom.* He has translated many American and English Poets, including Ezra Pound, Ronald Firbank, and Edmund White, and he has received several literary prizes, among them the Kościelski Foundation Prize and the Kazimiera Iłłakowiczówna Prize.

ERIC SPINOY (b. 1960) was born in Aalst, Belgium. Among his poetry collections are *The hunters in the snow, Bad wolves, L,* and *I.* Together with Dirk van Bastelaere and Patrick Peeters, he is editor of the journal *Freespace, Nieuwzuid.* He teaches modern Dutch literature at the University of Liège, Belgium.

SAVIANA STĂNESCU (b. 1967), born in Bucharest, Romania, is a poet and playwright and the author of three books of poetry in Romanian: *Love on Barbed Wire, Advice for Housewives and Muses,* and *Outcast.* Diary of Clone, translated with Adam J. Sorkin, appeared in 2004 from Spuyten Duyvil/Meeting Eyes Bindery. Her plays have been produced in Bucharest, Paris, Vienna, and New York, by troupes including the Lark Theatre Company and La MaMa Theatre. Stănescu won a Fulbright to NYU in 2001–2002. In the fall of 2006, Vinea Publishing released her new book of poems in English, *Google Me!*

ALEŠ ŠTEGER (b. 1973) studied comparative literature and German at the University of Ljubljana and is now widely considered one of Slovenia's foremost young poets. His books include the poetry collections *Kashmir* and *Protuberances,* and a prose book on Peru—*January in the Middle of Summer.* He lives in Ljubljana, Slovenia.

STEPHANOS STEPHANIDES (b. 1949) was born in Trikomo, now in Turkish territory. He was raised and educated in the UK, but returned to Cyprus in 1991 to serve as a founding member of the University of Cyprus. Since then, he has been active in establishing links between Greek Cypriot and Turkish Cypriot poets. He is the author of *Blue Moon in Rajashthan* and a literary-cultural study, *Translating Kali's Feast: The Goddess in Indo-Caribbean Ritual and Fiction.* He writes in English.

MILE STOJIĆ (b. 1955) was born in Dragicina in Bosnia-Herzegovina and lives in Sarajevo. He is a prominent Bosnian and Croatian poet, essayist, and journalist. He has published numerous poetry books and received many prestigious awards for his literary work in Bosnia and Croatia, including, most recently, the Goran's Wreath award for his valuable contribution to Croatian contemporary verse.

ULF STOLTERFOHT (b. 1963), born in Stuttgart, Germany, now resides in Berlin. A formally steeped experimental poet, he has been writing a series of poems under the title *jargons,* collected in two volumes *jargons X-XVIII* and *jargons I-IX.* Much acclaimed since 1994, he has been awarded the 2005 Anna Seghers Prize, the 2003 Ernst Meister Literature Förderpreis from the City of Hagen, and the 2001 Christine Lavant Poetry Prize.

EDVIN SUGAREV (b. 1953) was a dissident samizdat publisher in the 1980s who became a prominent political figure during Bulgaria's transition toward democracy in 1989, and served as a member of the Bulgarian parliament and ambassador to Mongolia and India. In 2005, Ivy Press Princeton published a collection of his poems in translation, *Secret Senses.* A second translated volume, *Kaleidoscope,* is forthcoming.

DARYA SUKHOVEI (b. 1977) graduated from St. Petersburg University. She is the author of two collections of poetry.

ANNI SUMARI (b. 1965) has published nine books, primarily of poetry. In 1998, she was awarded the Dancing Bear Prize from Yleisradio (Finland's equivalent of the BBC). She has also worked as a translator, translating Beckett and Robert Antoni among others. Her poems also appear in English translation in *The Other Side of Landscape: An Anthology of Nordic Poetry.*

DARIUSZ SUSKA (b. 1968) was born in Silesia and studied physics at Wrocław University. He has worked as a journalist for the national newspaper *Gazeta Wyborcza* and is now a scriptwriter for the TV channel TVN in Warsaw. He has published four volumes of poetry: *Things that were the world, DB 6160221, All Our Dear Ones in the Grave,* and *All Covered in Sand.*

MARCIN ŚWIETLICKI (b. 1961) was born in Lublin and studied at Jagiellonian University in Krakow. In 1995 he founded the post-punk band Świetlicki, to whose accompaniment he sometimes recites his poetry. He has received a number of awards for his work, including the Trakl Prize and the Kościelski Foundation Prize, and he has been nominated several times for the prestigious NIKE Prize. His collections include: *Cold countries, Schism, Third Half, 37 Poems on Vodka and Cigarettes,* and *Songs of a Profaner.*

ÁKOS SZILAGYI (b. 1950) was born in Budapest and studied Hungarian and Russian at the University of Budapest. He is a poet, translator, essayist, editor, literary historian, and an expert on Russian culture and politics. He specializes in what is called "sounding poetry," or perhaps a "poetry of noises," i.e., a singsong repetition of meaningless and/or onomatopoetic words. The recipient of several awards, he also writes "normal" poetry and poetry for children, and has published two dozen books of poetry, essays, and criticism.

ARTUR SZLOSAREK (b. 1968), born in Krakow, is a poet and translator from German. He studied Polish literature in Krakow and comparative literature at the University of

Bonn, and he currently lives in Berlin. His collections include *Written Poems, Various Poems, Ashes and Honey, Camera obscura, Letter to the Wall,* and *Under a Foreign Sky.* He has received the Kościelski Foundation Prize and was nominated for the NIKE Prize.

NOVICA TADIĆ (b. 1949) was born in a small village in Montenegro and has lived in Belgrade for most of his life. The author of numerous collections, he is one of the most celebrated Serbian poets today. *Night Mail: Selected Poems,* a book of his poems translated into English by Charles Simic, is available from Oberlin College Press.

PIA TAFDRUP (b. 1952), from Denmark, published her first book in 1980. She has published many books of poetry, a volume of poetics, and two plays; two of her books have appeared in English: *Spring Tide,* translated by Anne Born, and *Queen's Gate,* translated by David McDuff. In 1989, she was inducted into the Danish Academy; in 1999, she won the Nordic Council Prize for Literature; and in 2006, the Swedish Academy's Nordic Prize.

HABIB TENGOUR (b. 1947) was born in Mostagenem, Algeria. A poet and anthropologist, he divides his time between France and Algeria. His most recent collection of poems, *Etat de choses (State of Affairs)* was published in 2006, and Karthala Editions has just released a critical book on his work.

SIGURBJÖRG THRASTARDÓTIR (b. 1973) is the author of three poetry collections, four theater pieces, and a novel. She is also a columnist for the Icelandic newspaper *Morgunbladid.* She lives and works on the road, and in Reykjavkik.

ILPO TIIHONEN (b. 1950) is the author of four books of poems: *Yes ketchup!, A Short Ode to Everything: Selected Poems 1975–2000, Eros,* and *Largo.* His awards include two Government Awards in Literature and the Dancing Bear Prize.

EUGENIUSZ TKASZYSZYN-DYCKI (b. 1962) was born in Wólka Krowicka, studied Polish literature at the Marie Curie-Skłodowska University in Lublin, and worked as a schoolteacher before taking up an editorial position at the literary journal *Tworczosc* in Warsaw. His books of poetry include *Nenia and Other Poems, Peregrinary, A Young Man of Impeccable Manners,* and *Guide for the Homeless Regardless of Place of Residence,* as well as a selection of his work from 1987–1999 published as *Stone Full of Nourishment.* He has been awarded the Kazimiera Iłłakowiczówna Prize and the Barbara Sadowska Prize.

CHRISTIAN UETZ (b. 1963) lives in Zurich. He is the author of, among other volumes, *Don San Juan* and *The Constellation Sings.* He is also active on the spoken word and performance poetry circuit and has recorded his work on two CDs.

TOR ULVEN (1953–1995), from Norway, published his first book of poems in 1977; five more followed, including one published posthumously, and then his collected poems (2000). He also published seven books in other genres: fiction, memoirs, and essays. He was the recipient of the Hartvig Kiran Memorial Prize (1990), the Obstfelder Prize (1993), and the Dobloug Prize of the Swedish Academy (1995).

JOZEF URBAN (1964–1999) was a poet, journalist, songwriter, and literary editor who was considered one of the most talented writers in what's become known as the "Barbarian Generation" of Slovak literature. His collections, starting with *Small, Furious Robinson* (1985) and *The Book of the Half-Dead* (1992), won numerous literary prizes. Urban was killed in a car accident at the age of thirty-four.

KIRMEN URIBE (b. 1970) is from Ondarroa, in Spain's Basque Country. After receiving his university degree in Basque philology, he studied comparative literature in Italy. He currently writes a weekly column for the Basque-language daily *Berria,* and has published essays, stories, comics, translations, and a children's book. In collaboration with the musicians Mikel Urdangarin and Bingen Mendizabal, he has worked on multimedia projects, which have been documented in the CD-books *Bar Puerto* and *Too Old, Too Small, Maybe.* His first collection of poems, *Meanwhile Take My Hand,* won Spain's 2001 Critic's Prize, and has been translated into Spanish, Portuguese, and English.

RAPHAEL URWEIDER (b. 1974) was born in Bern, Switzerland, where he continues to live. He has published two collections of poetry, *The Opposite of Flesh* and *Lights in Menlo Park.* An active musician, he also plays and composes music for stage and has appeared several times with the Bern hip-hop group LdeeP. Among the several awards he has received for his poetry are the 2001 Bremen Literature Prize Förderpreis and the 1999 Leonce and Lena Prize.

ALEXANDRU VAKULOVSKI (b. 1978) was born in Antoneşti/Suvarov (now called Ştefan Vodă), Basarabia, in what is now the Republic of Moldova. With his brother Mihail, he is the founding editor of the prominent web journal *Tiuk!* A poet, essayist, writer of fiction, and translator, he has published widely in Romania and Moldova. He has published two books of poetry, *ecstasy* and *Oedipus: King of Freud's Mother,* as well as a play, *The Break,* and *Cunty,* a widely popular novel.

NILS ASLAK VALKEAPÄÄ (1943–2001), from Sápmi, was a prolific musician, artist, and poet who served as a cultural ambassador of the Sami people. Three of his books have appeared in English: *Greetings from Lappland: The Sami, Europe's forgotten people,* translated by Beverley Wahl; *Trekways of the Wind,* illustrated by the author and translated by Ralph Salisbury, Lars Nordström, and Harald Gaski; and *The Sun, My Father,* translated by Ralph Salisbury, Lars Nordström, and Harald Gaski.

ANDRÉ VELTER (b. 1945) was born in the Ardennes; now he makes his home in Paris, where he is an editor at Gallimard and director of the Poésie Gallimard pocket paperback series. A poet, essayist, and radio journalist, he divides his time between voyages to India, Afghanistan, Tibet, Mexico, and elsewhere, and the promotion of world poetries in France. He is the author of fifteen books of poems and six books of essays. *Extreme Love,* published by Gallimard in 2000, is a series of elegies for his life partner, the mountain climber Chantal Mauduit, killed in an avalanche in the Himalayas.

ELO VIIDING (b. 1974), born in Tallinn, is the third poet in her family; both her father and grandfather were important and influential Estonian poets. Elo Viiding is the author of several books of poetry, include *Axis, The Casket's Closeness, In the Light of Debt,* and *First Wish.*

HARIS VLAVIANOS (b. 1957) was born in Rome and grew up in Athens. He was educated in philosophy at the University of Bristol and in politics at Oxford. He is the editor of the influential journal *Poiisi* and the literary publishing house Nefeli, and has translated Whitman, Pound, Stevens, and Ashbery, among others. His six collections of poetry include *Adieu, The Angel of History,* and *Afterwards the End of Omorphia.* He writes poems in both Greek and English.

PIERRE VOÉLIN (b. 1949) grew up in Courgenay in northwestern Switzerland and studied art history and literature at the universities of Geneva and Freiburg. He lives today in Nyon, where he teaches French language and literature in a lycée. His collections of poems include *On Brief Death, Slow Passages of the Shade, Calm Wood, Word and Famine, The Light and Not the Others,* and *In the Millenial Eye.*

MARJOLEINE DE VOS (b. 1957) studied Dutch literature at the University of Amsterdam, and she is currently an editor at the Dutch newspaper, *NRC Handelsblad,* for which she writes mainly on art, literature, and cuisine, and has a biweekly column in the opinion section. Her first poetry collections, *Seal Please,* was nominated for the 2000 VSB Poetry Prize. In the same year a selection of her columns, *Now and Always: Reflections,* was published. Her second collection, *Snow Cat,* appeared in 2003.

JAN WAGNER (b. 1971) was born in Hamburg and lives in Berlin. Poet, translator, and critic, his collections of poetry include *A Trial Drill in the Sky* and *Guericke's Sparrow.* For his 2004 translation of James Tate's poetry, *The Wrong Way Home,* he received the 1999 Translation Prize from the City of Hamburg. Among the most recent accolades for his poetry are the Alfred Gruber Award (2004), the Mondsee Poetry Award, the Anna Seghers Award (2004) and the Ernst Meister Award for Poetry (2005).

ELISABETH WANDELER-DECK (b. 1939) was born in Zurich, where she runs her own gestalt analysis practice. Poet and musician, she routinely works with other musicians and composers on her own texts. She has published several poetry collections, among them *Hanging . . . , contro-bond,* and *contro-cantos.* Since 1990, she has received several awards and grants from the City and Canton of Luzerne, the Canton of Zurich, the Swiss Cultural Foundation Pro Helvetica and the Cassinelli Vogel Foundation.

PETER WATERHOUSE (b. 1956) was born in Berlin and lives in Vienna. Since 1975, he has published numerous theater pieces, critical essays, and poems. Among his books of poetry are *passim* and *Prospero's Land.* Also a prolific translator from Italian and English, he has translated the work of Seamus Heaney, Michael Hamburger, Andrea Zanzotto, and Biagio Marin, among many others. In 1994, he was awarded the Förderungspreis from the Austrian State Arts and Education Ministry; in 1993, the European Poetry Prize from the Münster International Poetry conference; and the Manuskript Prize in 1989.

ADAM WIEDEMANN (b. 1967), born in Krotoszyn, is a poet, prose writer, and music critic. He studied Polish literature at Jagiellonian University in Krakow and did graduate work there in literature and musicology. His poetry collections include *Male, Animal Fables, Starter, Cream Cakes,* and *Calypso,* which was nominated for the 2004 NIKE Prize.

NACHOEM M. WIJNBERG (b. 1961) studied law and economics in Amsterdam and received a doctorate in management from Erasmus University in Rotterdam. He is currently professor of management at the University of Amsterdam. Since the publication of his first book, *The Simulation of Creation,* he has published eleven volumes of poetry and four novels, and has been the recipient of the Herman Gorterprijs for the collection *Gifts.* He has also received the Paul Snoek Poetry Prize for *Birds,* and his collection *First This Then That* was nominated for the prestigious VSB Prize. A selection of his work, *From 10,* appeared in 2007.

MAGNUS WILLIAM-OLSSON (b. 1960), born in Bromma, is a poet, literary critic, and translator who has published seven volumes of poetry, three books of essays on poetry, and a book of autobiographical short stories. He has translated poetry from ancient and modern Greek (Sappho and Cavafy), Spanish (Antonio Gamoneda and Concho García), and Danish (Pia Tafdrup) into Swedish. His new and collected poems is called *The moment for Pindar is a small space in time.*

ØYSTEIN WINGAARD WOLF (b. 1958), from Norway, published his first book in 1983. He has since published some twenty-five books: mainly poetry, but also several novels and a children's book. He has also been active as a songwriter and cabaret singer; he issued his first CD, *Møt meg på halvveien [Meet Me Halfway]*, in 1998.

ULJANA WOLF (b. 1979) was born in Berlin. Her first book of poems, *kochanie ich habe brot gekauft* won the 2006 Peter-Huchel-Preis and the Dresdner Lyrikpreis.

ROGER WOLFE (b. 1962) was born in Westerham, Kent (UK), and has lived in Spain since 1966. He has published nine poetry collections, including *Talking about Painting with a Blind Man, Messages in Broken Bottles, Five Years in Bed, The Invention: Selected Poems,* and *Art in the Era of Consumption.* He has also published five collections of prose fiction and essays.

OKSANA ZABUZHKO (b. 1960), born in Kyiv, holds a PhD in the philosophy of arts and works as an associate scholar for the Institute of Philosophy of the Ukrainian Academy of Sciences. She is also Distinguished Professor of Creative Writing at Kyiv Shevchenko University. In 1994, she was a Fulbright Fellow to the U.S. Today, she is the most famous writer in Ukraine, thanks to her autobiographical novel, *Field Research in Ukrainian Sex.* She is also the author of several widely translated collections of poetry.

ANKA ŽAGAR (b. 1954), born in Zamost, Croatia, graduated in Croatian and comparative literature at the University of Zagreb, and currently works as a librarian. Among the most acclaimed of Croatia's poets, she has published six volumes of poetry.

BENJAMIN ZEPHANIAH (b. 1958) is a novelist, poet, and playwright. He grew up in Jamaica and Birmingham, England. Among his many books are *Gansta Rap, Too Black, Too Strong,* and *Refugee Boy.*

SERHIY ZHADAN (b. 1974), the author of eight books of poetry, was born in the Lyhansk region in eastern Ukraine. Generally considered the best poet of his generation, he lives in Kharkiv and writes poetry and prose.

VISAR ZHITI (b. 1952) was born in Durrës, Albania, and after college began teaching in the town of Kukës. In 1973, when he had just submitted his first poetry collection for publication, his work was suddenly denounced and in 1979 he was arrested and sentenced to thirteen years in prison. He was released in 1987, and in 1991–1994 he lived in Italy, Germany and the United States before returning to Albania after the fall of Albanian communism. Zhiti's first collection of poems was published in 1993, and he has subsequently published several more volumes, including a translation of *The Condemned Apple,* published in English in 2005 by Green Integer and translated by Robert Elsie.

MUSTAFA ZIYALAN (b. 1959) graduated from the medical school at the University of Istanbul, and for a number of years worked as a general practitioner and coroner in rural Anatolia. He has resided in the United States, where he works as a doctor, since 1990. His works include *Nigger of New York, Between Yesterday and Tomorrow,* and the book of short stories *Water Cats.*

UROŠ ZUPAN (b. 1963) grew up in Trbovlje, Slovenia, and graduated in comparative literature from the University of Ljubljana. He is the author of eight books of poetry, most recently *Oil and Locomotives*. He has received numerous awards for his work, and has translated a number of poets, including Yehuda Amichai and John Ashbery, into Slovenian.

VIKTAR ŽYBUL (b. 1978) lives and works in Belarus. He is the author of four volumes of poetry, and his work has been published abroad in Germany, the Czech Republic, and several other countries.

ABOUT THE TRANSLATORS

ED ADAMS (Polish) is one of the principal translators of Piotr Sommer's *Things to Translate*.

DONALD ADAMSON (Finnish) is a poet and translator lecturing in Finland. He has translated poems for *How to Address the Fog: XXV Finnish Poems 1978–2002* and cofounded the Scottish arts magazine *Markings*. His poem "Fause Prophets," which in 1999 won the Herald Millenniun Poetry Competition, is buried in a time capsule under the walls of the Scottish Poetry Library.

RICHARD ADANG (Estonian) is a poet from Seattle, Washington. He was a member of the U.S. Peace Corps in Estonia and taught at Rapla Ühisgümnaasium. In Estonia, he has published a collection of his own poems: *The Light in Estonia in 2001*.

AMMIEL ALCALAY (Bosnian) has recently cotranslated Shimon Ballas's *Outcast*. Among his own recent books are *Scrapmetal: Work in Progress and From the Warring Factions*.

EUGENIJUS ALIŠANKA (Lithuanian) is also a poet whose work appears in this anthology. His biography is on page 331.

STEFANIA ALLEN (Slovak) is, with James-Sutherland Smith, the cotranslator of *Not Waiting for Miracles,* the first anthology of contemporary Slovak poets to be published in English.

RADU ANDRIESCU (Romanian) is also a poet whose work appears in this anthology. His biography is on page 332.

LJUBICA ARSOVSKA (Macedonian) has recently translated (with Peggy Reid) Lidija Dimkovska's *Do Not Awaken Them with Hammers.* She is editor in chief of the quarterly *Kulturen Zivot,* the leading cultural magazine in Macedonia, and translator of numerous other books, plays, and poems.

JOHN ASHBERY (Polish) was born in Rochester, New York, in 1927. He is the author of more than twenty books of poetry. A former chancellor of the Academy of American Poets, Ashbery is currently the Charles P. Stevenson, Jr., Professor of Languages and Literature at Bard College.

VYT BAKAITIS (Lithuanian) is an American translator, editor, and poet born in Lithuania and living in New York City. His most significant collection of poetry is *City Country.*

GREGORY BALL (Flemish) studied graphic design and art teaching and moved to Flanders in 1977. After working in the theater, he now translates Dutch to English in the field of arts and culture.

BRIAN BARKER (Spanish) studied at Virginia Commonwealth University, George Mason University, and the University of Houston, where he received an Academy of American Poets Prize and several poetry fellowships. His collection *The Animal Gospels* won the Editors' Prize at Tupelo Press. He is assistant professor at Murray State University.

JUDITH BAUMEL (Italian) is the author of *The Weight of Numbers* and *Now.* She is associate professor of English and director of creative writing at Adelphi University.

FRANK BERGON (Spanish) is a novelist and professor of English at Vassar College. His novels include *Wild Game, The Temptations of St. Ed & Brother S*, and *Shoshone Mike*. He also edited the Penguin Nature Classics edition of *The Journals of Lewis and Clark*. He is currently writing a novel set in Chiapas, Mexico.

HOLLY ST. JOHN BERGON (Spanish) is a poet and a professor of English at Dutchess Community College in Poughkeepsie, New York. Her poems have appeared in several journals and anthologies, including *Ploughshares, College English, Pequod, Terra Nova, Travelers' Tales*, and *Prayers for a Thousand Years*.

BRUCE BERLIND (Hungarian) has published a dozen books as author, coauthor, translator, or editor. His most recent are *Charon's Ferry: Fifty Poems of Gyula Illyés*. His poems, translations, essays, and reviews have appeared in numerous journals, including *Poetry, Kenyon Review, New Letters, Amercan Poetry Review, Grand Street, Partisan Review*, and *Paris Review*. For his translations of contemporary Hungarian poetry he has received the Hungarian PEN Memorial Medal. He is Dana Professor Emeritus of English at Colgate University.

ADRIA BERNARDI (Italian) received the 2007 Raiziss/De Palchi Translation Award from the American Academy of Poets to complete work on a translation of Raffaello Baldini's poetry, *Small Talk*. Her novel, *Openwork*, was published in 2007.

CINZIA SARTINI BLUM (Italian) is associate professor of Italian at the University of Iowa. Her publications include *Rewriting the Journey: Figures of Subjectivity in Progress*; *The Other Modernism: F. T. Marinetti's Futurist Fiction of Power*; *Contemporary Italian Women Poets: A Bilingual Anthology* (in collaboration with Lara Trubowitz); and a translation of Carlo Michelstaedter's *Persuasione e rettorica* (in collaboration with Russell Valentino and David Depew).

JAMES BRASFIELD (Ukrainian) teaches at Pennsylvania State University's English Department. A Fulbright Scholar to Ukraine in 1993–1994, his translations have appeared widely and won such accolades as the PEN Center Award for Literature in Translation.

ALEXANDRA BÜCHLER (Czech) is the founding director of Literature Across Frontiers, a program of international literary exchange and policy debate based at the University of Wales. She has translated over twenty-five works, including books by authors such as J. M. Coetzee, David Malouf, Jean Rhys, Janice Galloway, and Rhea Galanaki into Czech. She has also edited and cotranslated a number of anthologies, including *A Fine Line: New Poetry from Eastern and Central Europe*.

UKZENEL BUÇPAPA (Albanian) is an Albanian writer and translator living in Tirana, Albania. His translations into Albanian include "The Waste Land" and "Howl," as well as poems by Rudyard Kipling, Robert Frost, Ezra Pound, Octavio Paz, and Yehuda Amichai. In 1992, he was a Fulbright Scholar and resident at the Iowa International Writers Program. His books include *My Daughter Speaks, Weeps, and Laughs with Chez Aba* and *Grey Days*.

EDWARD CAREY (Polish) was born in 1970 in England. Five of his plays have been produced in London, Romania, and Lithuania. He has also worked as a set designer and illustrator. His first novel, *Observatory Mansions*, was published in 2001. He lives in London.

KEVIN CAREY (Russian) is a poet and translator. He was born in 1952 in Ohio and educated at Williams College and Georgetown University. For some years he was a member of the U.S. diplomatic corps then, later, worked for the church in Jerusalem.

ILIJA ČAŠULE (Macedonian) is a professor of linguistics at Macquarie University in Australia. In addition to publications in linguistics, he has edited and translated (with Thomas Shapcott) *Island on Land,* an anthology of Macedonian poetry published by Macquarie University Press.

INARA CEDRINS (Latvian) is an artist, writer, and translator. She edited an issue of the online magazine *Omega* featuring Latvian poets (accessible at www.howlingdogpress .com).

WAYNE CHAMBLISS (Russian) has published work in *Jubilat, Fence, Germ, Drunken Boat,* and many other publications.

VITALY CHERNETSKY (Ukrainian) teaches Slavic and comparative literature at Miami University of Ohio. He has coedited the anthology *Crossing Centuries: The New Generation in Russian Poetry.*

DAVID CONNOLLY (Greek) is associate professor of translation studies at the Aristotle University of Thessaloniki. He has translated over twenty-five books of works by leading twentieth-century Greek poets and novelists. His translations have won awards in Greece, the UK, and the U.S.

HELEN CONSTANTINE (French) has translated *Mademoiselle de Maupin* by Theophile Gautier and *Dangerous Liaisons* by Choderlos de Laclos for Penguin, and *Paris Tales* for Oxford University Press. She coedits the international poetry magazine *Modern Poetry in Translation* with David Constantine.

ALFRED CORN (French) is the author of nine books of poetry, including *Contradictions* (2000) and *Stake* (1999), a novel, *Part of His Story,* and *The Poem's Heartbeat,* a book on English prosody, to be reissued in 2008.

SEAN COTTER (Romanian) is a widely published translator of Romanian literature into English, appearing in both Romanian and American journals and several books: Nichita Danilov's *Second-Hand Souls,* Liliana Ursu's *Goldsmith Market,* and Nicolae Tzone's *Balkan Aphrodite,* translated with Ioana Ieronim. A critic and theorist of translation and a specialist in translations by Ezra Pound, T. S. Eliot, and Lucian Blaga, Cotter is assistant professor of literature and translation studies at the University of Texas at Dallas.

PETER COVINO (Italian) is a regional editor for this anthology. His biography appears on page 381.

BILL COYLE (Swedish) is an American poet and translator living in Boston, Massachusetts. His poetry has appeared in *The Hudson Review, The New Republic,* and *Poetry,* and his translations in *Ars Interpres* and *PN Review.* His first collection of poems, *The God of This World to His Prophet,* won the New Criterion Poetry Prize and was published in 2006 by Ivan R. Dee.

ANNA CROWE (Catalan) is a poet, translator, and creative writing tutor living in St. Andrews, Scotland. She has been artistic director of the annual StAnza poetry festival in St. Andrews. Her first collection, *Skating Out of the House,* was published in 1997 by Peterloo Poets, followed by *A Secret History of Rhubarb* and *Punk with Dulcimer.* Some of her poems have been translated into Catalan and were included in the collection *L'ànima del teixidor.*

CHAD DAVIDSON (Italian) is a regional editor for this anthology. His biography appears on page 381.

SARAH DEATH (Swedish) has translated into English works of Swedish writers of various eras, including Fredrika Bremer, Victoria Benedictsson, Kerstin Ekman, Sven Lindqvist, Ellen Mattson, Inger Edelfeldt, and Carl-Johan Vallgren. In the UK she has twice won the George Bernard Shaw Prize for translation from Swedish and is also the editor of *Swedish Book Review*.

ERICA JOHNSON DEBELJAK (Slovenian) is a writer and translator from Slovenia. She is author of the recently published *The Poet and I*, on the life of Slovenian poet Srecko Kosovel. She contributes regularly (short fiction and essays) to American, European, and Slovenian literary journals. She is translator of Dane Zajc's *Barren Harvest: Selected Poems* and lives in Ljubljana.

JENNIFER K. DICK (French) is the author of *Fluorescence* and *Retina/Rétine*, and has translated poems by Rémi Boutthonier, Christophe Lamiot Enos, and Albane Gellé among others. She is a doctoral candidate at Paris III, where she teaches at the École Polytechnique and WICE, and co-organizes the IVY writers reading series.

ERIC DICKENS (Estonian) is a full-time literary translator from the Estonian. His recent translations of the novels *Treading Air* by the leading Estonian author Jaan Kross, and *Things in the Night* by Estonian theater director and postmodernist novelist Mati Unt, appeared in 2003 and 2006, plus a book of Gothic symbolist short stories by Friedebert Tuglas in 2007. His translation of another novel by Mati Unt, *Brecht Appears by Night*, will be published by the Dalkey Archive Press in 2008.

KRISTIN DIMITROVA (Bulgarian) is also a poet whose work appears in this anthology. Her biography is on page 336.

THEO DORGAN (Slovenian) is the author of *Sailing for Home, Sappho's Daughter*, and *Rosa Mundi*, among others. He has also translated Barbara Korun's *Songs of Earth and Light*.

SASHA DUGDALE (Russian) is the author of *The Estate* and *Notebook*. She received the Eric Gregory Award for her writing in 2003.

ANDREW DUNCAN (German) was born in 1956. His books of poetry include *Anxiety Before Entering a Room: Selected Poems 1977–1999* and *Savage Survivals*.

ROBERT ELSIE (Albanian) is a prolific translator, editor, and scholar of Albanian literature and history, with nearly twenty books to his name—most recently, a translation of Visar Zhiti's *The Condemned Apple*. Originally from Vancouver, he currently lives in the Eiffel Mountains in Germany.

CLIFFORD ENDRES (Turkish) lives in Istanbul and teaches at Kadır Has University. With Selhan Savcıgil-Endres, he has published translations in *Agenda, Massachusetts Review, Quarterly West, Seneca Review, Near East Review, The Turkish PEN*, and other journals. Endres also is the author of books on country music and Latin poetry.

D. J. ENRIGHT (Polish) was born in Leamington, Warwickshire, England, in 1920. He taught English literature for twenty-five years, mainly in Egypt, Japan, and Singapore. He was subsequently poetry editor and director of Chatto and Windus (1974–1982). In addition to writing poetry, he was a prose writer (fiction for adults and children, memoir, and criticism) and edited various anthologies. He died in 2002.

KATHRYN FARRIS (Belarusian, Russian) has work in *Runes* and *Web Del Sol Review of Books*. She is the recipient of fellowships from Port Townsend Writers' Conference and Upright Hall Residency for Writers.

JULIE FAY (French) divides her life between Raleigh, North Carolina, and Languedoc, France, with her teenage daughter and their dog, Rocks. Her poetry collections include *Blue Scorpion* and *The Woman Behind You*. A recent recipient of a Fulbright Senior Research Award, she is currently translating the work of Occitan author Max Rouquette. She is professor of English at East Carolina University.

MARELLA FELTRIN-MORRIS (Italian) is a regional editor for this anthology. Her biography appears on page 381.

DEBORAH FFOULKES (Dutch) is a performance poet who writes and performs her work in English, German, and Dutch. After living in Amsterdam for ten years, she moved to Cologne in 1992 and cofounded Germany's first "Open Mike." She has translated her own work and that of a number of other poets between her three languages.

KALINA FILIPOVA (Bulgarian) is on the faculty of the Department of English at Sofia University in Bulgaria. In addition to translating such writers as Petar Tchouhov, Georgi Gospodinov, and Steven Kissyof, she has also published scholarly work on James Joyce.

PETER FILKINS (German) is the translator of Ingeborg Bachmann's collected poems, *Darkness Spoken*, as well as the author of two volumes of his own poetry. He has been a recipient of a Berlin Prize Fellowship and currently teaches writing and literature at Bard College at Simon's Rock. His latest translation is of a novel called *The Journey*, by H. G. Adler, which will be published in 2009.

EVALD FLISAR (Montenegrin) is a leading Slovenian playwright and author. His *The Sorcerer's Apprentice* and *Travels in Shadowlands* have won him near-universal acclaim. Among many other honors, he has received the Prešeren Fund Prize, the highest Slovenian literary award.

TONY FRAZER (German) is editor of *Shearsman* magazine and publisher of Shearsman Books in Exeter, England. He translates poetry from German and Spanish, and is editor of *Spanish Poetry of the Golden Age, in contemporary English translations*.

STUART FRIEBERT (Czech) is the author of numerous collections of poetry, the most recent of which is *Near Occasions of Sin*. Among the many poets he's translated are Judita Vaičiūnaitė, Karl Krolow, and Sylva Fischerová.

AMAIA GABANTXO (Basque) is a literary translator, writer, and reviewer. Her work has appeared in many journals and newspapers, including the *Times Literary Supplement* and the *Independent*, as well as in *An Anthology of Basque Short Stories* and *Spain: A Traveler's Literary Companion*. Her translation of Anjel Lertxundi's *Perfect Happiness* is forthcoming from the University of Nevada Press. She moonlights as a flamenco dancer.

ZUZANA GÁBRIŠOVÁ (Czech) has published translations of Petr Hruška in *Kosmas* and *Cento* magazine.

MARGITA GAILITIS (Latvian) was born in Riga, Latvia, and is a writer, poet, and translator. Her poetry has been published in various periodicals and has been awarded both Ontario and Canada Council grants.

IAIN GALBRAITH (German) is a poet, essayist, and translator. His most recent books include, as editor, the anthologies *Intime Weiten. Schottishe Gedichte* and *The Night Begins with a Question. XXV Austrian Poems 1978–2002*, as well as a German edition of Michael Hamburger's prose, *Pro Domo: Selbstauskünfte, Rückblicke und andere Prosa*, and, as translator, Alfred Kolleritsch's *Selected Poems*.

RACHEL GALVIN (Russian) has published poems and translations in *Gulf Coast, Spinning Jenny, Gargoyle, Del Sol Review,* and *Nimrod.* Her first book of poems, *Of Pulleys & Locomotion,* is forthcoming from Black Lawrence Press. She recently completed a translation of Raymond Queneau's *Courir les rues* and is now translating César Vallejo's *Poemas Humanos.*

HARALD GASKI (Sami) is professor of Sami literature at the University of Tromsø, Norway. He has published fiction as well as translations, anthologies, and numerous scholarly works. Four of his books have appeared in English: *In the Shadow of the Midnight Sun: Contemporary Sami Prose and Poetry; Sami Culture in a New Era: The Norwegian Sami Experience; Biejjien baernie—Sami Son of the Sun;* and *Time Is a Ship That Never Casts Anchor: Annotated collection of Sami proverbs.*

IRMA GIANNETTI (Romanian) grew up in Cluj-Napoca (to Hungarians, Kolozsvár), speaking both Hungarian and Romanian. She was a graduate student in comparative literature at Penn State and now works in technology support at the university. Her cotranslations have appeared in a dozen literary magazines.

DANA GIOIA (Italian) is chairman of the National Endowment for the Arts and is a prolific poet, critic, editor, translator, and librettist. Among his recent books are *Disappearing Ink: Poetry at the End of Print Culture* and *Interrogations at Noon.*

JOHANNES GÖRANSSON (Swedish) is the coeditor of Action Books and the new online quarterly *Action, Yes.* In 2005, Action Books published *Remainland: Selected Poems of Aase Berg,* which he translated from Swedish. Göransson was recently a guest editor of the winter 2006 special Swedish issue of the journal *Typo,* which featured substantial selections of work by major Swedish-language Modernists and contemporary poets.

OLIVER GRANNIS (German) writes and translates poetry. He is professor emeritus of English language and linguistics at the University of Osnabrück. He has retired to upstate New York.

ROGER GREENWALD (Norwegian, Danish) is a regional editor of this anthology. His biography appears on page 381.

JENNIFER GROTZ (Polish) is the author of *Cusp,* winner of the Bakeless Prize for Poetry and the Natalie Ornish Prize. Her poems, translations, essays, and reviews have appeared in the *Kenyon Review, New England Review, Ploughshares, TriQuarterly, Best American Poetry 2000, Virginia Quarterly Review,* and the *Washington Post.* Currently she works as the assistant director of the Bread Loaf Writers' Conference and teaches at the University of North Carolina at Greensboro.

MARILYN HACKER (French) is a regional editor of this anthology. Her biography appears on page 381.

VICTORIA HÄGGBLOM (Swedish) is a writer and translator residing in Berkeley, California. For her own fiction as well as for her translations of Swedish writers Rynell and Öijer she has received grants and awards from the Fine Arts Work Center in Provincetown, PEN American Center, the Santa Fe Arts Institute, the Swedish Institute, the American-Scandinavian Foundation, and the Witter Bynner Foundation for Poetry, among other places. Her work has appeared in *Shenandoah, Cutbank,* and *Oakland Review.*

C. B. HALL (Finnish), who was born in 1952, began translating professionally in 1988. Since then he has translated a great variety of texts from Finnish and Swedish into English. He lives on Lopez Island, Washington, in the United States.

MICHAEL HAMBURGER (German) was born in 1924 in Berlin. His family emigrated to England in 1933 and eventually settled in London. A noted translator, poet, and academic, Hamburger has published over twenty volumes of poems, several collections of essays, and numerous translations. Among the many German-language writers whose work he has translated are Buchner, Celan, Enzensberger, Goethe, Grass, Hölderlin, Huchel, Rilke, and Trakl. Among the recognition he received for his translations were the Schlegel-Tieck Prize (1978 and 1981), the European Translation Prize (1990), the Hölderlin Prize (1991), and the Order of the British Empire (1992). Michael Hamburger died in June 2007.

SARKA HANTULA (Finnish) has an MA in English from the University of Oulu, Finland, and teaches at Helsinki Polytechnic University. Her translations of Finnish poetry and drama appear widely.

BARBARA J. HAVELAND (Danish) was born in Scotland in 1951. She has lived in Denmark since 1988—though with three years in Norway. She translates from Danish and Norwegian into English: primarily literary fiction, but also nonfiction, poetry, and screenplays. She has translated work by such leading Danish and Norwegian authors as Peter Høeg, Ib Michael, Jan Kjærstad, and Linn Ullmann.

CHRISTIAN HAWKEY (German) is the author of two books of poems: *Citizen Of* (2007) and *The Book of Funnels* (2004), both from Wave Books.

GARY HAWKINS (Spanish) is a poet, essayist, and teacher. His work collects around his concerns of beauty, identity, and democracy. He lives in Black Mountain, North Carolina.

PATRICK HENRY (Russian) is government editor at Bloomberg's Moscow bureau. He holds a PhD in Russian literature from the University of California–Berkeley.

ELLEN HINSEY (French) is the author of *Cities of Memory, The White Fire of Time*, and *Update on the Descent*, and her translations of contemporary French fiction and memoir have been published with Riverhead/Penguin Books. Her honors include a Berlin Prize Fellowship from the American Academy in Berlin and Poetry's Union League Civic and Arts Poetry Prize for translation. She teaches and lives in Paris.

STEFANIA HIRTOPANU (Romanian) was born in Romania in 1968 and left after 1989 in search of adventure and eager to leave the communist legacy behind. While living in Cork, Ireland, she was approached to do a literal translation for an anthology of ten Romanian poets into English edited by John Fairleigh, *Sorescu's Choice: Young Romanian Poets*. Hirtopanu now lives and works in London.

MICHAEL HOFMANN (German) was born in Freiburg, Germany, in 1957 and currently lives in London. His published poetry includes *Nights in the Iron Hotel*, which won the Cholmondeley Award; *Acrimony*, which won the Geoffrey Faber Memorial Prize; *Corona, Corona*; and *Approximately Nowhere*. Hofmann has translated more than thirty books from the German, mainly novels. Among others, he has won for his translations the Helen and Kurt Wolff Translator's Prize and (twice) the Schlegel-Tieck Prize (Translators' Association).

ANSELM HOLLO (Finnish), poet and literary translator, is a professor in the Jack Kerouac School of Disembodied Poetics at Naropa University in Boulder, Colorado. His most recent books are *Notes on the Possibilities and Attractions of Existence: Selected Poems 1965–2000* which won the San Francisco Poetry Center's Best Book Award for 2001, and *Guests of Space*.

MADELAINE HRON (Slovak) has translated Róbert Gál's *Signs and Symptoms*. She earned her PhD in comparative literature from the University of Michigan and is now on the faculty of Wilfrid Laurier University in Canada.

SIRI HUSTVEDT (Norwegian) is a writer who lives in Brooklyn, New York. She has published three novels, *The Blindfold*, *The Enchantment of Lily Dahl*, and *What I Loved*, as well as two books of essays, *A Plea for Eros* and *Mysteries of the Rectangle*. Her work has been translated into twenty-five languages.

JOHN IRONS (Flemish) studied French, German, and Dutch at Cambridge, where he wrote a doctorate on the poetry of the Dutch poet P. C. Boutens; beginning in 1968 he has lived in Scandanavia, where he studied English and German. He taught literature at Odense University in Denmark for a number of years. Since 1974 he has been teaching English at the Odense College of Education. He has been a professional translator since 1997 and has translated Danish as well as Dutch poetry into English.

HENRI ISRAELI (Albanian) is the author of a book of poems, *New Messiahs*, and translator of Luljeta Lleshanaku's *Fresco*. In 2002, he received an NEA translation grant, and he has received grants from the Canada Council on the Arts and the MacDowell Colony.

KATARZYNA JAKUBIAK (Polish) is a translator and a scholar. Her translations of Polish poetry have appeared in the anthology *Carnivorous Boy, Carnivorous Bird* and in American and British magazines, including *Poetry Wales*, *Gulf Coast*, and *Lyric*. She has collaborated with Ewa Sonnenberg on the bilingual collection *Pisane na piasku/Written on Sand* (Ha-art, 2007). Her Polish translations of Yusef Komunyakaa's poetry won the "New Voices" award from the magazine *Literatura nas'wiecie* in 2006. She teaches English at Millersville University in Pennsylvania.

HALINA JANOD's (Polish) first publication as a translator was Piotr Sommer's *Continued*.

BILL JOHNSTON (Polish) is associate professor of second language studies and comparative literature at Indiana University, Bloomington. Working in both prose and poetry, he has translated such authors as Witold Gombrowicz *(Bacacay)*, Tadeusz Różewicz *(New Poems)*, Magdalena Tulli *(Dreams and Stones and Moving Parts)*, Andrzej Stasiuk *(Nine)*, Krzysztof Kamil Baczyński *(White Magic and Other Poems)*, and Juliusz Słowacki *(Balladina)*. He has held fellowships from the National Endowment for the Arts and the National Endowment for the Humanities. In 2005, his translation of Magdalena Tulli's *Dreams and Stones* won the AATSEEL Translation Award.

PIERRE JORIS's (French) newest poetry publications include the CD *Routes, not Roots* (with Munir Beken, oud; Mike Bisio, bass; Ben Chadabe, percussion; and Mitch Elrod, guitar), issued by Ta'wil Productions; *Aljibar* (a bilingual volume of poems with French translations by Eric Sarner); and *Meditations on the Stations of Mansour Al-Hallaj 1-21*. Recent translations include *Paul Celan: Selections* and *Lightduress* by Paul Celan, which received the 2005 PEN Poetry Translation Award. With Jerome Rothenberg he edited the award-winning anthologies *Poems for the Millennium* and, most recently, *Pablo Picasso, The Burial of the Count of Orgaz & Other Poems*.

ILYA KAMINSKY (Belarusian, Russian) is a regional editor for this anthology. His biography appears on page 381.

STINA KATCHADOURIAN (Finland-Swedish) is a literary translator and writer who grew up as a member of the Swedish-speaking minority in Finland. A resident of the United States since the late 1960s, among her many translations from Swedish are books by Edith Södergran *(Love and Solitude)* and Märta Tikkanen *(Love Story of the Century)*. For a selection of her Tua Forsström translations she received the Leif and Inger Sjöberg Translation Prize from the American-Scandinavian Foundation. She has also published two books based on the American experience in Ottoman Turkey. She lives in Stanford, California.

CATRIONA KELLY (Russian) is professor of Russian at Oxford University. She is the author of *A History of Russian Women's Writing* and several other books.

MEL KENNE (Turkish) lives in Istanbul, Turkey, where he teaches in the American Literature and Culture Department at Kadır Has University. Three books of his poetry have been published, one of which, *South Wind,* won the 1984 Austin Book Award. Working with Saliha Paker, he translated into English the novel *Dear Shameless Death,* by the Turkish writer Latife Tekin. Kenne's poems and his translations of poems by Turkish poets have appeared in many magazines in America and Turkey.

JASCHA KESSLER (Hungarian) is a regional editor of this anthology. His biography appears on page 382.

KERRY SHAWN KEYS (Lithuanian) lives in Vilnius, Lithuania, where he taught translation theory and creative composition from 1998 to 2000 as a Fulbright lecturer at Vilnius University. He currently freelances as a poet, translator, and cultural liaison.

KATIE KING (Spanish) is a writer, lecturer, and media consultant in Washington, D.C. She has worked as a PBS documentary producer, a foreign correspondent for Reuters in Latin America, and a global Internet news executive for Reuters New Media. She studied Spanish literature and journalism at the University of Seville, the University of Washington in Seattle, and Columbia University in New York. She received a Nieman Fellowship from Harvard University in 1994.

ROULA KONSOLAKI (Greek) has, with Chrisopher Bakken, recently translated *The Lion's Gate: Selected Poems of Titos Patrikios.* Her translations from Greek have also appeared in *Modern Poetry in Translation, Two Lines, Pleiades,* and elsewhere.

MÁRIA KŐRÖSY (Hungarian) was, until her retirement, English secretary of the Hungarian PEN Club in Budapest. She has assisted dozens of American, Canadian, Irish, and English poets who learned to value Hungarian poetry and chose to devote their talents to translating it. Her consequent importance to Hungarian letters is considerable.

BILIANA KOURTASHEVA (Bulgarian) is a scholar and translator active in Bulgaria.

MILJENKO KOVAČIĆEK (Bosnian, Croatian) (1955–2004) was a translator and poet. He translated into English a voluminous anthology of contemporary Croatian poetry titled *Exclamations,* edited by Tonko Maroević, and published by the Croatian Writers' Association in 2001.

KALJU KRUUSA (Estonian) is the author of *Frame of Mind,* which was awarded the Betti Alver Literary Prize for best debut of the year. He studied English language and literature and semiotics at the University of Tartu. Kruusa has translated Umberto Saba's poetry from Italian into Estonian, and poems of his friends into English and Finnish.

TOMISLAV KUZMANOVIĆ (Serbian, Montenegrin, Bosnian, Croatian) is the translator of *A Castle in Romagna* (with Russell Valentino) by Igor Stiks and *The Death of the*

Little Match Girl by Zoran Ferić. His translations of fiction and poetry and other writings have appeared in various publications in the U.S. and Croatia, among others the *Iowa Review, 91st Meridian, eXchanges, Poetry International Web, Transcript, Relations, Quorum,* and *Frakcija.* He is a graduate of Zagreb University and the Translation Workshop at the University of Iowa and currently teaches English and translation studies at Zadar University, Croatia.

KAREN LEEDER (German) is reader in German and fellow and tutor at New College, Oxford. She has published widely on modern German poetry and translates a number of contemporary writers: most recently, Michael Krüger, *Scenes from the Life of a Bestselling Author*; Raoul Schrott, *The Desert of Lop*; and Evelyn Schlag, *Selected Poems,* for which she won the Schlegel-Tieck Prize for Translation in 2005.

RIKA LESSER (Swedish) is a regional editor for this anthology. Her biography appears on page 382.

ALEXIS LEVITIN (Portuguese) is a regional editor for this anthology. His biography appears on page 382.

CLAUDIA LITVINCHIEVICI (Romanian) is a graduate of the Faculty of Letters of the University of Cluj, from the English-German Department. She is one of Adam J. Sorkin's cotranslators of Ruxandra Cesereanu's *Lunacies.*

HERBERT LOMAS (Finnish), poet, translator, and critic, was born in the Pennines. His *Letters in the Dark* was an *Observer* Book of the Year, and he has received Guinness, Arvon, and Cholmondeley awards. His *Contemporary Finnish Poetry* won the Poetry Society's 1991 biennial translation award, he is a member of the Finnish Academy, and he was made Knight First Class, Order of the White Rose of Finland, for his services to Finnish literature.

TOM LOŽAR (Slovenian) has written and translated for the *Canadian Forum, Maisonneuve, AGNI, Prostor in Cas, Mladina,* and *Razgledi.* He is a columnist for the Maribor daily, *Vecer.*

BRANDON LUSSIER (Estonian) has published translations in *Circumference, eXchanges, Sirena,* and other journals and anthologies. He was a Fulbright Fellow to Estonia in 2003 and since has received grants and fellowships from the American Literary Translators Association, the Minnesota State Arts Board, and the Jerome Foundation. Lussier has also spoken about the translation of Estonian poetry at Princeton University and at the American Literary Translators Association's national conference.

ELIZABETH MACKLIN (Basque) is the author of two books of poetry, *A Woman Kneeling in the Big City* and *You've Just Been Told.* A recipient of a 1994 Guggenheim Fellowship in Poetry, the 1999 Amy Lowell Poetry Traveling Scholarship, and a 2005 PEN Translation Fund grant for *Meanwhile Take My Hand* by Kirmen Uribe, she is currently at work on a third poetry collection. She lives in New York City.

NORA MAKHOUL (French) is a doctoral candidate in comparative literature at the CUNY Graduate Center.

W. MARTIN (Polish) is a doctoral student in comparative literature at the University of Chicago. He edited a *New Polish Writing* issue of the *Chicago Review* in 2000 and as an editor and translator has been instrumental in introducing many younger Polish poets and prose writers to English-speaking readers, including Natasha Goerke, Adam

Wiedemann, Michał Witkowski, and Marzanna Bogumiła Kielar. He also translates from the German.

DAVID MASON (Greek) is the author of *Ludlow, Arrivals* and *The Poetry of Life and the Life of Poetry,* among others. He has also edited several influential poetry anthologies.

CHRISTOPHER MATTISON (Russian) is the translation editor for *Zoland Poetry Annual.* He lives in Princeton, New Jersey.

OLIVIA MCCANNON (French) is currently working on a new version of Balzac's *Old Goriot* for Penguin Classics. Recent translations include French plays for the Royal Court, and Jean Follain for *Modern Poetry in Translation.* A selection of her own poems will appear in the 2007 *Oxford Poets Anthology.* She was awarded a Hawthornden Fellowship in 2005.

DAVID MCDUFF (Swedish, Icelandic, Russian, Finnish) has lived in London since 1981. Among his Swedish translations published by Bloodaxe are *Edith Södergran: Complete Poems* and *Karin Boye: Complete Poems.* His translation of Gösta Ågren's *A Valley in the Midst of Violence* won the Shaw/TLS Prize in 1994, and he was recently awarded the Grand Prize of the Finland-Swedish Writers' Association. His translations of four novels by Dostoyevsky are available in Penguin Classics.

MIRIAM MCILFATRICK-KSENOFONTOV (Estonian) worked as a teacher and teacher trainer in Portugal from 1983 to 1992 and also ran teacher-training courses in Spain, Italy, Romania, and Estonia. She has translated poems by Indrek Hirv, Doris Kareva, Kalev Kesküla, Triin Soomets, and Elo Viiding.

RICHARD MCKANE (Russian) is a prolific translator of Russian poetry, including Anna Akhmatova's *Selected Poems* and, with Elizabeth McKane, Osip Mandelshtam's *The Moscow Notebooks* and *The Voronezh Notebooks.*

JAMIE MCKENDRICK (Italian) is a writer and translator whose most recent book of poems is *Ink Stone.* His selected poems *Sky Nails* was published in 2001.

HARITA MEENEE (Greek) is the author of several books, among them *The Sacred Feminine and Mary Magdalene* and *The Women's Olympics and the Great Goddess.* With Don Schofield, she has translated the work of Kiki Dimoula, Nicos Focas, and Liana Sakelliou into English. She lives in Athens, Greece.

ASKOLD MELNYCZUK (Ukrainian) is the founder of *AGNI,* an influential literary magazine at Boston University. He is responsible for bringing many new Ukrainian voices to the attention of the U.S. literary community.

PHILIP METRES (Russian) is the author of *Primer for Non-Native Speakers* and *Instants.* His first full-length collection of poems in English is *To See the Earth.* Visit him at www.philipmetres.com.

IAN MILNER (Czech) has published translations of Vladimír Holan, Sylva Fischerová, Josef Hanzlik, and others. He is one of the principal translators of Miroslav Holub's *Poems Before & After.*

JARMILA MILNER (Czech) has published translations of the work of numerous poets, including Vladimír Holan, Sylva Fischerová, and Josef Hanzlik. She is one of the principal translators of Miroslav Holub's *Poems Before & After.*

ANTHONY MOLINO (Italian) has translated several books of poetry, including *Echoes of Memory: Selected Poems of Lucio Mariani,* Antonio Porta's *Melusine: A Ballad* *and a Diary,* and *Kisses from Another Dream,* as well as *Nearsights: Selected Poems of Valerio Magrelli.*

MICHAEL MOLNAR (Russian) is the translator of *Paradise: Selected Poems of Elena Shvarts.*

VALZHYNA MORT (Belarusian, Ukrainian, Russian) is also a poet whose work appears in this anthology. Her biography is on page 348.

ERÍN MOURE (Galician) was born in Calgary, Alberta, in 1955. She attended the University of Calgary and the University of British Columbia. She now lives in Montreal. Mouré worked as a technical writer for VIA Rail until recently; she now makes her living as a writer. In 1988, Mouré won the Governor General's Literary Award in the poetry category for her book *Furious.*

PAUL MULDOON (Irish) is the author of *Horse Latitudes, Moy Sand and Gravel,* and *Poems 1968–1998,* among others.

MICHAEL M. NAYDAN (Ukrainian) is one of the most prolific translators of poetry from Ukrainian language at work today. He is a professor of Slavic languages at Pennsylvania State University.

MURAT NEMET-NEJAT (Turkish) is a regional editor for this volume. His biography appears on page 382.

MIROSLAV NIKOLOV (Bulgarian) is the son of Lyubomir Nikolov, whose work he has translated for this anthology. His translations have also appeared in *Modern Poetry in Translation.*

LARS NORDSTRÖM (Sami) was born in Stockholm, attended the University of Stockholm, Portland State University in Portland, Oregon, and Uppsala University, Sweden, where he received his PhD in American literature in 1989. He has published numerous volumes of poetry, nonfiction, and translations.

GREGORY O'DONOGHUE (Bulgarian) is the author of *Kicking; The Permanent Way;* and *Making Tracks.* He has also translated Kristin Dimitrova's *A Visit to the Clockmaker.* He died in Cork in 2005.

EWALD OSERS (Bulgarian, Czech) is a leading translator. Among the many authors he's rendered into English are Jirí Mucha, Egon Hostovsky, Miroslav Holub, Karel Capek, Ivan Klíma, Zdeněk Svěrák (Kolja), Arnošt Lustig, and the 1984 Nobel laureate Jaroslav Seifert (as well as the Irish Nobel laureate Seamus Heaney into Czech).

EUGENE OSTASHEVSKY (Russian) is the author of *Iterature* and editor of *OBERIU: An Anthology of Russian Absurdism.*

SALIHA PAKER (Turkish) is professor of translation studies at Boğaziçi University, Istanbul. She edited and cotranslated *Ash Divan: Selected Poetry of Enis Batur. Swords of Ice,* her most recent cotranslation (with Mel Kenne) of Latife Tekin's novel, came out from Marion Boyars in 2007.

MICHAEL PALMA (Italian) is the author of *A Fortune in Gold* and other poetry collections. In addition to Franco Buffoni, he has translated volumes of poetry by ten other modern and contemporary Italian poets, as well as a fully rhymed translation of Dante's *Inferno.*

BENJAMIN PALOFF (Polish) is a poetry editor for *Boston Review.* His poems have appeared in *The Antioch Review, Faultline,* the *New Republic,* the *Paris Review, A Public*

Space, and elsewhere. He received his MFA from the University of Michigan, where he received two Hopwood Awards, and now teaches. He received a PhD from Harvard in 2007. His most recent translations are Dorota Masłowska's *Snow White and Russian Red* and Marek Bieńczyk's *Tworki.*

DAVID PERRY (German) is the author of one book of poetry, *Range Finder,* and two chapbooks, *Knowledge Follows* and *New Years.* He currently lives in Shanghai and Kansas City, Missouri.

FRANK PERRY (Swedish) is a writer and literary translator living in London. For his translations of contemporary Swedish drama and modern poetry, he was awarded the Swedish Academy prize in 2004. In addition to recent work providing English versions of Swedish plays and fiction for children and young people, he has translated Bodil Malmsten's novel *The Price of Water in Finistère* and Jonas Hassen Khemiri's play *Invasion.*

NOVICA PETROVIĆ (Serbian) works in the English Department of the Faculty of Philology of Belgrade University, where he currently holds the post of a senior lecturer and teaches third-year students translation from English into Serbian and text analysis. In 2005 he received his PhD, having defended his PhD thesis entitled *Man and the Universe in the Work of Arthur C. Clarke and Stanislaw Lem.*

WANDA PHIPPS (Ukrainian) has published in *AGNI, Hanging Loose, Transfer, Exquisite Corpse,* and many other journals. She has received awards from the New York State Council on the Arts.

KATERINA PINOSOVÁ (Czech) is also a poet whose work appears in this anthology. Her biography is on page 350.

MICHAEL PISARO (German) was born 1961 in Buffalo, New York, and is a composer and performer. A member of the Wandelweiser Composers Ensemble, he teaches at the California Institute of the Arts and lives in Southern California. He has composed over eighty works for a great variety of instrumental combinations and has taken part in festivals throughout the world with extended composer residencies in Germany.

GABRIELE POOLE (Italian) is of American Italian background. He holds a PhD in English from the University of Notre Dame and is currently assistant professor in English language and translation at the University of Cassino, Italy. He has worked extensively as translator and has recently translated a selection of poems by the American poet John Matthias.

LUDMILLA G. POPOVA-WIGHTMAN (Bulgarian) has translated Konstantin Pavlov's *Capriccio for Goya* and Danila Stoianova's *Memory of a Dream.*

JUSTIN QUINN (Czech) is an Irish poet and translator. His poetry collections include *The 'O'o'a'a' Bird, Privacy, Fuselage,* and *Waves & Trees.*

G. J. RACZ (Spanish) has had his translation of Benito Pérez Galdés's *Gerona* published by the Edwin Mellen Press. He teaches at Long Island University in Brooklyn.

GRAHAM W. REID (Macedonian) coedited (with Milne Holton) the influential collection *Reading the Ashes: An Anthology of the Poetry of Modern Macedonia.* He has translated numerous Macedonian writers, including Kocho Ratsin, Grigor Prlichev, and Zoran Ančevski.

PEGGY REID (Macedonian) has recently translated (with Ljubica Arsovska) Ludija Dimkovska's *Do Not Awaken Them with Hammers.* In 1994, she received the Macedonian

Literary Translators' Society Award; she has also won first prize at the Avon Poetry Festival, UK, twice for her own poetry. She teaches English at the University of SS. Cyril and Methodius, Skopje.

VERA RICH (Belarusian) is a prolific translator from the Belarusian and Ukrainian. She was awarded the Ivan Franko Prize, one of the most prestigious awards for literary translation in Ukraine.

MAURICE RIORDAN (Maltese) is the author of the poetry collections *The Holy Land* and *Floods,* among others. His translation of Immanuel Mifsud's *Confidential Reports* was published by Southword Editions in 2005.

MICHAEL RITTERSON (German) is associate professor of German at Gettysburg College, Pennsylvania.

SCOTT ROLLINS (Dutch), born in 1952 in the United States, has lived in the Netherlands since the early 1970s. A prolific translator of Dutch poetry and fiction, he is also the author of *Borderlines—Selected Poems and Fictions: 1972–1992.*

KATHRYN RONNAU-BRADBEER (Dutch) is a lecturer in the Dutch department at University College London.

RALPH SALISBURY (Sami) is a poet and fiction writer of Cherokee descent who grew up in Iowa. He is the author of two books of short fiction and seven books of poetry and is now professor emeritus at the University of Oregon.

SELHAN SAVCİĞIL-ENDRES (Turkish) lives in Istanbul and teaches at Kadir Has University. With Clifford Endres, she has published translations in *Agenda, Massachusetts Review, Quarterly West, Seneca Review, Near East Review, The Turkish PEN,* and other journals. She has also written on Orhan Pamuk and Paul Auster, among others.

ALINA SAVIN (Romanian) was born in 1980 and studied philology (French-English) and history of the Jews in Iaşi, Romania. She received a master's degree in multimedia in Poitiers, France, and currently works as an editor and translator.

DON SCHOFIELD (Greek) has poems, essays, and translations in numerous American journals, including *Partisan Review, New England Review,* and *Poets & Writers,* as well as in journals in Europe and Asia. In addition, he is the author of *Approximately Paradise.* A resident of Greece for more than twenty-five years, he currently lives in Thessaloniki.

BERNARD SCUDDER (Icelandic) lives in Reykjavík as a full-time translator. His translations encompass sagas, ancient and modern poetry, and leading contemporary novels and plays.

STEVEN SEYMOUR (Russian) is a translator and interpreter of Russian, Polish, French, and Spanish. He has served with the U.S. Army, then with the U.S. Department of State in Geneva, Switzerland (nuclear disarmament talks), and with the U.S. Embassy, Moscow. Mr. Seymour lives in New York City.

THOMAS SHAPCOTT (Macedonian) is a prolific Australian novelist, short story writer, and poet. Among his many books is the anthology of Macedonian poetry *Island on Land,* coedited and translated with Ilija Čašule.

ANDREW SHIELDS (German) has published a chapbook of poems, *Cabinet d'Amateur,* and a number of translations from the German, including the poetry collection *Tussi Research* by Dieter M. Gräf. His blog is at andrewjshields.blogspot.com.

AURA SIBIŞAN (Romanian) is not only a translator but also a lecturer at the University of Brasov in Romania, where she teaches American studies.

AMELA SIMIĆ (Bosnian) is the translator of Goran Simić's *From Sarajevo with Sorrow* and *Immigrant Blues* and, with Zoran Mutić, translator of Ferida Duraković's *Heart of Darkness.*

CHARLES SIMIC (Serbian) is the author of many books, most recently, *The Voice at 3:00 A.M.: Selected Late and New Poems* and *My Noiseless Entourage.* He has been the recipient of the Pulitzer Prize for poetry, and is currently the U.S. Poet Laureate.

ANNA SKUCIŃSKA (Polish) is an editor of *Przekładaniec: A Journal of Literary Translation* and an editor and translator of *Carnivorous Boy, Carnivorous Bird: A Bilingual Anthology of Contemporary Polish Poetry.* She lives in Krakow.

DOUGLAS BURNET SMITH (Ukrainian) is the author of twelve books of poetry. He teaches creative writing at St. Francis Xavier University in Nova Scotia, Canada, and at the American University of Paris. *Sister Prometheus: The Marie Curie Poems* will appear in 2008 from Wolsak & Wynn Publishers, Toronto.

ROD SMITH (French) is the author of several books of poetry, including the upcoming *The Good House & Other Poems.* He is currently editing the correspondence of Robert Creeley for the University of California Press and is the founder and editor of Edge Books and *Aerial* magazine. He lives in Washington, D.C.

ADAM J. SORKIN (Romanian) is a regional editor for this anthology. His biography appears on page 382.

LAIMA SRUOGINIS (Lithuanian), a poet and translator, has published an anthology of Lithuanian poetry in translation. A Fulbright lecturer at Vilnius University in 1997, she is now an assistant professor of English at the University of Southern Maine.

BOGDAN ŞTEFĂNESCU (Romanian) is an associate professor in English at the University of Bucharest who currently teaches courses in British literature and critical theory. He has taught as a Fulbright Lecturer at Penn State University and has received research grants from the British Council, University of London, University of Stuttgart, and New Europe College.

STEPHANOS STEPHANIDES (Greek) is also a poet whose work appears in this anthology. His biography is on page 356.

DONNA STONECIPHER (French, German) is the author of three books of poetry, most recently *The Cosmopolitan,* which won the 2007 National Poetry Series, selected by John Yau. Her translations of French and German poets have been published widely.

MARIO SUŠKO (Croatian), a poet in his own right (with twenty-five poetry collections, five of them in English), is also a prolific editor and translator, having edited and translated Walt Whitman's deathbed edition of *Leaves of Grass*; also, works by Saul Bellow, William Styron, Bernard Malamud, Donald Barthelme, Theodore Roethke, and e. e. cummings, among others. He lives in the U.S. and is an associate professor at Nassau Community College in Garden City, New York.

JAMES SUTHERLAND-SMITH (Slovak) is a prolific poet and translator. His recent poetry books include *In the Country of Birds* and *At the Skin Resort.* With Viera Sutherland-Smith, he has translated numerous volumes, including *Selected Poems of Mila Haugová, Selected Poems of Ján Buzassy,* and *Selected Poems of Ivan Laučik.*

VIERA SUTHERLAND-SMITH (Slovak) is a prolific translator and has, with James Sutherland-Smith, translated (among many others) *Selected Poems of Mila Haugová, Selected Poems of Ján Buzassy,* and *Selected Poems of Ivan Laučik.*

ELIN SÜTISTE (Estonian) studied at the University of Tartu. She translates and writes scholarly research on Japanese haiku.

COLE SWENSEN (French) is the author of several volumes of poetry, including *The Glass Age* and *Ours*. She translates contemporary French poetry, prose, and art criticism and edits La Presse Books. She teaches at the Iowa Writers' Workshop.

GEORGE SZIRTES (French) is the author of thirteen books of poetry, including *Reel,* which won the T. S. Eliot Prize for poetry in 2004. He is normally a translator of Hungarian poetry and fiction and has won various awards for his work in that field.

ULVIJA TANOVIĆ (Montenegrin, Bosnian) is a freelance translator based in Sarajevo, Bosnia and Herzegovina. She graduated from the English Department of the University in Sarajevo and completed the American Studies Diploma Program at Smith College. Her translations of prose and poetry have appeared in the literary magazines *Odjek, Lica,* and *Diwan,* as well as the anthology *Words Without Borders.*

VIRLANA TKACZ (Ukrainian) is the founding director of Yara Arts Group, a resident company at La MaMa Experimental Theatre group in New York. She is a recipient of a National Endowment for the Arts Fellowship.

J. C. TODD (Latvian) is the author of *What Space This Body* and *Nightshade and Entering Pisces* and has poems and translations in the *American Poetry Review,* the *Paris Review, Prairie Schooner,* the *Wild River Review,* and other journals. She is a visiting lecturer in creative writing at Bryn Mawr College.

LARA TRUBOWITZ (Italian) is assistant professor of English at the University of Iowa. She is coeditor of *Contemporary Italian Women Poets: A Bilingual Anthology* (with Cinzia Sartini Blum), coeditor of *Antisemitism and Philosemitism in the Twentieth and Twenty-first Centuries: Representing Jews, Jewishness, and Modern Culture* (with Phyllis Lassner), and is currently completing a manuscript entitled *Conspiring to Be Civil: Antisemitism, Philosemitism, and the Modernist Moment.*

MICHAEL TWEED (French) is an artist comfortable in various mediums and is author of numerous books, including poetry, prose, art criticism, philosophical musings, and theater. His translations can also be found in the *Yale Anthology of Twentieth-Century French Poetry* and elsewhere. Samples of his visual art and writings can be seen at www.pensum.ca.

ALISSA VALLES (Polish, Dutch) is a regional editor for this anthology. Her biography appears on page 383.

ANDREW WACHTEL (Croatian) is Bertha and Max Dressler Professor in the Humanities at Northwestern University, where he serves as dean of the Graduate School and director of the Roberta Buffett Center for International and Comparative Studies. His most recent books are *Remaining Relevant After Communism: The Role of the Writer in Eastern Europe* and *Plays of Expectations: Intertextual Relations in Russian 20th-Century Drama.*

DEREK WALCOTT (Russian) has received the Nobel Prize for Literature. His most recent book is *Selected Poems.* He teaches at Boston University.

ROSMARIE WALDROP (German) was born in Germany in 1935 and lives in Providence, Rhode Island, where she coedits Burning Deck Press with her husband, Keith Waldrop. Her newest poetry volume, *Curves to the Apple,* binds together the trilogy *The Reproduction of Profiles, Lawn of Excluded Middle,* and *Reluctant Gravities.* She has translated the work of Edmond Jabès, Jacques Roubaud, Emmanuel Hocquard, Friederike Mayröcker, Elke Erb, Ernst Jandl, Oskar Pastior, and many others. Her work is widely anthologized, and she is the recipient of numerous international fellowships and awards.

ROBERT WELCH (Slovak) is a prolific writer and translator. Among his many publications are *The Abbey Theatre, 1899–1999: Form and Pressure, The Blue Formica Table* (poems), and *Groundwork* (a novel). In 2005, Southword Editions published his translation of Dana Podracká's *Forty Four.*

ELŻBIETA WÓJCIK-LEESE (Polish) has taught contemporary literature in English, translation, and comparative literature since 1991. In 1999–2000, as a Fulbright scholar, she studied the Elizabeth Bishop Manuscripts at Vassar College. Her translations of Polish poets have appeared in, among others, *Poetry Review, Poetry London, Poetry Wales, Modern Poetry in Translation, Poetry Ireland,* and elsewhere. She coedits *Przekladaniec: A Journal of Literary Translation.* She also translates from the English; her publications include poetry by Carol Ann Duffy, Denise Riley, Gillian Allnutt, and Nuala Ní Dhomhnaill.

MARC WOODWORTH (Slovak) is an editor at *Salmagundi,* a lecturer in the English department at Skidmore College in Saratoga Springs, New York, and the author of *Bee Thousand,* a volume in the 33⅓ series, as well as *Arcade,* a book of poems. As a 2006 Fulbright lecturer in Slovakia, he met and began working with Bratislava-based poet Martin Solotruk.

ELIZABETH OEHLKERS WRIGHT (German) is a regional editor for this anthology. Her biography appears on page 383.

FRANZ WRIGHT (Belarusian) received the Pulitzer Prize in poetry for *Walking to Martha's Vineyard.* His other recent books include *Earlier Poems, God's Silence, The Beforelife,* and *Ill Lit: New and Selected Poems.*

MATVEI YANKELEVICH (Russian) is the editor of the Eastern European Poets Series at Ugly Duckling Presse. He is the author of *The Present Work.*

ANDREW ZAWACKI (Slovenian) is the author of *By Reason of Breakings: Poems* and *Anabranch* and editor of *Afterwards: Slovenian Writing 1945–1995.*

JONAS ZDANYS (Lithuanian) is an award-winning poet and a leading Lithuanian American translator. He is the author of more than twenty books, including collections of his own poetry and translations of work by modern Lithuanian poets and prose writers.

RICHARD ZENITH (Portuguese) lives in Lisbon, Portugal, where he works as a freelance writer, translator, and researcher in the Fernando Pessoa Archives. His recent publications include *A Little Larger Than the Entire Universe: Selected Poems of Fernando Pessoa* and *Education by Stone: Selected Poems of João Cabral de Melo Neto,* which won the 2006 translation award from the Academy of American Poets.

ABOUT THE EDITORS

CHRISTOPHER BAKKEN is the author of two books of poems, *Goat Funeral* and *After Greece*, and cotranslator of *The Lions' Gate: Selected Poems of Titos Patrikios*. He teaches at Allegheny College.

PETER COVINO is an assistant professor of English and creative writing at the University of Rhode Island. He is the author of the poetry collection *Cut Off the Ears of Winter*, winner of the PEN/Osterweil Award for emerging poets and a finalist for the Thom Gunn Award and the Paterson Poetry Prize. His chapbook, *Straight Boyfriend*, won the 2001 Frank O'Hara Prize.

CHAD DAVIDSON is the author of a book of poems, *Consolation Miracle*, and his translations from Italian, in collaboration with Marella Feltrin-Morris, have appeared widely. He teaches at the University of West Georgia.

MICHAEL DUMANIS, born in the Soviet Union, is the author of *My Soviet Union*, winner of the Juniper Prize for Poetry, and coeditor of *Legitimate Dangers: American Poets of the New Century*. He is an assistant professor of English at Cleveland State University and director of the Cleveland State University Poetry Center.

MARELLA FELTRIN-MORRIS is an assistant professor of Italian studies in the Modern Languages and Literatures Department of Ithaca College. She has translated from the Italian several books of philosophy, and her collaborative translations with Chad Davidson appear in numerous literary magazines.

ROGER GREENWALD attended the City College of New York, the St. Marks in the Bouwerie Poetry Project workshop, and the University of Toronto. He has published one book of poems, *Connecting Flight*, and several volumes of poetry and fiction translated from Scandinavian languages, most recently *North in the World: Selected Poems of Rolf Jacobsen*. He has won the CBC Radio/*Saturday Night* Literary Award for poetry, as well as numerous awards for his translations.

MARILYN HACKER is the author of eleven books of poems, most recently *Essays on Departure: New and Selected Poems*, and eight collections of translations, including *Charlestown Blues*, poems by Guy Goffette, and *Nettles*, poems by Vénus Khoury-Ghata. Her translation of *King of a Hundred Horsemen* by Marie Étienne won the Robert Fagles Translation Prize.

BRIAN HENRY is the author of five books of poems, most recently *The Stripping Point*, which appeared in both the United States and England. A professor at the University of Richmond, he edits the magazine *Verse*.

JOHN ISLES is the author of *Ark* and has a new book of poems coming out in the fall of 2008. He lived in Estonia for a number of years, where he taught English through the Peace Corps. He currently teaches at the City College of San Francisco.

ILYA KAMINSKY, originally from Odessa, Ukraine, now lives in San Francisco. He is the author of a poetry collection, *Dancing in Odessa*, and teaches at San Diego State University.

JASCHA KESSLER, professor emeritus at UCLA, has received numerous awards for his translations from a number of different languages—especially Hungarian. He has published seven books of poetry and fiction and six books of translations.

JOHN KINSELLA, originally from Perth, Western Australia, is professor of English at Kenyon College. He has published more than thirty books, and, among other editing endeavors, is editor of *Salt*.

RIKA LESSER is the author of four books of poetry, most recently *Questions of Love: New & Selected Poems*. She has published books of poetry in translation—by Claes Andersson, Gunnar Ekelöf, Hermann Hesse, Rainer Maria Rilke, and Göran Sonnevi—as well as translations of various works of Swedish or German fiction and non-fiction. Among the many grants and awards she has received are the Amy Lowell Poetry Traveling Scholarship and the Poetry Translation Prize of the Swedish Academy.

ALEXIS LEVITIN has translated twenty-four books, including Clarice Lispector's *Soulstorm* and Eugenio de Andrade's *Forbidden Words*. His most recent book is Astrid Cabral's *Cage*. His awards include two NEA translation fellowships. He is currently working on an anthology of Brazilian short stories.

WAYNE MILLER teaches at the University of Central Missouri, where he is editor of *Pleiades: A Journal of New Writing*. He is the author of a book of poems, *Only the Senses Sleep*, and cotranslator of *I Don't Believe in Ghosts*, by Albanian poet Moikom Zeqo.

MURAT NEMET-NEJAT, poet, essayist, and translator, born in Istanbul, has lived in the United States since 1959. He is the editor of *Eda: An Anthology of Contemporary Turkish Poetry*. His books include the poetry collections *The Bridge, Turkish Voices, Vocabularies of Space, Io's Song, Aishe Series and Other Harbor Poems,* and *The Structure of Escape;* the translation from the Turkish poets Orhan Veli and Ece Ayhan, *I, Orhan Veli* and *A Blind Cat Black* and *Orthodoxies;* and the essays, *The Peripheral Space of Photography,* "Ideas Towards a Theory of Translation in *Eda*," "Questions of Accent," and "Eleven Septembers Later: Readings of Benjamin Hollander's *Vigilance*."

D. A. POWELL is the author of three books of poems, most recently *Cocktails*. He is a professor of English at the University of San Francisco.

KEVIN PRUFER is the author of four books of poems, most recently *National Anthem*, and editor of *The New Young American Poets* and *Dark Horses: Poets on Overlooked Poems*. He teaches at the University of Central Missouri, where he is editor of *Pleiades: A Journal of New Writing*.

ADAM J. SORKIN has translated more than thirty books from the Romanian, and he has won numerous prizes for his work. He is Distinguished Professor of English at Penn State Brandywine.

IGOR ŠTIKS was born in 1977, in Sarajevo, Bosnia and Herzegovina. His fiction, literary criticism, and essays have appeared widely in journals and reviews of the former Yugoslavia. He is a coeditor of an anthology of contemporary Croatian fiction and an anthology of international short fiction in English. His novel, *A Castle in Romagna,* received the "Slavic" Best First Book Award in 2000 and has been translated into German, Spanish, and English. His second novel, *Elijah's Chair,* received both the Gjalski Award and the Kiklop Award for the Best Fiction Book of the Year in Croatia. The German, Dutch, Spanish, Hungarian, Macedonian, and Slovenian editions are forthcoming.

He is a doctoral candidate at Institut d'Études Politiques de Paris and Northwestern University, and currently lives in Chicago.

JOVANKA ULJAREVIĆ was born in Kotor, Montenegro. She studied at the Faculty of Philosophy in Belgrade and has authored several books of poetry, including *Before the Flies, Masquerade of Prostheses,* and *In Rosin Sandals.* The latter was published simultaneously in Slovenian and its original Montenegrin. She is coeditor of the renowned Montenegrin magazine for literature, culture, and social issues *Ars* and the founder and coordinator of *Cyber Art Centre.*

ALISSA VALLES, originally from Amsterdam, studied languages, history, writing, and literature in London, St. Petersburg, and Houston. She is editor and translator of Zbigniew Herbert's *The Collected Poems: 1956–1998.*

SAM WITT is the author of two collections of poems, most recently *Sunflower Brother.* He was a Fulbright scholar to St. Petersburg, and has participated in literary festivals in Vilnius, Lithuania.

ELIZABETH OEHLKERS WRIGHT's translations of contemporary German poets have appeared in journals such as the *Seneca Review, AGNI, Another Chicago Magazine, Zoland Poetry* and the *PIP Anthology of World Poetry of the Twentieth Century,* vol. 7. Her translations of Zafer Şenocak's poetry will appear with Zephyr Press in fall 2008 under the title *Door Languages.*

PERMISSION ACKNOWLEDGMENTS

Every effort has been made to trace the ownership of copyrighted material and to make full acknowledgment of its use. The editors and Graywolf Press regret any errors or omissions, which will be corrected in subsequent editions upon notification in writing to the publisher. Thank you to the many publishers, translators, and poets who generously granted permission to reprint the poems in this volume.

"Five untitled poems," translated from the Norwegian of **Bjørn Aamodt**. English translation copyright 2008 by Roger Greenwald. First published in Norwegian in *Samlede dikt 1973–1994*. Published with the permission of Roger Greenwald.

Inga Ābele's "Autumn Recipe": translated by Inara Cedrins. English translation copyright 2008 by Inara Cedrins. Printed here with permission of Inara Cedrins and Inga Ābele.

Neringa Abrutyte's "The Beginning": translated by Jonas Zdanys. Translation copyright 2008 by Jonas Zdanys. Printed here with the permission of Jonas Zdanys and the rights holder.

Kurt Aebli's "An Old Gaping Wound Wheedling Out An Unmasked Smile": translated by Elizabeth Oehlkers Wright. Translation copyright 2008 by Elizabeth Oehlkers Wright. First published in German in *Ameisenjagd. Gedichte* (Suhrkamp Verlag, 2004). Printed with permission of Elizabeth Oehlkers Wright and Suhrkamp Verlag.

"Orpheus" and "Relativity," translated from the Catalan of **Anna Aguilar-Amat**. English translation copyright 2008 by Anna Crowe. First published in Catalan in *Música i escorbut,* published by Edicions 62 Empúries. Published with the permission of Anna Crowe and Anna Aguilar-Amat Castillo.

"Extinction," by **Mimoza Ahmeti**, translated from the Albanian of Mimoza Ahmeti. English translation copyright 2008 by Robert Elsie. Published with the permission of Robert Elsie and Mimoza Ahmeti.

Marigo Alexopoulou's "Chinese Woman's Spirit," "Manuscripts of Autumn," "Small Prayer," and "One Night with Seferis": translated from the Greek by Roula Konsolaki. English translations copyright 2008 by Roula Konsolaki. "One Night with Seferis" and "Chinese Woman's Spirit" from *Faster Than Light* (Kedros ed., 2000); "Small Prayer" from *Which Day Is Missing* (Kedros ed., 2003); "Manuscripts of Autumn" from *Poetry,* Athens, 2005. Reprinted with the permission of Roula Konsolaki and the rights holders.

Eugenijus Ališanka's "from the case of bones": translated by Kerry Shawn Keys. Translation copyright 2008 by Kerry Shawn Keys. Reprinted with permission of Kerry Shawn Keys and Eugenijus Ališanka.

Urs Allemann's "For the Lyre": translated by Elizabeth Oehlkers Wright. Translation copyright 2008 by Elizabeth Oehlkers Wright. Reprinted with permission of Elizabeth Oehlkers Wright and Urs Engeler.

Gabrielle Althen's "Rooms": translated by Marilyn Hacker. "Rooms" originally appeared in this translation in *Chelsea*. English translation copyright by Marilyn Hacker. Printed with permission of Marilyn Hacker and the rights holders.

Moniza Alvi's "Fish" from *Carrying My Wife,* copyright 2000 by Bloodaxe Books. Reprinted with permission of Bloodaxe Books.

"What's Slouching" by **Zoran Ancevski**, translated by Graham Reid, Peggy Reid, and the author: All best efforts have been made to secure permission for this use.

"Bloody Bad Shit," translated from the Romanian of **Radu Andriescu**. English translation copyright 2008 by Adam J. Sorkin. First published in Romanian in *Punţile Stalinskaya,* published by Editura Brumar. First published in English in *Metamorphosis*. Published with the permission of Adam J. Sorkin, Radu Andriescu, and Editura Brumar.

"Jamaica the Cossack," translated from the Ukrainian of **Yuri Andrukhovic**. English translation copyright 2008 by Valzhyna Mort. Published with the permission from Valzhyna Mort and Yuri Andrukhovic.

Antonella Anedda's "from *Winter Dwellings*": translated by Chad Davidson. English translation copyright 2008 by Chad Davidson. Originally published in *Residenze invernali* (Crocetti, 1992). Reprinted with permission of Chad Davidson and Nicola Crocetti. Antonella Anedda's "Earth": translated by Jamie McKendrick. English translation copyright 2008 by Jamie McKendrick. First published in Italian in *Il catalogo della gioia* (Donzelli, 2003). This translation first appeared in *The Faber Book of 20th-Century Italian Poems*, edited by Jamie McKendrick (Faber & Faber, 2004). Reprinted with permission of Jamie McKendrick and Faber & Faber.

"Walls," translated from the Albanian of **Lindita Arapi**. English translation copyright 2008 by Robert Elsie. First published in Albanian in *Ndodhi në shpirt*, published by Onufri. Published with the permission of Robert Elsie and Lindita Arapi.

Simon Armitage's "Kid": from *The Shout: Selected Poems* by Simon Armitage. Copyright 2005 by Harcourt, Inc. Reprinted by permission of Harcourt, Inc.

"Life" and "The Tale of the Hedgehog," translated from the Basque of **Bernardo Atxaga**. English translation copyright 2008 by Amaia Gabantxo. First published in *Poemas y Híbridos*, published by Visor. Published with the permission of Amaia Gabantxo and Bernardo Atxaga.

Krešimir Bagić's "a house": translated by Miljenko Kovačićek. First published in *Exclamations: An Anthology of Croatian Poetry 1971–1994* (The Bridge/Croatian Writers Association, 2001). Reprinted with permission of Krešimir Bagić.

"[creating a homer is less complicated than you might imagine]," translated from the Belarusian of **Mikhas Bajaryn**. English translation copyright 2008 by Valzhyna Mort. Published with the permission of Valzhyna Mort and Mikhas Bajaryn.

Raffaello Baldini's "The Knife": translated by Marella Feltrin-Morris. English translation copyright 2008 by Marella Feltrin-Morris. First published in Italian *La naiva Furistír Ciacri*, Turin: Einaudi, 2000. Printed with the permission of Marella Feltrin-Morris. Raffaello Baldini's "Picking": translated by Adria Bernardi. English translation copyright 2004 by Adria Bernardi. First published in Italian in *La naiva Furistír Ciacri*, Turin: Einaudi, 2000. This translation first appeared in *Two Lines*. Printed with permission of Adria Bernardi and Einaudi Publishers.

"You'll Shrivel Up You'll Be an Exotic Fruit," translated from the Romanian of **Daniel Bănulescu**. English translation copyright 2008 by Adam J. Sorkin. First published in Romanian in *Republica federală*, published by Editura Vinea. Published with the permission of Adam J. Sorkin, Daniel Bănulescu, and Editura Vinea.

"Manuscript Found by Natasha Rostova During the Fire," translated from the Russian of **Polina Barskova**. English translation copyright 2008 by Ilya Kaminsky. Published with the permission of Ilya Kaminsky and Polina Barskova. "to A.K.," translated from the Russian of Polina Barskova. English translation copyright 2008 by Ilya Kaminsky, Kathryn Farris, and Rachel Galvin. Published with the permission of Ilya Kaminsky and Polina Barskova.

"The nightingale sings," translated from the Albanian of **Eqrem Basha**. English translation copyright 2008 by Robert Elsie. First published in Albanian in *Zogu i zi*, published by Flaka e vëllazërimit. Published with the permission of Robert Elsie and Eqrem Basha.

Enis Batur's "F Minor—D-940," "Dear Bartleby," and "Face-to-Face Conversation IX": "F Minor—D-940" and "Face-to-Face Conversation" translated by Saliha Paker and Mel Kenne; "Dear Bartleby" translated by Clifford Endres and Selhan Savcıgil. All poems first appeared in English in Enis Batur's *Ash Divan: Selected Poems of Enis Batur* (Talisman House, 2006). Reprinted with the permission of Talisman House Press, Enis Batur, and the translators.

Sami Baydar's "Gigi" and "Here It's Coming": translated by Murat Nemet-Nejat. Translation copyright 2004 by Murat Nemet-Nejat. This translation first appeared in *Eda: An Anthology of Contemporary Turkish Poetry* (Talisman, 2004). Reprinted with permission of Murat Nemet-Nejat.

Aleksandar Bečanović's "Pessoa: On Four Addresses": translated by Tomislav Kuzmanović. Translation copyright 2008 by Tomislav Kuzmanović. Printed with permission of Aleksandar Bečanović and Tomislav Kuzmanović.

Dario Bellezza's "[I believe I should have a child]" and "[I lick you between dirty sheets,]": translated by Peter Covino. English translation copyright 2008 by Peter Covino. Printed with permission of Peter Covino.

Marcel Beyer's "Snow", translated by Michael Hofmann. Reprinted with permission from the translator.

"Hotel Central," translated from the Ukrainian of **Natalka Bilotserkivets**. English translation copyright 2008 by Michael M. Naydan. Published with the permission of Michael M. Naydan and Natalka Bilotserkivets.

Béla Bodor, "What to Expect": translated by Jascha Kessler. Translation copyright 2008 by Jascha Kessler. Printed with permission of Jascha Kessler and and Béla Bodor.

"the men of my country," translated from the Ukrainian of **Andriy Bondar**. English translation copyright 2008 by Vitaly Chernetsky. First published in Ukrainian in *Prymityvni formy vlasnosti*, published by LA "Piramida." Published with the permission of Vitaly Chernetsky and Andriy Bondar.

"[We do what? We are involved in space,]," translated from the Czech of **Petr Borkovec**. English translation copyright 2008 by Justin Quinn. First published in English in *PN Review*. Published in *From the Interior: Poems 1995–2005*, by Seren Books. Reprinted with the permission of Justin Quinn, Petr Borkovec, and Seren Books.

"Everyday Occurrence," translated from the Czech of **Ivana Bozdechová**. English translation copyright 2008 by Ewald Osers. First published in English in *Modern Poetry in Translation*. Published with the permission of Ewald Osers and Ivana Bozdechová.

Rosa Alice Branco's "Mornings on the Ground," "The Highest Branch," and "Between Yesterday and Your Mouth": translated by Alexis Levitin. Translation copyright 2008 by Alexis Levitin. Printed with permission of Alexis Levitin and Rosa Alice Branco.

Ronalds Briedis' "Silence" and "Before addressing the people": translated by Margita Gailitis and J. C. Todd. Copyright 2008 by Margita Gailitis and J. C. Todd. Printed here with permission of Margita Gailitis, J. C. Todd, and Ronalds Briedis.

Balša Brković's "The Babylon Song": translated by Ulvija Tanović. Translation copyright 2008 by Ulvija Tanović. Reprinted with permission of Balša Brković and Ulvija Tanović.

"The Year 1981," translated from the Albanian of **Flora Brovina**. English translation copyright 2008 by Robert Elsie. First published in Albanian in *Mat e çmat*, published by Rilindja. Published with the permission of Robert Elsie and Flora Brovina.

Helwig Brunner's "[Reading into the face how the skin]": translated by Andrew Duncan. Translation copyright 2008 by Andrew Duncan. Reprinted with permission of Andrew Duncan and the rights holder.

Franco Buffoni's ["techniques of criminal investigation]" and "[If you don't know what it means in English to maroon]": translated by Michael Palma. English translations copyright 2008 by Michael Palma. Reprinted here with permission of Michael Palma and Gradiva Publications.

"Excuse and Explanation," translated from the Russian of **Evgenii Bunimovich**. English translation copyright 2008 by Patrick Henry. First published in English in *Crossing Centuries: The New Generation in Russian Poetry*. Published with the permission of Patrick Henry and Evgenii Bunimovich.

"De Humani Corporis Fabrica" from *The Good Neighbour* by **John Burnside**, Copyright 2005 by Jonathan Cape. Reprinted by permission of The Random House Group Ltd.

Marius Burokas's "Simpleton": translated by Kerry Shawn Keys. Translation copyright 2008 by Kerry Shawn Keys. Reprinted with permission of Kerry Shawn Keys and Marius Burokas.

Rui Pires Cabral's "Polish Restaurant," "Lost Friends," "This Way Out," "Our Turn," and "City of the Missing": translated by Alexis Levitin. Translations copyright 2008 by Alexis Levitin. Printed with permission of Alexis Levitin and Rui Pires Cabral.

"60 Minutes," translated from the Norwegian of **Pedro Carmona-Alvarez**. English translation copyright 2008 by Roger Greenwald. First published in Norwegian in *Helter*. Published with the permission of Roger Greenwald, Pedro Carmona-Alvarez, and the Cappelen Agency.

Ciaran Carson's "The Words": from *Opera et Cetera* (1996), copyright by The Gallery Press and Wake Forest University Press. Reprinted by kind permission of the author, Wake Forest University Press, and The Gallery Press, Loughcrew, Oldcastle, Country Meath, Ireland.

Patrizia Cavalli's "[To simulate the burning of the human heart, the humiliation]" and "[The rain brings me back]": translated by Judith Baumel. The English translations first appeared in *New Italian Poets* (Story Line Press, 1991). Reprinted with permission of Judith Baumel and Patrizia Cavalli. Patrizia Cavalli's "[Almost always he who is content is also vulgar]": translated by Peter Covino. English translation copyright 2008 by Peter Covino. Printed here with permission of Peter Covino and Patrizia Cavalli.

Branko Čegec's "Eyes, Ears, Mirror": translated by Miljenko Kovačiček. Translation copyright 2008 by the estate of Miljenko Kovačiček. First published in *Exclamations: An Anthology of Croatian Poetry 1971–1994* (The Bridge/Croatian Writers Association, 2001). Reprinted with permission of Branko Čegec.

"The Killer," translated from the Romanian of **Ruxandra Cesereanu** by Adam J. Sorkin and Claudia Litvinchievici, with Ruxandra Cesereanu. English translation copyright by Adam J. Sorkin. First published in English in *Lunacies* by Meeting Eyes Bindery. Printed with permission of Adam J. Sorkin.

Zehra Cirak's "Friendly Fire": translated by Elizabeth Oehlkers Wright. Translation copyright 2008 by Elizabeth Oehlkers Wright. This poem appeared in German in *Vogel auf dem Rücken eines Elefanten. Gedichte*, by Zehra Cirak, copyright 1991 by Verlag Kiepenheuer & Witsch. Printed with permission of Elizabeth Oehlkers Wright and Verlag Kiepenheuer & Witsch.

Yiorgos Chouliaras's "Occupied City," "Refugees," "Borges in Crete," and "Pencil in the Bread" by Yiorgos

Chouliaras, translated from the Greek by David Mason and the author. English translation copyright 2008 by David Mason and the author. First published in Greek in *The Treasure of the Balkans* (Ypsilon, 1988), *Gramma* (Ypsilon, 1995), and *Fast Food Classics* (Ypsilon, 1992). Reprinted with the permission of David Mason and Yiorgos Chouliaras.

William Cliff's "Ballade of the Mouse": translated by Alfred Corn. Original language copyright Alfred Corn. First published in French in *L'État Belge*, Éditions de La Table Ronde, Paris, 2000. Printed with permission of Alfred Corn and Éditions de La Table Ronde.

"A Scottish Assembly" from *A Scottish Assembly*, by **Robert Crawford**. Copyright 1990 by Chatto & Windus. Reprinted by permission of the Random House Group Ltd.

Maurizio Cucchi's "[From the Cairo to Loreto]" and "[He left throwing us]": translated by Peter Covino. English translations copyright 2008 by Peter Covino. These poems first appeared in Italian in *L'ultimo viaggio di Glenn* (Mondadori, 1999). Maurizio Cucchi's "Letter and Prayer" and "[Why do you breathe on my head?]": translated by Peter Covino. English translations copyright 2008 by Peter Covino. These poems first appeared in Italian in *La luce del distacco* (Mondadori, 1996). All best efforts have been made to secure permission for this use.

"Practicing Ballerina" translated from the Norwegian of **Henning Kramer Dahl**. English translation copyright 2008 by Roger Greenwald. First published in Norwegian in *Dansestykker for legeme og stillhet*. Published with the permission of Roger Greenwald and Henning Kramer Dahl.

Dragan Jovanović Danilov's "On a Sunday Afternoon, a Soul Is a Fascinating Fascist": translated by Tomislav Kuzmanović. Translation copyright 2008 by Tomislav Kuzmanović. Printed with permission of Tomislav Kuzmanović and Dragan Jovanović Danilov.

Paul de Roux's "Figure in a village," "Waiting (1)," and "Waiting (2)": translated from the French by Helen Constantine. English translation copyright 2008 by Helen Constantine. First published in French in *Allers et Retours* by Editions Gallimard, 2002. Published with permission of Helen Constantine.

Aleš Debeljak's "Cast Vote": Translated by Andrew Zawacki and the author. English translation copyright 2008 by Andrew Zawacki and the author. Reprinted with the permission of Andrew Zawacki and the author.

"Theory of Recruiting," translated from the Russian of **Regina Derieva**. English translation copyright 2008 by Kevin Carey and Regina Derieva. First published in English in *Modern Poetry in Translation*. Published with the permission of Regina Derieva. "Dark Thoughts" and "[From a land of institutes to a land of prostitutes.]," translated from the Russian of Regina Derieva. English translation copyright 2008 by Valzhyna Mort. Published with the permission from Valzhyna Mort and Regina Derieva.

Nuala Ní Dhomhnaill's "The Language Issue": Translated by Paul Muldoon. From *Pharaoh's Daughter* (1990), copyright by The Gallery Press and Wake Forest University Press. Reprinted by kind permission of the author, Wake Forest University Press, and The Gallery Press, Loughcrew, Oldcastle, Country Meath, Ireland.

"A Visit to the Clockmaker," by **Kristin Dimitrova**, translated by Gregory O'Donoghue, from *A Visit to the Clockmaker*, copyright Kristin Dimitrova. Reprinted by permission of Kristin Dimitrova and Southword Editions.

"Decent Girl," translated from the Macedonian of **Lidija Dimkovska** by Ljubica Arsovska and Peggy Reid, from *Do Not Awaken Them with Hammers*, copyright Ugly Duckling Presse. Reprinted by permission of Ugly Duckling Presse.

"The Nth Day of the Nth Month," translated from the Danish of **Adda Djørup**. English translation copyright 2008 by Roger Greenwald. First published in Danish in *Monsieurs monologer*. Published with the permission of Roger Greenwald and Adda Djørup.

Michael Donhauser's "The Apple": translated by Elizabeth Oehlkers Wright. Translation copyright 2008 by Elizabeth Oehlkers Wright. This poem first appeared in *Akzente*. Reprinted with permission of Elizabeth Oehlkers Wright and Urs Engeler.

Milan Đordević's "Far Away from Forest Sounds": translated by Tomislav Kuzmanović. Translation copyright 2008 by Tomislav Kuzmanović. Printed with permission of Tomislav Kuzmanović and Milan Đordevic.

Ulrike Draesner's "hyacinth colic": translated by Iain Galbraith. Translation copyright 2008 by Iain Galbraith. First published in German in *Für die nacht geheuerte zellen* (Luchterhand Literaturverlag, 2005). Printed with permission of Iain Galbraith, Ulrike Draesner, and Luchterhand Literaturverlag.

Kurt Drawert's "Disoriented": translated by Elizabeth Oehlkers Wright. Translation copyright 2008 by Elizabeth Oehlkers Wright. First published in *Frühjahrskollektion* (Suhrkamp Verlag, 2002). Printed with permission of Elizabeth Oehlkers Wright and Suhrkamp Verlag.

Ariane Dreyfus's "Rosas 1998": translated by Donna Stonecipher. Translation copyright 2008 by Donna

Stonecipher. This poem originally appeared in *Les Compagnies Silencieuses* (Flammarion, 2001). Printed with permission of Donna Stonecipher and the original-language rights holder.

Sylviane Dupuis's "from *Musicales*": translated by Ellen Hinsey. Translation copyright 2008 by Ellen Hinsey. First published in *Géométrie de l'illimité* (La Dogana, Geneva, 2000). Printed here with permission of Ellen Hinsey and Sylviane Dupuis.

Ferida Duraković's "Paper Tea": translated by Amela Simić from *Heart of Darkness* (White Pine Press, copyright 1999). Reprinted with permission of White Pine Press.

Daiva Èepauskaitė's "Love, a Last Glance": translated by Vyt Bakaitis. Translation copyright 2008 by Vyt Bakaitis. Printed by permission of Vyt Bakaitis and Daiva Èepauskaitė.

Oswald Egger's "[Only, sometimes coast herons fly in a low V"]" from *Room of Rumor: Tunings*, translated from the German by Michael Pisaro. Copyright 2004. Reprinted with permission of Green Integer Books, www .greeninteger.com.

Gyrdir Elíasson's "Nocturne": translated from the Icelandic by Bernard Scudder. English translation copyright 2008 by Bernard Scudder. "Nocturne" first appeared in *Brushstrokes of Blue: The Young Poets of Iceland* (Shad Thames Books, 1994). Reprinted with the permission of Bernard Scudder, Gyrdir Elíasson, and Shad Thames Books.

Martin Enckell's "Saint Petersburg": translated by David McDuff. Translation copyright 2008 by David McDuff. Printed with permission of David McDuff and the rights holders.

Haydar Ergülen's "Pomegranate": translated by Murat Nemet-Nejat. Translation copyright 2008 by Murat Nemet-Nejat. This translation first appeared in *The Translation Review 68*. Reprinted with permission of Murat Nemet-Nejat and the original-language rights holder.

Seyhan Erözçelik's "from *Rosestrikes*": translated by Murat Nemet-Nejat. Translation copyright 2008 by Murat Nemet-Nejat. These translations first appeared in *Bombay Gin*. Reprinted with permission of Murat Nemet-Nejat and Seyhan Erözçelik.

"[Dip us in fire or water,]," translated from the Russian of **Alexander Aremenko**. English translation copyright 2008 by Matvei Yankelevich. First published in Russian in *Gorizontalnaya Strana* [Horizontal Country], published by Pushkinsky Dom, 1999. Published with the permission of Matvei Yankelevich and Aleander Eremenko.

Marie Étienne's "from *The Ebony Mare*": translated by Marilyn Hacker. English translation copyright 2008 by Marilyn Hacker. Printed with permission of Marilyn Hacker and the rights holders.

Daniel Falb's "a social still life in the line of vermeer": translated by Donna Stonecipher. Translation copyright 2008 by Donna Stonecipher. Printed here by permission of Donna Stonecipher and the original-language rights holders.

Gerhard Falkner's "You sleep": translated by Elizabeth Oehlkers Wright. Translation copyright 2008 by Elizabeth Oehlkers Wright. First published in German in *X-te Person Einzahl* (Suhrkamp Verlag, 1996). Reprinted with permission of Elizabeth Oehlkers Wright and Suhrkamp Verlag.

"Eggs, Newspaper, and Coffee," translated from the Czech of **Sylva Fischerová**. English translation copyright 2008 by Stuart Friebert. First published in English in *Field*. Published with the permission of Stuart Friebert and Sylva Fischerová. "The Language of the Fountains," translated from the Czech of Sylva Fischerová. English translation copyright 2008 by Stuart Friebert. First published in English in *The Literary Review*. Published with the permission of Stuart Friebert and Sylva Fischerová. "The Only Place," translated from the Czech of Sylva Fischerová. First published in English in *The Tremor of Racehorses* by Blooaxe Books, translated by Jarmila and Ian Milner. Published with the permission of Sylva Fischerová.

Mark Ford's "We Crave": from *Soft Sift* (Faber & Faber, 2001). Reprinted with permission of Faber & Faber, Ltd., and Harcourt, Inc.

Tua Forsström's "It's beautiful in Sicily in the spring when the lemon trees are in bloom": translated from the Finland-Swedish by Stina Katchadourian. English translation copyright 2008 by Stina Katchadourian. Published in Finland-Swedish in *Jag studerade en gång vid en underbar fakultet*, copyright Tua Forsström, Söderströms (Helsinki), 2003. Published in English translation in *I studied once at a wonderful faculty* (Bloodaxe Books, 2006). Reprinted with the permission of Bloodaxe Books, Stina Katchadourian, and Tua Forsström. Tua Forsström's "*from Minerals*": translated from the Finland-Swedish by David McDuff. English translation copyright 2008 by David McDuff. Published in Finland-Swedish in *Jag studerade en gang vid en underbar fakultet*, copyright Tua Forsström, Söderströms (Helsinki), 2003. Published in English translation in *I studied once at a wonderful faculty* (Bloodaxe Books, 2006). Reprinted with the permission of Bloodaxe Books, David McDuff, and Tua Forsström.

"Conspiracies" and "In the Californian Back Yard," translated from the Danish of **Niels Frank**. English translation copyright 2008 by Roger Greenwald. First published in Danish in *Tabernakel*. Published with the permission of Roger Greenwald and Niels Frank.

Katarina Frostenson's "Echo's Gorge": translated from the Swedish by Frank Perry and Sarah Death. English translation copyright 2008 by Frank Perry and Sarah Death. First published in Swedish in *Korallen*, published by Wahlström & Widstrand, 1999. Published with the permission of Frank Perry, Sarah Death, and Katarina Frostenson. This English translation first appeared in *Swedish Book Review*. Katarina Frostenson's "Sonnet from Shadow of a Gift": translated from the Swedish by Frank Perry. English translation copyright 2008 by Frank Perry. First published in Swedish in *Karkas, fem linjer*, published by Wahlström & Widstrand, 2004. Published with the permission of Frank Perry and Katarina Frostenson.

Inga Gaile's "The wind smooths out all the wrinkles and lights beacon in our eyes" and "To leave, flee, lope, swim away with": translated by Inara Cedrins. English translation Copyright 2008 by Inara Cedrins. Printed here with permission of Inara Cedrins and Inga Gaile.

"*from* Epigraffiti," translated from the Slovak of **Róbert Gál**. English translation copyright 2003 by Madelaine Hron. First published in Slovak in *Epigraffiti* by Vetus Via. First published in English in *Signs and Symptoms* (Twisted Spoon Press).

"Pietà (Ivy on the Cross)," translated from the Romanian of **Emilian Galaicu-Păun**. English translation copright 2008 by Adam J. Sorkin. First published in Romanian in *Gestuar*, published by Editura AXA. Published with the permission of Adam J. Sorkin and Emilian Galaicu-Păun.

"At the Virgin's Breast," translated from the Romanian of **Mihail Gălățanu**. English translation copyright 2008 by Adam J. Sorkin. First published in Romanian in *Poetus Captivus*, published by Editura Dominus. First appeared in English in *Arson*. Published with the permission of Adam J. Sorkin and Mihail Gălățanu.

"To My Mother," translated from the Russian of **Sergey Gandlevsky**. English translation copyright 2008 by Philip Metres. First published in English in *Tin House*. Published with the permission of Philip Metres and Sergey Gandlevsky.

"Ford" and "Father," translated from the Spanish of **Pablo García Casado**. English translation copyright 2008 by Brian Barker. Published with the permission of Brian Barker and Pablo García Casado.

Luis García Montero, "Poetics" and "Poetry," translated by Katie King. © Katie King. Published in *Words Without Borders* [www.wordswithoutborders.org]. By permission of *Words Without Borders,* an online magazine for international literature hosted by Bard College and supported by the National Endowment for the Arts.

Gür Genç's "Kiss My Corpse": translated from the Turkish by the poet and Stephanos Stephanides. English translation copyright 2008 by the poet and Stephanos Stephanides. First published in Turkish in *Ye* (Isik Kitabevi, 1994). English translation published with the permission of Gür Genç and Stephanos Stephanides. Gür Genç's "I Worshipped Too Many Gods": translated from the Turkish by the poet and Stephanos Stephanides. English translation copyright 2008 by the poet and Stephanos Stephanides. First published in Turkish in *Augur* (B/6, 2005). English translation published with the permission of Gür Genç and Stephanos Stephanides.

Claire Genoux's "from *Saisons du corps*": translated by Ellen Hinsey. Translation copyright 2000 by Ellen Hinsey, translated from *Saisons du corps* (Editions Empreintes, 1999). This translation originally appeared in *Frank: an International Journal of Contemporary Writing and Art*, #18, Paris, 2000. Reprinted here with permission of Ellen Hinsey and Editions Empreintes.

"Leda" and "Fed Up," translated from the Dutch of **Eva Gerlach**. English translation copyright 2008 by Alissa Valles. Published with the permission of Alissa Valles and Eva Gerlach.

Guy Goffette's "So Many Things": translated by Julie Fay. English translation copyright 2008 by Julie Fay. First published in French in *Le Pêcheur d'Eau*, published by Gallimard. Published with the permission of Julie Fay and Guy Goffette. An earlier version of this translation originally appeared in *Prairie Schooner*. Guy Goffette's "Around the Flames" and "The Number": translated by Marilyn Hacker. English translations copyright 2008 by Marilyn Hacker. Printed with permission of Marilyn Hacker and the rights holders.

"Passing the Church of the French Consulate," translated from the Russian of **Dmitry Golynko**. English translation copyright 1998 by Eugene Ostashevsky. First published in Russian in *Homo Scribens*, published by Borey-Art. First published in English in *Shark*. Published with the permission of Eugene Ostashevsky and Dmitry Golynko.

Pavle Goranović's "Great Preparations": translated by Evald Flisar. English translation copyright 2008 by Evald Flisar. Published with the permission of Evald Flisar and the rights holder.

"The Love Rabbit," translated from the Bulgarian of **Georgi Gospodinov** by Kalina Filipova. English translation copyright 2008 by Georgi Gospodinov. Published with the permission of Georgi Gospodinov. "The Ritual," translated from the Bulgarian of Georgi Gospodinov. English translation copyright 2008 by Bilyana

Kourtasheva. First published in Bulgarian in *Pisma do Gaustin* by Zhanet Press. Published with the permission of Bilyana Kourtasheva and Georgi Gospodinov.

Dieter M. Gräf's "While Dancing: A Paradigm": from *Tousled Beauty: Selected Poems*, translated from the German by Andrew Shields. Copyright 2005. Reprinted with permission of Green Integer Books, www.greeninteger.com.

Gintaras Grajauskas's "World in Your Pocket" translated by Kerry Shawn Keys and Eugenijus Ališanka. Translation copyright 2008 by Kerry Shawn Keys and Eugenijus Ališanka. Reprinted with permission of Kerry Shawn Keys, Eugenijus Ališanka, and Gintaras Grajauskas. Gintaras Grajauskas's "The Night Watchman": translated by Laima Sruoginis. Translation copyright 2008 by Laima Sruoginis. Printed with permission of Laima Sruoginis and Gintaras Grajauskas.

Bruno Grégoire's "White Siestas" ("Siestes blanches") and "Sanctuary" ("Sanctuaires"): translated by Ellen Hinsey. Translation copyright 2008 by Ellen Hinsey. First published in *l'Usure l'étoile* (Obsidiane, 1998). Reprinted with permission of Ellen Hinsey and Obsidiane.

Vona Groarke's "The Riverbed": Reprinted by kind permission of the author and The Gallery Press, Loughcrew, Oldcastle, County Meath, Ireland, from *Shale* (1994). Published in the USA in *Flight and Earlier Poems* (2003), copyright by Wake Forest University Press. Reprinted by kind permission of the Wake Forest University Press.

Tatjana Gromača's "I Like It When You Come Around with Your Friends": Translation copyright 2008 by Andrew Wachtel. Reprinted with permission of Andrew Wachtel and Tatjana Gromača.

"Selected Exercises in Case Law II" and "The Law Is the Mediterranean," by **Cathrine Grøndahl**, translated from the Norwegian of Cathrine Grøndahl. English translations copyright 2007 and 2008, respectively, by Roger Greenwald. First published in Norwegian in *Lovsang*. "Selected Exercises in Case Law II" first published in English in *AGNI*. Published with the permission of Roger Greenwald and Cathrine Grøndahl.

"In the Provinces 2 (In Gotland)" from *Ashes for Breakfast* by **Durs Grünbein**, translated by Michael Hofmann. Translation copyright © 2005 by Michael Hofmann. Reprinted by permission of Farrar, Straus and Giroux, LLC.

Tobias Grüterich's "5 aphorisms": translated by Elizabeth Oehlkers Wright. Translation copyright 2008 by Elizabeth Oehlkers Wright. Printed with permission of Elizabeth Oehlkers Wright and Tobias Grüterich.

Ulla Hahn's "Respectable Sonnet": translated from the original German ("Anständiges Sonett") by Oliver Grannis from the collection *Herz Über Kopf* (Deutsche Verlags-Anstalt, 1981) Translation copyright 2008 by Oliver Grannis. This translation first appeared in *Modern Poetry in Translation*, no. 16. Reprinted with permission of Oliver Grannis.

"To Withstand Evil" and "Alpha Centauri," translated from the Slovak of **Mila Haugová**. English translation copyright 2008 by James Sutherland-Smith and Viera Sutherland-Smith. First published in English in *Scent of the Unseen*, by Arc Publications. Published with the permission of James Sutherland-Smith, Viera Sutherland-Smith and Mila Haugová.

Kerstin Hensel's "At the Flea Market": translated by Elizabeth Oehlkers Wright. Translation copyright 2008 by Elizabeth Oehlkers Wright. Original published in German in *Bahnhof verstehen: Gedichte 1995–2000* (Luchterland Literaturverlag). Printed with permission of Elizabeth Oehlkers Wright and Luchterland Literaturverlag.

W. N. Herbert's "Scaldfoot": from *The Laurelude*, copyright 1998 by Bloodaxe Books. Reprinted with permission of Bloodaxe Books.

Stefan Hertmans's "Death on a Pale Horse," "First Steps," and "While sketching": translated by Gregory Ball. These poems first appeared in Flemish in *Muziek voor de overtocht. Gedichten 1975–2005*. De Bezige Bij, Amsterdam 2006. These translations first appeared in *Absinthe*. Printed with permission of Stefan Hertmans, Gregory Ball and De Bezige Bij.

Selima Hill's "North Carolina": from *A Little Book of Meat*, copyright 1993 by Bloodaxe Books. Reprinted with permission of Bloodaxe Books.

Emmanuel Hocquard's "from *The Invention of Glass*": translated by Cole Swensen and Rod Smith. Translation copyright 2008 by Cole Swensen and Rod Smith. Published in French in *L'invention du verre* (P.O.L., Paris, 2005). Printed with permission of Cole Swensen, Rod Smith, and P.O.L.

"Door" and "At the Claws," translated from the Czech of **Petr Hruška**. English translation copyright 2008 by Zuzana Gábrišová. Published with the permission of Zuzana Gábrišová and Petr Hruška.

Flóra Imre's "Snow Covers the Garden": Traslated by Jascha Kessler. Translation copyright 2008 by Jascha Kessler. Printed with permission of Jascha Kessler and Flóra Imre.

Küçük İskender's "from *souljam*": translated by Murat Nemet-Nejat. Translation copyright 2004 by Murat

PERMISSION ACKNOWLEDGMENTS 391

Nemet-Nejat. This translation first appeared in *Eda: An Anthology of Contemporary Turkish Poetry* (Talisman, 2004). Reprinted with permission of Murat Nemet-Nejat.

"Apologetic Telegram," translated from the Bulgarian of **Mirela Ivanova**. English translation copyright 2008 by Ewald Osers. First published in Bulgarian in *Samotna Igra*. First published in English in *Modern Poetry in Translation*. Published with the permission of Ewald Osers and Mirela Ivanova.

Ann Jäderlund's "Three poems from *Soon into Summer I Will Walk Out*": translated from the Swedish by Johannes Göransson. English translation copyright 2008 by Johannes Göransson. First published in Swedish in *Snart gar jag i sommaren ut*, published by Albert Bonniers Förlag, 1990. Published with the permission of Johannes Göransson and Ann Jäderlund. These poems first appeared in English translation in *Fourteen Hills* ("Into a field . . ." and "Out of the throat . . .") and *Typo 7* ("The big valley . . .").

"Sèma" and "[Not to be is Nothing's only quality.]" translated from the Norwegian of **Cornelius Jakhelln**. English translation copyright 2008 by Roger Greenwald. First published in Norwegian in *Yggdraliv*. Published with the permission of Roger Greenwald and Cornelius Jakhelln.

Kathleen Jamie's "Wee Wifey": from *Mr and Mrs Scotland are Dead: Poems 1980–1994*, copyright 2002 by Bloodaxe Books. Reprinted with permission of Bloodaxe Books.

Franck André Jamme's "How Long?": translated by Michael Tweed. Translation copyright 2008 by Michael Tweed. Translation first published in *Another Silent Attack* (Black Square Editions, 2006). Originally published in *Encore une attaque silencieuse* (Draguignan, 1999). Published with the permission of Michael Tweed and the original-language rights holders.

"*from* Picnic on the Spiral Staircase," translated from the Dutch of **Esther Jansma**. English translation copyright 2008 by Scott Rollins and Katheryn Ronnau-Bradbeer. Published with the permission of Katheryn Ronnau-Bradbeer and Esther Jansma.

Saša Jelenković's "Fortress": translated by Tomislav Kuzmanović. Translation copyright 2008 by Tomislav Kuzmanović. Printed with permission of Tomislav Kuzmanović and Saša Jelenković.

Miljenko Jergović's "Feldwebel Zorn's Motorcycle": translated by Tomislav Kuzmanović. Translation copyright 2008 by Tomislav Kuzmanović. Printed with permission of Tomislav Kuzmanović and Miljenko Jergović.

Arne Johnsson's "from *Changes*: Sketch XXV": translated from the Swedish by Rika Lesser. English translation copyright 2008 by Rika Lesser. Published in Swedish in *Förvandlingar* by Brutus Östlings Bokförlag Symposion, 1985, 2005. English translation published with the permission of Rika Lesser and Arne Johnsson. Arne Johnsson's "*from* Part of this and separate as everyone": translated from the Swedish by Rika Lesser. English translation copyright 2008 by Rika Lesser. Published in Swedish in *Del av detta och avskild som alla* by Brutus Östlings Bokförlag Symposion, 2002. English translation published with the permission of Rika Lesser and Arne Johnsson.

Elísabet Jökulsdóttir's "The Divorce Children": translated from the Icelandic by David McDuff. English translation copyright 2008 by David McDuff. "The Divorce Children" first appeared in *Brushstrokes of Blue: The Young Poets of Iceland* (Shad Thames Books, 1994). Reprinted with the permission of David McDuff, Elísabet Jökulsdóttir, and Shad Thames Books.

"Novel," translated from the Danish of **Pia Juul**. English translation copyright 2004 by Barbara J. Haveland. First published in Danish in *Forgjort*, published by Tiderne skifter. First published in English in *Exile: The Literary Quarterly*. Published with the permission of Barbara J. Haveland, Pia Juul, and Tiderne skifter.

Hédi Kaddour's "Spiritual Distress" and "Treason" translated by Marilyn Hacker. "Treason" first appeared in this translation in *American Poetry Review* and *Ambit* (UK). "Spiritual Distress" was first published in this translation in *Poetry International* and *PN Review* (UK). English translations copyright by Marilyn Hacker. Reprinted with permission of Marilyn Hacker and the rights holders.

"Parting makes simple sense" by **Katia Kapovich**, translated from the Russian by Richard McKane. English translation copyright 2002 by Richard McKane. First published in English in *Modern Poetry in Translation*. Published with the permission of Katia Kapovich.

Zvonko Karanović's "Melancholy": translated by Tomislav Kuzmanović. Translation copyright 2008 by Tomislav Kuzmanović. Printed with permission of Tomislav Kuzmanović and Zvonko Karanovic.

Laurynas Katkus's "Later on" and "Žvėrynas in Winter": translated by Kerry Shawn Keys. Translation copyright 2008 by Kerry Shawn Keys. Reprinted with permission of Kerry Shawn Keys and Laurynas Katkus.

Jackie Kay's "Virus": from *Off Colour*, copyright 1999 by Bloodaxe Books. Reprinted with permission of Bloodaxe Books.

"Dream of the Meaning of Dreams," translated from the Polish of **Bozena Keff**. English translation copyright 2008 by Alissa Valles. Published with the permission of Alissa Valles and Bozena Keff.

"Commedia," translated from the Belarusian of **Andrej Khadanovich**. English translation copyright 2008 by Valzhyna Mort. Published with the permission of Valzhyna Mort and Andrej Khadanovich.

"Ghazal" by **Mimi Khalvati**: from *The Meanest Flower*, copyright Carcanet Press. Reprinted with permission of Carcanet Press.

"[Frost ropes in the ditch: nothing could break through],"translated from the Polish of **Marzanna Bogumiła Kielar**. English translation copyright 2002 by W. Martin. First published in English in *Verse*. Published with the permission of W. Martin and Marzanna Bogumiła Kielar. "Winter Elegy," translated from the Polish of Marzanna Bogumiła Kielar. English translation copyright 2000 by W. Martin. First published in English in *Chicago Review*. Published with the permission of W. Martin and Marzanna Bogumiła Kielar. "Early Spring," translated from the Polish of Marzanna Bogumiła Kielar. English translation copyright 2000 by W. Martin. First published in English in *Chicago Review*. Published with the permission of W. Martin and Marzanna Bogumiła Kielar.

Thomas Kling's "Stratum I" and "Stratum III": translated by Peter Filkins. These translations first appeared in *Poetry* magazine. Translations copyright 1998. Reprinted with permission of Peter Filkins and Suhrkamp Verlag.

Marija Knežević's "On-Site Investigation V": translated by Tomislav Kuzmanović. Translation copyright 2008 by Tomislav Kuzmanović. Printed with permission of Tomislav Kuzmanović and Marija Knežević.

Nicolai Kobus's "anna": translated by Elizabeth Oehlkers Wright. Translation copyright 2008 by Elizabeth Oehlkers Wright. Printed with permission of Elizabeth Oehlkers Wright and Nicolai Kobus.

"[A new language: the language]" and "[Two columns of smoke]," translated from the Polish of **Krzysztof Koehler**. English translation copyright 2008 by Bill Johnston. Published in Polish in *Na krancu dlugiego pola i inne wiersze z lat 1988–1998* by Biblioteka Frondy. Published with the permission of Bill Johnston and Krzysztof Koehler.

Uwe Kolbe's "Never now anywhere": translated by Michael Hamburger. English translation copyright 2008 by Michael Hamburger. Reprinted with permission of Michael Hamburger and the rights holder.

"Skin Is a Wrapping of Bones," translated from the Slovak of **Ivan Kolenič**. English translation copyright 2008 by James Sutherland-Smith. First published in English in *Not Waiting for Miracles* (Moudry Peter). Published with the permission of James Sutherland-Smith and Ivan Kolenič.

Anise Koltz's "from *The Fire Eater*": translated by Pierre Joris. English translation copyright 2008 by Pierre Joris. First published in French in *L'avaleur de feu* (Editions PHI, 2003). Published with permission of Pierre Joris and the rights holders.

"Heavy Burden, Your Fragile Body," translated from the Albanian of **Abdullah Konushevci**. English translation copyright 2008 by Robert Elsie. First published in Albanian in *Pikat AD*, published by Rilindja. Published with the permission of Robert Elsie and Abdullah Konushevci.

Barbara Korun's "Every Breath You Take": translated by Theo Dorgan. First published in English in Barbara Korun's *Songs of Earth and Light*, Southword Editions, copyright 2008. Reprinted with the permission of Southword Editions.

"Adam," translated from the Albanian of **Gazmend Krasniqi**. English translation copyright 2008 by Robert Elsie. First published in Albanian in *Ungjilli sipas diallit*, published by Revista Letrare Shqiptare Ars. Published with the permission of Robert Elsie and Gazmend Krasniqi.

Angela Krauss's "Leipzig, 1999": translated by Michael Ritterson. English copyright 2008 by Michael Ritterson. This translation first appeared in *International Poetry Review*. Reprinted here with permission of Michael Ritterson and Angela Krauss.

Ursula Krechel's "My Mother" translated by Elizabeth Oehlkers Wright. Translation copyright 2008 by Elizabeth Oehlkers Wright. Published in German in *Ungezürnt: Gedichte, Lichter, Lesezeichen* (Suhrkamp Verlag, 2002). Printed with permission of Elizabeth Oehlkers Wright and Suhrkamp Verlag.

"Bronchitis (a psychopoem)," translated from the Macedonian of **Kata Kulavkova**. English translation copyright 2008 by Ilija Čašule. First published in Macedonian in *Nova pot*. First published in English in *Time Difference*, published by Zumpres; Blesok Publishing. Published with the permission of Ilija Čašule and Kata Kulavkova.

Asko Künnap's "O night, my car": translated by the author with Eric Dickens and Richard Adang. English language copyright 2004 the author with Eric Dickens and Richard Adang. This poem originally appeared in *Asko Künnap and Karl Martin Sinijärv* (Näo kirik, 2004). Reprinted with permission of Eric Dickens, Richard Adang, and the rights holders.

Vivian Lamarque's "At Vacation's End" and "To Pasolini": translated by Peter Covino. English translations copyright 2008 by Peter Covino. These poems first appeared in Italian in *Una quieta polvere* (Mondadori,

"There was a man" and "Button Box" translated from the Dutch of **Tonnus Oosterhof**. English translation copyright 2008 by Deborah Ffoulkes. Published with the permission of Tonnus Oosterhof. "Secret Agent," translated from the Dutch of Tonnus Oosterhof. English translation copyright 2008 by Alissa Valles. Published with the permission of Alissa Valles and Tonnus Oosterhof.

Imre Oravecz's "The Hole" and "Soldiers' Graves": translated from the Hungarian by Bruce Berlind and Mária Kőrösy. English translation copyright 2008 by the translators. Both translations first appeared in *Grand Street*. Published with permission from Bruce Berlind and the rights holders.

Lauri Otonkoski's "Herbal Wisdom" and "from *The Poetry Track*": translated by Anselm Hollo. English translations copyright 2008 by Anselm Hollo. Printed here with permission of Anselm Hollo and the rights holders.

Jean-Baptiste Para's "Svetla" ("Svetla") and "Tomorrow" ("Demain"): translated by Olivia McCannon. English translation copyright 2008 by Olivia McCannon. First published in French in *La Faim Des Ombres* by Obsidiane. Published with the permission of Olivia McCannon, Jean-Baptiste Para, and Obsidiane.

Bert Papenfuss's "on edge": translated by David Perry. English translation copyright 2008 by David Perry. Printed here with permission of David Perry and Bert Papenfuss.

Alexei Parshchikov, "Estuary," translated by Wayne Chambliss. © 2007 by Wayne Chambliss. Published in *Words Without Borders* [www.wordswithoutborders.org], July 2007. By permission of *Words Without Borders*, an online magazine for international literature hosted by Bard College and supported by the National Endowment for the Arts. First published in Russian in *Dneprovsky August*, by Molodaya Guardiya (1986).

"An Elliptical Stylus" copyright 2001 by **Don Paterson**. Reprinted from *The White Lie: New and Selected Poetry* with the permission of Graywolf Press.

"[you can't see the battle because it's far off, in Eritrea]," translated from the Galician of **Chus Pato**. English translation copyright 2007 by Erín Moure. First published in Galician in *m-Talá*, by Edicións Xerais de Galicia (©2000). First published in English in *Jacket* (jacketmagazine.com). Published with the permission of Erín Moure and Chus Pato. "[and now the panopticon is a ruin]," translated from the Galician of Chus Pato. English translation by Erín Moure. First published in Galician in *Charenton*, by Edicións Xerais de Galicia (© 2005). The English language edition of *Charenton*, translated by Erín Moure, is published by Shearsman Books (© 2007) in the UK and USA and Buschek Books (© 2007) in Canada. Printed with the permission of the publishers, Erín Moure, and Chus Pato.

"Four Poems," translated from the Russian of **Vera Pavlova**. English translation copyright 2008 by Steven Seymour. First published in English in *The New Yorker*. Published with the permission of Steven Seymour and Vera Pavlova.

Andras Petöcz's "The Lake at Dawn," "A Banal Poem. Subject: Love," and "In Praise of the Sea": translated by Jascha Kessler. Translations copyright 2008 by Jascha Kessler. Printed with permission of Jascha Kessler and Andras Petöcz.

"The Evening," translated from the Spanish of **José Manuel del Pino**. English translation copyright 2008 by G. J. Racz. First published in Spanish in *Los altos oleajes*, by Fundación Animación Cultural Antequera. First published in English in *Absinthe: New European Writing*. Published with the permission of G. J. Racz and José Manuel del Pino. "The Sweet Arms of Inspiration," translated from the Spanish of José Manuel del Pino. English translation copyright 2008 by G. J. Racz. First published in Spanish in *Los altos oleajes*, by Fundación Animación Cultural Antequera. First published in English in *Absinthe: New European Writing*. Published with the permission of G. J. Racz and José Manuel del Pino.

"from *Lake Poems*," by **Katerina Pinosová**. Copyright 2001 by Katerina Pinosová. Published with the permission of Katerina Pinosová.

"Green Line" by **Lysandros Pitharas**: All best efforts have been made to secure permission for this use.

"A Diary," by **Dana Podracká**, translated by Robert Welch, from *Forty Four: Poems*, copyright © Dana Podracká. Reprinted by permission of Southword Editions.

"Madi's Laugh," translated from the Romanian of **Simona Popescu**. Published with the permission of Sean Cotter and Simona Popescu.

Steffen Popp's "Silvae (lit)": translated by Donna Stonecipher. Translation copyright 2008 by Donna Stonecipher. Printed here by permission of Donna Stonecipher and the original-language rights holders.

Jean Portante's "from *The Desert*": translated by Pierre Joris. English translation copyright 2008 by Pierre Joris. First published in French in *Ouvert Fermé* (Editions PHI, 1994). Published with permission of Pierre Joris and the rights holders.

"A Certain Tree in Powązki Cemetery," "Space" and "Don't Sleep, Take Notes" from *Continued* © 2005 by Piotr Sommer and reprinted by permission of Wesleyan University Press.

"Internal Manifesto I" and "Uncertainty," translated from the Polish of Ewa Sonnenberg. English translation copyright 2008 by Katarzyna Jakubiak. "Internal Manifesto I" first published in Polish in *Smycz* by Astrum, 2000; "Uncertainty" first published in Polish in *Plonacy Tramwaj* by Zielona Sowa Publishers, 2001. Published with the permission of Katarzyna Jakubiak and Ewa Sonnenberg.

"Five Fathoms Down" translated from the Polish of Andrzej Sosnowski. English translation copyright 2008 by Benjamin Paloff. First published in Polish by Stowarzyszenie Literackie "Kresy" in *Stancje*. Published with the permission of Benjamin Paloff. "Errata" translated from the Polish of Andrzej Sosnowski. English translation copyright 2008 by Benjamin Paloff. First published in Polish by Pomona in *Konwój. Opera*. Published here with the permission of Benjamin Paloff.

Erik Spinoy's "from *Susette*": translated by John Irons. Translation copyright 2008 by John Irons. "from *Susette*" appeared originally in this translation in *Modern Poetry in Translation*. Reprinted here with permission of John Irons, Eric Spinoy, and *Modern Poetry in Translation*.

"The Infanta Augustina" and "The Infanta Margherita," translated from the Romanian of Saviana Stănescu by Adam J. Sorkin, Aura Sibişan, and the poet. English translation copyright by Adam J. Sorkin. First published in English in *Diary of a Clone* by Meeting Eyes Bindery. Reprinted with permission of Adam J. Sorkin.

Aleš Šteger's "The Returning of What Is to Come": translated by Tom Ložar. Translation copyright 2002 by Tom Ložar. This translation first appeared in *Ten Slovenian Poets of the Nineties* (Slovene Writers Association, 2002). Reprinted with permission of Aleš Šteger and the Slovene Writers Association.

Stephanos Stephanides' "Ars Poetica: Sacred or Daemonic" first appeared in *Blue Moon in Rajasthan* (Kochlias Publications, 2005). Reprinted with permission of the author.

Mile Stojić's "A House on Ice": translated by Miljenko Kovačiček. First published in *Exclamations: An Anthology of Croatian Poetry 1971–1994* (The Bridge/Croatian Writers Association, 2001). Reprinted with permission of Mile Stojić.

Ulf Stolterfoht's "Jargons IV (2)": translated from the German by Rosmarie Waldrop. English translation copyright 2002 by Rosmarie Waldrop. First published in *Aufgabe 2* (Spring, 2002). Translated from "Fachsprachen IV (2)", in Ulf Stolterfoht, *Fachsprachen I–IX*, Basel/Weil am Rhein: Urs Engeler Editor, 1998. Published with permission of Rosmarie Waldrop and Ulf Stolterfoht.

"Liminal Moments," translated from the Bulgarian of Edvin Sugarev by Ludmilla G. Popova-Wightman, from *Secret Senses*, copyright © 2005 by Ivy Press. Reprinted by permission of Ludmilla G. Popova-Wightman and Ivy Press.

"Spring Scales," translated from the Russian of Darya Sukhovei. English translation copyright 2008 by Christopher Mattison. First appeared in English in *Modern Poetry in Translation*. Published with the permission of Christopher Mattison and Darya Sukhovei.

Anni Sumari's "Fete": translated by Sarka Hantula. First published in English in *The Other Side of Landscape: An Anthology of Contemporary Nordic Poetry*, Slope Editions, 2006. Translation copyright 2006 by Sarka Hantula. Reprinted with permission of Anni Sumari, Slope Editions, and Sarka Hantula.

"Light" and "Death is the top player in our playground," translated from the Polish of Dariusz Suska. English translation copyright 2008 by Alissa Valles. Published with the permission of Alissa Valles and Dariusz Suska.

"Preface" and "Song of the Ill," translated from the Polish of Marcin Świetlicki. English translation copyright 2005 by Elżbieta Wójcik-Leese. First published in English in *Orient Express*. Published with the permission of Elżbieta Wójcik-Leese and Marcin Świetlicki.

Ákos Szilagyi's "O!" and "You Think": translated by Jascha Kessler. Copyright 2008 by the translators. Printed here with permission of the translator.

"Imagination," translated from the Polish of Artur Szlosarek. English translation copyright 2008 by Jennifer Grotz. First published in Polish in *Pod Obcym Niebem*, by Wydawnictwo Literackie 2005. Published with the permission of Jennifer Grotz and Artur Szlosarek. "Temptation," translated from the Polish of Artur Szlosarek. English translation copyright 2006 by Jennifer Grotz and Anna Skucińska. First published in *AGNI Online*, 2006. First published in Polish in *Pod Obcym Niebem*, by Wydawnictwo Literackie 2005. Published with the permission of Jennifer Grotz, Anna Skucińska, and Artur Szlosarek.

Novica Tadić's "Antipsalm": translated by Charles Simic. Originally published in English in *The Horse Has Six Legs: Contemporary Serbian Poetry*, edited by Charles Simic. Graywolf Press, 1992.

"A Thousand Times Recalled," translated from the Danish of Pia Tafdrup. English translation copyright

Peter Waterhouse's "About What Is a Hand And What Is in the Hand": translated from the German by Rosmarie Waldrop. English translation copyright 1999 by Rosmarie Waldrop. First published in Peter Waterhouse, *Where Are We Now,* Sausalito, CA: Duration Press, 1999. Translated from "Über das, was die Hand ist, und das, was der Hand ist," in *passim,* Reinbek bei Hamburg: Rowohlt Verlag, 1986. Published with the permission of Rosmarie Waldrop and Peter Waterhouse.

Adam Wiedemann, "Calypso," translated by W. Martin. © by W. Martin. Published in *Words Without Borders* [www.wordswithoutborders.org], September 2005. By permission of *Words Without Borders,* an online magazine for international literature hosted by Bard College and supported by the National Endowment for the Arts. "Notable Essay: Music," translated from the Polish of Adam Widemann. English translation copyright 2008 by Alissa Valles. Published with the permission of Alissa Valles and Adam Wiedemann.

"I Am a Doctor," "Psalm 22," and "In the dream of an angel," translated from the Dutch of Nachoem M. Wijnberg. English translation copyright 2008 by Alissa Valles. Published with the permission of Alissa Valles and Nachoem M. Wijnberg.

Magnus William-Olsson's *"(Analogia)"*: translated from the Swedish by Rika Lesser. English translation copyright 2008 by Rika Lesser. Published in Swedish in *Ögonblicket är för Pindaros ett litet rum i tiden: Nya dikter och de gamla* by Wahlström & Widstrand, 2006. English translation published with the permission of Rika Lesser and Magnus William-Olsson. This translation of *"(Analogia)"* first appeared in *Words Without Borders: The Online Magazine for International Literature.*

"The Soapmaker" and "[Your left hand]" translated from the Norwegian of Øystein Wingaard Wolf. English translation copyright 2008 by Roger Greenwald. "The Soapmaker" first published in Norwegian in *Wolf i utvalg.* "[Your left hand]" first published in Norwegian in *De gales kjemi* (Solum Forlag). Published with the permission of Roger Greenwald and Øystein Wingaard Wolf.

"Recovery Room," translated from the German by Christian Hawkey. English translation copyright 2008 by Christian Hawkey. First published in German in *kochanie ich habe brot gekauft* published by kookbooks, 2005. Published with the permission of Christian Hawkey, Uljana Wolf, and kookbooks.

"Wisdom," "Words," and "The Last Night of Earth," translated from the Spanish of Roger Wolfe. English translation copyright 2008 by Gary Hawkins. Published with the permission of Gary Hawkins.

"Letter from the Summer House," translated from the Ukrainian of Oksana Zabuzhko. English translation copyright 2008 by Douglas Burnet Smith. Published with the permission of Douglas Burnet Smith and Oksana Zabuzhko. "A Definition of Poetry," translated from the Ukrainian of Oksana Zabuzhko. English translation copyright 2008 by Michael M. Naydan and Askold Melnyczuk. Published with the permission of Michael M. Naydan and Oksana Zabuzhko.

Anka Žagar's "Journey": translated by Tomislav Kuzmanović. Translation copyright 2008 by Tomislav Kuzmanović. Printed with permission of Tomislav Kuzmanović and Anka Žagar.

Benjamin Zephaniah's "White Comedy": from *Propa Propaganda,* copyright 1996 by Bloodaxe Books. Reprinted with permission of Bloodaxe Books.

"Alcohol" translated from the Ukrainian of Serhiy Zhadan. English translation copyright 2004 by Virlana Tkacz and Wanda Phipps. First published in Ukrainian in *History of Culture at the Turn of This Century* published by Krytyka. First published in English in *Welcome to Ukraine* No. 3, 2004. Translation published with permission from Virlana Tkacz and Wanda Phipps.

"Hunger Strike," translated from the Albanian of Visar Zhiti. English translation copyright 2008 by Robert Elsie. First published in Albanian in *Hedh në kafkë,* by Naim Frashëri. First published in English in *The Condemned Apple* (Green Integer 2005). Published with the permission of Robert Elsie and Visar Zhiti.

Mustafa Ziyalan's "Days": translated by Murat Nemet-Nejat. Translation copyright 2004 by Murat Nemet-Nejat. This translation first appeared in *Eda: An Anthology of Contemporary Turkish Poetry* (Talisman, 2004). Reprinted with permission of Murat Nemet-Nejat and Mustafa Ziyalan.

Uroš Zupan's "May": translated by Erica Johnson Debeljak. English translation copyright 2008 by Erica Johnson Debeljak. First published in Slovenian in *Sutre,* by Aleph. Published here with the permission of Erica Johnson Debeljak and Uroš Zupan.

"[I don't want to be the navel of the Earth.]," translated from the Belarusian of Viktar Žybul. English translation copyright 2004 by Vera Rich. Previously published in Belarusian in *Vieshy na Svabodu.* First published in English in *Poems on Liberty* by Radio Free Europe/Radio Liberty. Published with the permission of Vera Rich and Viktar Žybul.

The text of *New European Poets* has been set in Adobe Garamond Pro, drawn by Robert Slimbach and based on type cut by Claude Garamond in the sixteenth century. This book was designed by Ann Sudmeier. Manufactured by Friesens on acid-free paper.